EDI DEVELOPMENT STUDIES

Curbing Corruption

*Toward a Model for
Building National Integrity*

The World Bank
Washington, D.C.

Copyright © 1999
The International Bank for Reconstruction
and Development / THE WORLD BANK
1818 H Street, N.W.
Washington, D.C. 20433, U.S.A.

The Economic Development Institute (EDI) was established by the World Bank in 1955 to train officials concerned with development planning, policymaking, investment analysis, and project implementation in member developing countries. At present the substance of the EDI's work emphasizes macroeconomic and sectoral economic policy analysis. Through a variety of courses, seminars, and workshops, most of which are given overseas in cooperation with local institutions, the EDI seeks to sharpen analytical skills used in policy analysis and to broaden understanding of the experience of individual countries with economic development. Although the EDI's publications are designed to support its training activities, many are of interest to a much broader audience. EDI materials, including any findings, interpretations, and conclusions, are entirely those of the authors and should not be attributed in any manner to the World Bank, to its affiliated organizations, or to members of its Board of Executive Directors or the countries they represent.

The material in this publication is copyrighted. Requests for permission to reproduce portions of it should be sent to the Office of the Publisher at the address shown in the copyright notice above. The World Bank encourages dissemination of its work and will normally give permission promptly and, when the reproduction is for noncommercial purposes, without asking a fee. Permission to copy portions for classroom use is granted through the Copyright Clearance Center Inc., Suite 910, 222 Rosewood Drive, Danvers, Massachusetts 01923, U. S. A.

The backlist of publications by the World Bank is shown in the annual *Index of Publications*, which is available from the Office of the Publisher.

Rick Stapenhurst is a public sector management specialist in the Regulatory Reform and Private Enterprise Division of the World Bank's Economic Development Institute.

Sahr J. Kpundeh is a consultant on governance and anticorruption issues in the Regulatory Reform and Private Enterprise Division of the World Bank's Economic Development Institute.

Library of Congress Cataloging-in-Publication Data

Curbing corruption : toward a model for building national integrity /
   edited by Rick Stapenhurst, Sahr J. Kpundeh.
     p.   cm.—(EDI development studies)
   Includes bibliographical references (p.   ) and index.
   ISBN 0-8213-4257-6
    1. Political corruption. 2. Political corruption—Case studies.
   3. Political corruption—Africa, Sub-Saharan—Case studies.
   I. Stapenhurst, Rick.   II. Kpundeh, Sahr John.   III. Series.
   JF1081.C87   1999
   364.1'323—dc21   98-38593
                                   CIP

Contents

Foreword

The link between governance and economic development is perhaps the most topical issue in the development arena today. The Economic Development Institute (EDI) of the World Bank is a leader in the practical applications of good government principles to development policy. As part of its Governance Program, EDI has facilitated various anticorruption workshops, seminars, and surveys in more than a dozen countries in Africa, Eastern Europe, Latin America, and the Middle East. Participants in these workshops have included politicians, public administrators, leaders from civil society, and representatives from international and bilateral agencies. Workshop and seminar participants have outlined innovative ways to increase transparency and accountability and also reported progress in more traditional reform activities in the civil service, budgeting, and financial management.

This volume contains selections by theorists and practitioners of governance work, with in-depth case studies of corruption in three countries—Tanzania, Uganda, and Sierra Leone. Part I presents lessons of experience. Highlighting the interaction between corruption and economic performance, the chapters discuss a broad range of problems and approaches to reform. Two examples of good practice are showcased—Hong Kong (China) and Singapore—along with the challenging case of Bolivia. Part II considers economic and institutional approaches to anticorruption efforts. It highlights some of the institutions that can play a role in curbing corruption and pays particular attention to the public sector and civil society, including the media. The final chapter in this part proposes a framework for analyzing and strengthening institutions that can curb corruption. Part III presents the three country case studies. Tanzania and Uganda are relative success stories, while Sierra Leone has failed to curb corruption. One noteworthy lesson is that a multifaceted strategy combining economic reforms and the strengthening of "national integrity" institutions is likely to have more success than piecemeal reforms, such as establishing an anticorruption agency without undertaking related reforms. Essential to any strategy, however, is political commitment.

The World Bank's commitment to working with governments to build clean and efficient public sectors is based on the premise that this endeavor is key to sustainable development. Governance thus is figuring prominently in country assistance strategies and in the dialogue between the Bank and its clients. Although strategies to promote good government must be country-specific, policy lessons learned in one setting may be transferable elsewhere. It is toward that end and in the spirit of sharing experience and knowledge that this volume of readings has been prepared. It is dedicated to those individuals seeking to improve economic welfare by creating a better informed and more empowered public.

Vinod Thomas
Director
Economic Development Institute

Acknowledgments

Special thanks are due to Susan Rose-Ackerman, Ladipo Adamolekun, Mark Schacter, Mike Stevens, and Gojko Vuckovic for their useful comments on earlier drafts of this volume and to Winfield Swanson, who provided editorial assistance.

Contributors

B. E. D. de Speville	Consultant; former Commissioner of the Independent Commission against Corruption, Hong Kong
Alan Doig	Professor of Public Service, Liverpool John Moores University
Michael Johnston	Professor of Political Science, Colgate University
Daniel Kaufmann	Manager, Regulatory Reform and Private Sector Development Division, Economic Development Institute, The World Bank
Mohammad M. Kisubi	Consultant; former Senior Advisor to the Ministry of Public Service, Uganda
Sahr J. Kpundeh	Consultant, Economic Development Institute, The World Bank
Petter Langseth	Senior Public Sector Management Specialist, Regulatory Reform and Private Sector Development Division, Economic Development Institute, The World Bank
Tan Ah Leak	Deputy Director, Corrupt Practices Investigation Bureau, Singapore

Alex Muganda   High Commissioner for Tanzania to Zimbabwe;
                        former Secretary to the Presidential Commission
                        against Corruption, Tanzania

Jeremy Pope   Director of Research and former Executive
                        Director, Transparency International, Berlin

Augustine Ruzindana   Chair, Public Accounts Committee, Ugandan
                        Parliament; former Inspector General, Uganda

Shahrzad Sedigh   Consultant, Economic Development Institute,
                        The World Bank

Antonio Sanchez   Senator and former Minister of Finance and
   de Lozada   Comptroller General, Republic of Bolivia

Rick Stapenhurst   Public Sector Management Specialist, Private
                        Sector Development and Regulatory Reform
                        Division, Economic Development Institute,
                        The World Bank

Introduction:
An Overview of the Costs of Corruption and Strategies to Deal with It

Rick Stapenhurst and Shahrzad Sedigh

Corruption is, in its simplest terms, the abuse of power, most often for personal gain or for the benefit of a group to which one owes allegiance. It can be motivated by greed, by the desire to retain or increase one's power, or, perversely enough, by the belief in a supposed greater good. And while the term "corruption" is most often applied to abuse of public power by politicians or civil servants, it describes a pattern of behavior that can be found in virtually every sphere of life.

Controlling corruption is emerging as one of the key concerns within the international community. On March 21, 1996, Latin American countries signed an anticorruption treaty; remaining members of the Organization of American States, including Canada and the United States, are expected to follow suit. The influential Organisation for Economic Co-operation and Development has also adopted a resolution calling for an end to tax breaks for companies that pay bribes in foreign markets. After years of being treated as a taboo subject, the issue has begun to attract serious attention from the aid donor community.

A review of the popular press points to one clear and overwhelming conclusion: corruption is a pervasive phenomenon that can be found in countries of widely varying ideology, economic conditions, and social de-

1

velopment. Although some societies may be more vulnerable than others and may suffer more devastating effects, no country in the world today is immune from corruption's corrosive influence.

Yet for all its seeming prevalence, there is no clear evidence that corruption has become more widespread today. It has been around, in one form or another, from the earliest days of social organization. What *has* changed is that information about corrupt practices has become more available as governments have become increasingly unable to conceal evidence of wrongdoing; the level of public tolerance for corruption has declined; and the spread of democracy seems to afford less fertile ground in which corruption can flourish.

Silvio Wasibord, professor of communications at Rutgers University, argues that "corruption is more visible because of new political and media conditions rather than because the governments of [selected countries] are more corrupt than their predecessors" (Toronto *Globe and Mail*, December 19, 1995). The growth of both the Internet and media conglomerates that are less fearful of taking on repressive regimes has forced corruption out into the open. In numerous countries, vigorous media campaigns have helped keep corruption front and center in the public eye.

Economic change—both domestically and internationally—has also diminished acceptance of corruption. In many developing countries, a growing middle class has shown itself considerably less deferential to authority than its peasant forebears were and less tolerant of the corruption that has traditionally benefited a few wealthy members of the elite while impoverishing the state. At the same time, although increasing economic ties between countries have expanded the opportunities for corruption and bribery, the harsh dictates of the global marketplace are a powerful force against corrupt practices. As ties between North and South multiply, media and other reports suggest that a growing number of businesses find themselves enmeshed in illegal, and costly, bidding wars that have little to do with real competitiveness or comparative advantage. International corporations that are willing to participate in corrupt practices are becoming more aware of the long-term costs of corruption, especially because many of today's chief whistle-blowers are private sector firms.

Where Corruption Occurs

Corruption in public life typically occurs in a few key arenas, regardless of a country's political structure or level of social and economic development.

In general, malfeasance is most likely to occur where the public and private sectors (broadly defined) meet, and especially where there is a direct responsibility for the provision of a desired service or the application of specific regulations or levies. This includes, for example, public procurement and contracting, licensing activities such as the granting of import or export permits, the rezoning of land, and the collection of revenue, whether through taxation or customs duties.

Systems to collect taxes and customs revenues are particularly susceptible to corruption, as the Tanzanian case study in chapter 11 demonstrates. Through bribery and other forms of patronage, a wealthy elite can escape a fair tax assessment or avoid paying taxes altogether. By the same token, customs officials can use the threat of delay or high levies—or the promise of low assessments—to extort funds from business.

Not surprisingly, given the opportunities public office affords the corrupt, corruption is also reported in the appointment or election of public officials of every rank. In some cases, corrupt politicians sell favors to their eager benefactors, regardless of the public good. Politicians may also use their position in power to extort bribes from companies that might otherwise be unwilling to engage in such practices.

Corruption finds expression as well in the appointment of family members, relatives, and friends to public organizations that have profitable monopoly positions in some area of private or public sector activity. Contracting and procurement are other affected areas of government, with those who award the contracts or procure goods and services routinely demanding bribes, kickbacks, percentages, or other "gifts" from those seeking government business and sales.

At a more petty level—but the one that most directly affects an aggrieved public—corruption involves countless underpaid or greedy civil servants who overcharge the public for services such as the granting of drivers' licenses, passports, and business permits. Often these same civil servants are, in turn, paying a perverse form of tithe to their superiors for the right to hold a public sector job and profit from the many opportunities it offers for extortion.

The Costs of Corruption

Clearly, activities like those just described, when practiced on a large enough scale, can significantly harm the social, political, and economic life of any society. Indeed, corruption is damaging if only for the simple reason that it distorts choice. In the public realm, decisions that should be made for the social good, with due regard to the norms of public sector efficiency and sound governance, are instead based on considerations of private gain, with little attention paid to the effects on the wider community. Corrupted decisionmaking distorts the public expenditure process, leading to the funding of inappropriate megaprojects. In effect, public decisionmaking is sold to the highest, best-connected bidder, thereby diverting public funds from more efficient uses and reducing the resources available for legitimate and more productive public use.

Corruption also damages the economic life of a society. Although some argue that it can help grease the wheels of a slow-moving and overregulated economy, there is little doubt that corruption increases the cost of goods and services, promotes unproductive investment in projects that are not economically viable or sustainable, contributes to a decline in standards (for example, in construction and transportation), and can even increase a country's indebtedness and impoverishment. Although the economic costs of corruption are difficult to measure, some studies suggest that they include:

- A 3 to 10 percent increase in the price of a given transaction to speed up the delivery of a government service
- Inflated prices for goods—as much as 15 to 20 percent higher—as a result of government-imposed monopolies
- A loss of as much as 50 percent of government tax revenues because of graft and corruption
- Excessive charges to governments for goods and services because of overbilling on procurement contracts or the purchase of expensive and unnecessary items, with governments paying 20 to 100 percent more than necessary.

Strategies to Deal with Corruption

Experience demonstrates that no single approach to curbing corruption is likely to be effective. Instead, success involves a wide range of strategies, working together as much as possible in an integrated fashion. In general, these strategies must include measures that reduce the opportunity for—and benefits of—corruption, increase the likelihood that it will be detected, and make punishment of transgressors more likely.

Anticorruption programs have essentially two strands. First, appropriate administrative, financial, and economic reforms can minimize the opportunities for corruption. Second, capacity building can strengthen the institutions—the media, parliament, watchdog agencies, and the judiciary, among others—that raise public awareness about corrupt behavior and its costs and/or investigate incidences of corruption.

A successful program often begins with recognition of the scope of the problem and a clear understanding of its causes. This means identifying those areas of public administration where corruption is most likely to occur and being able to isolate and remedy the conditions that have helped it flourish. In some cases, this involves sweeping public sector reform, as is now under way in Bolivia and Uganda. Such reform must include an array of initiatives on lesser and grander scales.

At the working level, reform might mean improved supervision of civil servants to ensure they are not abusing their positions for personal gain. Awareness campaigns that stress both the importance of public service and the costs of corruption (including punishment for offenders) can also be effective and have been successfully employed in a number of economies, including Hong Kong (China) and Singapore. Civil servants can be encouraged to report instances of corruption; however, if such reporting is to take place, it is vital to provide civil servants with appropriate channels for disclosing the misdeeds of their colleagues and superiors.

Another tactic is to limit the discretion available to public servants, so that their behavior—especially when it involves procurement or the granting of licenses and permits—is more subject to established rules and regulations. Procurement practices, which are often the most susceptible to wrongdoing, can also be simplified and made more open, transparent, and competitive. The rules and regulations should be communicated in simple, clear language and made easily accessible to the public and those seeking government services.

Also vital—as demonstrated by the case studies on Tanzania, Uganda, and Sierra Leone (chapters 11, 12, and 13)—is the need to ensure a decent wage for civil servants so that they do not seek to complement their earnings through bribery and extortion. Ensuring livable wages that are competitive with private sector remuneration also helps enable the civil service to attract the best possible pool of qualified people.

At the broader level, more fundamental public sector reforms are often required to reduce corruption, particularly in countries such as Tanzania, where the state has played an intrusive role in social and economic life. Programs with little public support or low policy priority should be eliminated, given that they often exist merely to support the corrupt activities of a few key public officials.

Reforms can also involve the privatization of inefficient parastatals that, because of their monopoly positions, are able to extract huge sums from the public coffers and the private sector. By reducing the degree of interaction between the private and public sectors, privatization directly reduces the opportunities for corrupt behavior. Moreover, the need to operate to a "bottom line" can be a powerful disincentive to engage in the inefficient corrupt practices that are endemic in many parastatals around the world. Deregulating and expanding markets, initiating tax reform, and improving public expenditure management also play a role.

Finally comes enforcement. Enforcement is, to some extent, one of the least efficient ways of reducing corruption because it addresses the problem only after it has occurred. However, enacting and enforcing laws can have a strong deterrent effect and are necessary complements to other preventive efforts.

The case studies of Tanzania, Uganda, and Sierra Leone highlight a variety of enforcement mechanisms and legal measures to deal with corruption, ranging from special bureaus with investigative powers (borrowing heavily from the experiences of Hong Kong [China] and Singapore) to codes of conduct that carry the weight of the constitution behind them. The legal measures designed to control corruption need not be complex, but they must provide for penalties whose costs outweigh the benefits of corruption. For example, they can forbid the awarding or enforcement of contracts, licenses, and permits for corrupt reasons, thereby giving those presented with such a situation a powerful incentive to report the misbehavior. Importantly, the legal system itself needs to be "clean" and perceived as enforcing anticorruption laws.

The examples of Tanzania, Uganda, and Sierra Leone further demonstrate that the organizations charged with investigation or punishment must be invested with the means—both human and financial—to fulfill their mandates. Optimally, they should also enjoy some form of arms-length or independent relationship with the state. The case studies show that organizations that ostensibly have sweeping powers to fight corruption can be rendered ineffective by insufficient resources—often directly related to government control of their budget allocations—and by reporting arrangements that leave them susceptible to central government control.

In all efforts to combat corruption, the commitment of senior elected representatives and other public officials is pivotal, as experience in Bolivia, Hong Kong (China), and Singapore demonstrates. If those who govern a society lack the political will to refrain from corruption and institute change, real reform is difficult to undertake and virtually impossible to sustain.

To some extent, creating this political will and sustaining the momentum for reform depend on a strong civil society that is willing and able to press for change. A strong and active civil society can be a powerful tool for expanding awareness of corruption and, often, a key source of information on corrupt practices. Some parts of civil society can make particularly vital contributions: professional associations of lawyers, accountants, and auditors have expertise in some of the major areas prone to corruption; the private sector can refuse to comply with corruption and report instances of bribery and extortion; and the press can act as a watchdog for the public by reporting frequently on the fight against corruption and exposing the prevalence and costs of wrongdoing. In the end, civil society and its institutions are perhaps the most powerful source of support for public leaders who are genuinely committed to reform and willing to pursue reform efforts in partnership with the many individuals and organizations within society.

Obstacles to Reform

If the elements of successful anticorruption campaigns are, by now, relatively well understood, they are also extraordinarily difficult to undertake and sustain. Any number of factors can contribute to their failure.

For example, the power of any given leader to enact change may be limited, particularly when an entrenched, corrupt elite has held de facto power for generations, is backed by influential factions in the army and the private sector, and possibly enjoys the support of foreign leaders. Moreover, where corruption is pervasive and infects the whole of government machinery, the opportunities to begin reform will be few and the array of obstacles bewildering.

In addition, pressure for reform that stems from the lower ranks of the bureaucracy can be stymied by the absence of political will or interest among higher-level public servants and political officials. At any step of the way, the absence of commitment at the top, or at the bottom, can effectively thwart efforts to reform. Moreover, reform can be imperiled if a recalcitrant elite or public service slows its progress, and if an expectant public interprets the delays as signs of an absence of real commitment to justice.

Just as reform efforts must be broadly supported, they must also be directed at all of those who engage in and benefit from corruption. Campaigns that aim at petty offenders or scapegoat a few members of the elite but do not systematically address corruption soon lose all legitimacy and, by force of example, encourage continued wrongdoing on the part of all members of society.

Reform can also be ineffective if undertaken in a disorganized, poorly coordinated, or ad hoc fashion, or if overreliance on law and enforcement leads to repression and the imposition of another powerful—and most likely corrupt—regime. Laws do have a role to play in punishing transgressors, but they need to be complemented by public awareness campaigns, education, and broadly based reform.

At the same time, organizations charged with enforcing the law, or with investigating corruption and recommending preventive measures, are essential and need adequate staffing and resources. As the example of Tanzania demonstrates, it is not enough to grant enforcement bodies all the formal powers needed to undertake far-reaching anticorruption campaigns. These organizations are ultimately ineffective if they are unable to attract and retain qualified staff or obtain sufficient funds to support investigations and ensure that their recommendations are implemented instead of being subject to the whims of the executive.

Although corruption in Tanzania, Uganda, and Sierra Leone has arisen against different backdrops—for example, Tanzania's relative stability stands in sharp contrast to Uganda's extreme repression and instability—some common threads are evident. It is clear that corruption thrives especially well in a few keys areas of government activity—procurement, revenue collection, the front-line provision of public services, and the daily operations of parastatal organizations. It is apparent as well that poor civil service wages, economic stagnation, authoritarian government, and a bloated state apparatus all induce corruption. Moreover, the three countries share similar obstacles to reform—entrenched elites, an absence of political will, and little understanding of the costs of corruption and the ineffectiveness of laws that cannot be enforced by underresourced anticorruption organizations with flawed mandates, structures, and reporting arrangements.

The strategies to control corruption comprise long-term processes that are as much about changing attitudes and behavior as they are about changing the institutions of a society. Curbing corruption is not merely about ethics and morality; it is about sound governance and the effective, efficient use of public resources for the public good.

Overview of This Volume

In chapter 1 Johnston and Doig consider the political and social context within which anticorruption programs operate. Johnston notes how countries can reach a "low-corruption equilibrium," while Doig highlights the linkages between corruption and development. In chapter 2 Kaufmann presents lessons from comparative analysis of recent literature, dispelling some myths and exposing some biases in anticorruption strategies. The rest of part I is devoted to the experiences of three countries. De Speville summarizes the experience of Hong Kong, China, in chapter 3, and Leak presents the case of Singapore in chapter 4. Both authors highlight the role of anticorruption agencies; de Speville also notes the importance of raising public awareness about the costs of corruption and involving civil society in the fight against corruption. In chapter 5 de Lozada focuses on Bolivia, discussing the linkage between democratic reforms and public accountability and emphasizing the role of the Office of Comptroller General and the importance of financial reforms.

Part II covers some of the key aspects of anticorruption strategies. In chapter 6 Kaufmann highlights the essential economic reforms that should be part of anticorruption strategies. Pope summarizes the main elements of successful strategies in chapter 7, and, in chapter 8, considers ways in which accountability can be enhanced within the public sector. In chapter 9 Kisubi underlines the importance of involving civil society, including the media. In chapter 10 Langseth, Stapenhurst, and Pope pull together these and other elements of an anticorruption strategy to enhance "national integrity systems."

Part III presents three country case studies. Chapters 11 and 12 cover, respectively, Tanzania and Uganda, where comprehensive anticorruption strategies are bringing positive results. Chapter 13 discusses Sierra Leone, where considerably less success has been achieved. The volume concludes with a summary of key lessons about corruption and the most effective means of combating it.

Part I

Lessons of Experience

1

Different Views on Good Government and Sustainable Anticorruption Strategies

Michael Johnston and Alan Doig

This chapter presents two different and sometimes opposing views on the constraints on anticorruption strategies that reformers might encounter. While Alan Doig focuses on the conflicts between and the conflation of good government, good governance, and economic development objectives, Michael Johnston emphasizes the wider political and economic situation that helps sustain a corrupt system as an equilibrium.[1] This equilibrium, argues Johnston in the first section, is endemic to weak institutions also linked to low economic growth. That is why leaders can take on bureaucratic corruption only under specific conditions, and why, if they want their reforms to show results, they should attack the vertical organization and horizontal coordination of corruption, institute checks and balances within government, and ensure adequate salaries for civil servants.

In the second section Doig underlines that although donors have increasingly focused on corruption as a core obstacle to the encouragement of good government, it is usually very difficult to effectively implement anticor-

---

1. Michael Johnston's contribution is a summary of Johnston (1997b). Alan Doig's contribution is based on Doig (1995). Elsa Pilichowski edited this chapter.

ruption strategies, particularly when longer-term political and economic reforms are being promoted at the same time and resources are limited. It is important that practicable, effective, and sustainable means are available to prevent, investigate, and reform corrupt practices.

What Can Be Done about Entrenched Corruption?
An Essay by Michael Johnston

Corruption is not a problem that "happens" to otherwise healthy societies, nor does it necessarily lead to collapse. It is one of a constellation of development problems, endogenous to a situation and often symptomatic of other difficulties. The most serious cases—entrenched political and bureaucratic corruption—are equilibria. They are tightly organized and internally stable, creating and being sustained by conditions of weak political competition, slow and uneven economic growth, and a weak civil society.

Conditions for Entrenched Corruption

Although political and bureaucratic corruption differ, they are both entrenched if they are pervasive, organized, and monopolistic. These three characteristics are not necessarily interrelated, but when they combine, corruption is particularly damaging.

Pervasive corruption is wrongdoing so common—throughout an entire country or a subunit—that there are few practical alternatives to dealing with corrupt officials. Organized corruption involves internal coordination, shared knowledge, and a vertical exchange of benefits. It facilitates an internal economy linking principals and agents. Principals provide protection, make major decisions, and control agents' discretion, powers, and access to shares of the take, while political or bureaucratic agents pay for their spoils through loyal support. Organized corruption closes off clients' political or bureaucratic alternatives, giving the organization more corrupt leverage. It creates a network of operatives sharing not only rewards but also risks; they thus have a stake in protecting corruption, increasing its proceeds, and freezing out critics and holdout agents and clients. Well-organized corruption is a sign that political opposition and bureaucratic checks and balances have been weak for some time. As for monopolistic corruption, it occurs when extensive corruption faces no meaningful political opposition or economic competition. Not only is monopolistic corruption harder to eradicate, but practitioners are able to produce maximum benefits over a considerable period of time.

Entrenched *political* corruption—corruption in mass politics and policy formation, including bribery, extortion, election fraud, abusive patronage, and official intimidation of opposition groups—features the domination of politics by a monopolistic organization or faction, in part through, and reaping large rewards from, corruption. Alam (1995) identifies three kinds of "countervailing actions" that losers from corruption might take: evasive actions to reduce dependency on corrupt officials, direct actions (such as protest and violence) that raise the cost or risk of corruption for officials, and illicit actions that fight corruption with corruption.

Entrenched *bureaucratic* corruption is different in that corrupt bureaucrats do not face full-blown competition from other governments or other agencies performing identical functions. Still, bureaucrats can create lasting and lucrative corruption that feeds on and helps sustain an environment of economic and political dependency. Vertical organization is a significant step toward entrenched corruption. Here, agents share a portion of their take with principals. Specialization can be a source of instability (an official may move to another administration to avoid paying a bribe), but if agencies collude, the result could be smaller individual payments but a much larger take over time.

Entrenched corruption is persistent and difficult to combat not only because of its inner workings, but also because it is embedded in a wider political and economic situation that helps sustain it as an equilibrium. It creates, and depends on, institutional monopolies and the shortage of economic and political alternatives they generate. Institutional monopolies with uncontested control of government—or, in the bureaucracy, collective monopolies (Shleifer and Vishny 1993)—preempt meaningful checks and balances and enjoy virtually unlimited discretion. A paucity of economic alternatives—whether resulting from an extensive state presence in the economy or the weakness of the private economy—means that most individuals, firms, and investors must deal with corrupt officials if they are to do business at all. A lack of political alternatives means that critics of corruption will find it difficult to demand accountability.

Together, such conditions constitute a powerful corruption-sustaining syndrome. Mauro (1997) shows that extensive corruption tends to depress investment and economic growth. Keefer (1996) finds that a lack of credible property and contractual rights—a plausible result of entrenched corruption—shifts investors' focus to quick returns, harming the prospects for sustainable economic development. Keefer and Knack (1995) argue that corruption is part of a syndrome of poor-quality institutions linked to low economic growth. Prolonged slow or negative growth perpetuates the scarcity of economic alternatives, inhibiting the development of new economic activities and political interests while preserving dependency on corrupt officials. Political monopoly power puts civil liberties at risk: elections and trials can be rigged. Intimidation and the perception that corruption is inevitable can deny mass support to reformers; they may conclude that they have nothing to gain and much to lose by remaining in opposition, and they may throw their lot in with the powerful. This state of political and economic fragility seriously weakens civil society, without which even a full set of democratic institutions will not produce accountability. The role of aid partners is definitely to revive civil society and take measures to enhance competition and institutions.

From Entrenched Corruption to a Low-Corruption Equilibrium

Entrenched corruption is not the only possible equilibrium. In some countries corruption is less serious, and opponents have real options. Resistance to corruption is based not just on fear of punishment but also on legitimate norms and traditions shared by contending interests in the economy and politics. Political and economic opportunities are sufficiently plentiful that there is less need to use wealth to buy political power, or to use power to extract wealth in order to get ahead (Huntington 1968; Johnston 1997a). Political officials who oversee bureaucrats know they may lose power because of corruption and ineffective policies. Supervision from above, scrutiny from outside, and structural checks and balances mean that individual officials and small groups do not possess monopoly discretion and find it difficult to organize and coordinate corruption on a large scale. As a result, although corruption occasionally arises, it does not become entrenched.

Countries can move from a high- to a low-corruption equilibrium. Although there is no quick recipe for this transition, it is of manageable scale. The goal is to encourage developments that undermine the monopolies and organization of entrenched corruption while strengthening the forces that elsewhere sustain the low-corruption alternative. Stronger political and economic competition can enhance accountability and create incentives for political leaders to move against corruption. Reduced corruption will encourage economic growth, further broadening economic alternatives and straightening interests in civil society while weakening the political and bureaucratic leverage underlying entrenched corruption.

Although such a process does not require a fully institutionalized democracy, a good start is to guarantee property and contract rights and meaningful civil liberties that allow an independent press and opposition to develop. To broaden political monopolies, one task is to establish independent avenues of appeal against corruption and other abuses, chiefly in the courts but also in the form of investigative agencies, inspectors general, and ombudsmen open to public complaints and scrutiny. In addition, political competition should be institutionalized, creating opportunities for political forces to win significant power through publicly visible processes—and lose power if they fail to act on corruption or other problems.

Although political and bureaucratic corruption can flourish independently, in practice the two are likely to coexist and be interlinked. In fact, the more serious the corruption in either arena, the less likely it is to exist alone. In an interlocked system of entrenched bureaucratic and political corruption, bureaucratic rents can be coordinated and shared across both realms, while monopoly power allows politicians to preempt opposition. Economic policies can maximize dependency on corruption while curtailing competition. There will be few opportunities for direct countervailing actions, short of taking on the entire regime, and illicit responses will require the indulgence of corrupt officials (Alam 1995).

In countries with deeply entrenched corruption, attempts to confront the issue directly are confined to small groups of dissidents willing to mount a fundamental critique of the political order (Johnston and Hao 1995). Where corruption is less entrenched, political leaders may take what McCubbins and Schwartz (1984) call the "fire-alarm" approach. That is, although officials may have both the formal duty and the political incentives to confront bureaucratic corruption, they may do so only sporadically and in response to compelling problems or crises. If networks are sufficiently organized and coordinated, corrupt bureaucrats can respond by covering up their dealings more effectively.

Whatever the model of oversight, political initiatives against bureaucratic corruption will depend on the balance of power between the two realms, and in this competition bureaucrats possess significant resources. For example, political leaders may well tolerate considerable bureaucratic corruption if they share in its spoils or if their own political position is weak or compromised. If bureaucratic corruption gives preference to favored political interests or helps buy off potential opponents, if it provides enough income to bureaucrats to make tax increases less necessary, if corruption cleanups seem likely to mobilize elite opposition, or if the organization and coordination of bureaucratic corruption helps paper over conflicts among bureaucratic factions, then, in the absence of compelling domestic or international pressure to confront corruption, political figures may do little. Reforms that break up the organization or coordination of corruption may produce a disorganized scramble (Elliott 1997) or the kind of independent-monopolies situation (Schleifer and Vishny 1993) likely to be damaging to the economy. Even a dedicated corruption fighter would have to be confident that reforms could survive such a crisis.

Political leaders who draw—and stand to lose—their mandates from institutionalized political competition, however, will have reasons to undertake bureaucratic reform as well as a stronger position from which to do so. Their determination to act may be reinforced if bureaucratic corruption protects a competing power outside the political process or makes the bureaucracy unresponsive and unaccountable.

Once they take on bureaucratic corruption, political leaders must do several things. If bureaucrats are paid so little that they steal to survive, their salaries need to be increased. Politicians should equalize civil servants' pay with what they would earn in the private sector, or use other means, such as a schedule of fees for services, to ensure adequate and fair compensation. Political leaders also need to attack the vertical organization and horizontal coordination of corruption, increasing the independence of agencies from each other or encouraging competition among them. Placing new managers at the head of each major agency and creating powerful inspectors general who are directly accountable to top political leadership might be a step against both vertical organization and horizontal coordination. Finally, leaders can institute checks and balances within government. They can separate routine powers, for example, or in parliamentary systems where full separation is not feasible, create independent courts, oversight bodies, and client advocates. If government can be made accessible to opposition politicians, journalists, and members of the public, then checks and balances will be not only an administrative mechanism to counter corruption but a mechanism with support from powerful forces in society.

Corruption, Good Government, Good Governance, and Economic Development: An Essay by Alan Doig

In December 1989 the United Nations sponsored an interregional seminar on corruption in government, noting that "the problem of corruption in government has come to be recognized universally as a major concern in public management" (United Nations 1990, p. 1). Participants discussed not only "new forms and dimensions of corruption, but also its pervasive effect on government performance, the use of public resources, the general morale in the public services and the legitimacy of the state and the law" (p. 1). Dealing with corruption is now perceived as crucially important: "Corrupt activities of public officials can destroy the potential effectiveness of all types of governmental programs, hinder development, and victimize individuals and groups" (United Nations 1993, p. 4).

Good government provides a responsive governmental and state administrative framework, which facilitates good governance. Although good governance and economic development must be longer-term goals than good government, the former will not be achievable without the latter. According to the British Council (1993), good government in practice would mean:

- A legitimate and representative government, thanks to democratic elections
- An accountable administration and a responsible government characterized by free-flowing information, separation of powers, effective internal and external auditing, low levels of corruption and nepotism, competent officials (including trained public servants), realistic policies, and low defense expenditure
- Governmental respect for human rights, as indicated by freedom of religion and movement, impartial and accessible criminal justice systems, and the absence of arbitrary government power.

Governance, defined as the "use of political authority and the exercise of control over society and the management of its resources for social and economic development," encompasses the "nature of functioning of a state's institutional and structural arrangements, decision-making processes, policy formulation, implementation capacity, information flows, effectiveness of leadership, and the nature of the relationship between rules and the ruled" (Serageldin and Landell-Mills 1991, p. 4). Governance therefore incorporates not only the integrity, efficiency, and economy of government but its effectiveness as measured by the ends to which government organization and activity are directed.

Every society, whether democratic or authoritarian, harbors some form of corruption. However, systemic corruption indicates that resources for public purposes are no longer managed effectively and are appropriated for private gain. Economic development is concerned with the restructuring of state activities and the promotion of macroeconomic policies that in turn provide a favorable environment for private sector investment, initiative, and growth:

- Deregulation to allow trade liberalization and private sector investment
- The removal of controls on inward investment and the promotion of capital market development
- Market-based pricing of the fruits of state-subsidized activities, including food, power, transport, and rents
- Reduced state support of public sector employment or wages and reduction and reorganization of public sector enterprises
- Privatization.

Whatever the source or focus of external pressure for reform, there appears to be a "remarkable consensus" among aid donors and creditors regarding "the need for democracy, less corruption, greater respect for human rights, and 'good governance' or 'good government'" (Riley 1992, p. 4). A synthesized hypothesis would recognize good government as the precondition for good governance and sustainable economic development.

Corruption and Good Government: Constraints on Change

Moves to promote and encourage good government face obstacles when there is no integrated donor approach and occasional conflict between, as well as conflation of, good government, good governance, and economic development objectives. Efforts to improve government may be further constrained by the existing political and economic conditions of countries to which they are directed: "The generation of adjustment out of crisis and donor pressure means that changes in the role and performance of government have to be managed under difficult circumstances where there are political tensions, resistance from the losers in the population, demoralization in the public sector and multiple changes occurring at the same time" (Batley 1994, p. 492).

Furthermore, the absence of a consensus among donors regarding the "best means to achieve policy objectives . . . may cause resentment and uncertainty among aid recipients . . . [and] may allow recipient governments to play donors off against one another. . . . Efforts to promote participation and democratization may also impede economic reform by generating unsustainable demands from newly mobilized interest groups" (Overseas Development Institute 1992, p. 4). Encouraging countries to undertake steps toward good government, therefore, may not be straightforward. The functions of the public sector, the complexities of economic development, and the roles of existing political leaderships have to be considered.

BLOATED PUBLIC SECTORS. Developing countries' state sectors are generally thought to be overstaffed and inefficient, weighed down by procedural and control functions. Critics argue that they employ large numbers of poorly paid, poorly trained officials who have few opportunities for legitimate promotion and financial improvement, and that senior levels are penetrated by special-interest economic groups and political influence. Furthermore, having a large state sector has allowed governments to absorb manpower and given them "a fundamental mechanism for gaining command of society. Broad groups in society had come to depend on the massive state enterprise. . . . The groups which were benefiting from the state enterprise became committed to the elite which was running it. In this sense the elite was creating the basis of its own indispensability" (Cooper 1982, p. 23). Measures to tie politically significant parts of the population to the state through employment have arisen in part from many governments' mistrust of market principles and an independent commercial sector, as well as from their preference for direction and control of the economy.

Developing countries are under pressure from donors to reduce state domination of gross national product and the labor market. Yet rapid retrenchment of personnel and cuts in public expenditure may "leave public enterprises short of funds for vital maintenance, equipment and supplies. . . . A balance must therefore be struck between improved efficiency and better management, on the one hand, and the requirements of proper maintenance and utilization of existing capacity and enterprises, on the other" (Abbott 1993, p. 23). Thus it may be generally accepted that

> governments have frequently and inappropriately overextended the public sector. . . . It would be counterproductive to push private sector expansion too fast and too far. Inefficiency in public monopolies does not necessarily create a case for private monopolies. The mix of state and private sector activity varies, and should vary, with the specifics of individual countries' economic, political and administrative structures. Indeed, many public sector enterprises were set up because the private sector offered inadequate services or no services at all. For external agencies to push national governments too far on this or other such issues, could risk the credibility of otherwise sound programmes. (Commonwealth Secretariat 1989, p. 59)

THE COMPLEXITIES OF ECONOMIC DEVELOPMENT. The assumption that economic development is hindered by the size and inefficiency of the state, as well as by its claims on resources and funding, should be balanced against weaknesses in the private sector's infrastructure and relations with the state, and the time and means necessary for both to evolve to a point where economic development is sustainable. For some countries "the fact that both domestic and overseas private investment, especially in the poorer developing countries, have often fallen rather than risen in response to cuts in public development expenditure" has been compounded by a "squeeze on public sector development spending" (Mosley, Harrigan, and Toye 1991, pp. 303–4). In such circumstances, the demands of economic liberalization may be counterproductive: "True structural adjustment requires the building up of the country's export sectors and associated infrastructure, which in the short term may require more rather than less intervention" (pp. 303–4).

In addition, the private sector may not be in the position to capitalize on economic liberalization. Even if it is, it may not welcome the volatility of the export market, particularly in agricultural or extractive commodities, much as it may not wish to take over state enterprises with their attendant problems of reducing work forces, retraining remaining employees, and replacing old equipment. Private firms may prefer instead to focus on high-value import or franchised brand-name goods or services or exploit the existing regulatory, license, and quota systems to provide short-term gains and, in the longer term, create a commercial class with little interest in good government or economic liberalization. Such constraints and uncertainties will discourage reinvestment and the accumulation of productive capital, as well as encourage corruption and other means of influence to avoid or seek accommodation with unreformed bureaucracies and the arbitrary use of political power.

In Sub-Saharan Africa overregulated and predatory state controls have encouraged entrepreneurial activities that result in fast, large returns intended to avoid penalization and provide the means to "maximise the influence or the power position of the owners" (Dia 1993, p. 23). In Latin America, according to Andreski (1970, pp. 112–13), the impact of fluctuations in the world prices of staple commodities "discourages long-term planning and sound business practices," while inconstant laws and regulations, together with the predilection for evasion, promote get-rich-quick firms over "solid" business. Excessive tariffs combined with uncontrollable mass smuggling create an environment where a majority of businesspeople can be implicated in illegal transactions and where employers are compelled to evade unrealistic social security laws. In Kenya, economic uncertainty has prompted employers to invest profits in land and housing rather than expansion (Cockcroft 1990, p. 160); in the Arab Republic of Yemen, Yemeni working abroad made similar investments because of minimal amounts of land for sale and minimal opportunities for investment in rural areas (Sultan 1993, pp. 381–82).

However, government policies that actively seek to promote economic development or a new economic class may themselves generate new problems. Although Malaysia's New Economic Policy was designed to enhance the role of indigenous Malays in the economy, many used it for immediate personal gain. This example underlines the limitations of private sector contributions for the system's good and the political gamble that policies that create public goodwill and loyalty may also increase the general propensity for rule breaking (Tharan 1979; Sivalingam 1983, p. 429). In the Arab Republic of Yemen the government's measures to deal with its economic problems increased the opportunities for corruption. For instance, officials and businesspeople operated their own market mechanisms to circumvent import restrictions, price controls, and the sale of food and other commodities by state companies to offset private sector exploitation (Sultan 1993, pp. 338–88). In Venezuela fraud hindered rational efforts by the government to stimulate exports through tax incentives; 20 companies were discovered to have claimed millions of dollars in tax credits on nonexistent exports (Little 1992, p. 55). More recently in China, government officials concerned with the stagnant economy and the need to revitalize society relinquished control over resource allocation, increased the autonomy of local authorities to manage investment, and decentralized management of economic enterprises. As a result, old patron-client networks revived, and new patterns of corruption emerged (Gong 1993, pp. 317, 323–24).

UNCOMMITED POLITICAL LEADERS. Another constraint to weeding out corruption may be political leaders who are ambivalent toward reform and its sustainability. Anticorruption rhetoric has been a routine feature of politics, invariably less as a precursor to longer-term reform than as a means to diffuse opposition to the incoming regime, placate external agencies, and secure tenure in office (Gillespie and Okruhlik 1991). As Williams (1987, p. 125) points out, "In too many cases, . . . far from attempting to improve the situation, governments, or at least major parts of them, are the problem. Anticorruption campaigns then degenerate into political rhetoric designed more to appease foreign donors and international financial institutions than to address the major issues."

Olowu (1993, p. 231) comments that in Nigeria "political actors often talk of accountability and integrity but this by itself does not translate into a genuine commitment to detect and penalize unethical behavior. Even when anticorruption agencies are created, they are usually denied the resources needed to achieve their stated purpose. . . . In many cases the codes of ethics they are asked to enforce have no broad-based popular understanding or support." Furthermore, "the preoccupation with panic measures and the creation of *ad hoc* panels and tribunals to replace non-functioning legal institutions for ensuring public accountability have not been particularly helpful." (Olowu 1987, p. 230).

Efforts to fight corruption in other countries, too, have often been only cosmetic. Mexico's government increasingly used anticorruption rhetoric during the 1980s to deflect attention from its economic difficulties. "Indeed, many of the outcries and mobilizations against corruption of the 1980s were staged or triggered by the government in a well-orchestrated effort to use corruption symbolically to divert attention away from the economic difficulties and rejuvenate popular faith in the government" (Morris 1991, p. 122). In Sierra Leone the military government of Valentine Strasser that took power in April 1992 proposed commissions of inquiry, anticorruption squads, and tough legislation. But the laws lacked specific enforcement measures, and plans to establish a permanent independent commission against corruption, revise salaries, provide incentives to public workers, and reorganize the civil service remained unfinished (Kpundeh 1993, p. 242).

Anticorruption rhetoric unmatched by sustainable reform will lead to indifference or cynicism among those outside the political system about the value and sustainability of reform. Where there is political reform— particularly in the short-term proliferation of the trappings of participatory government and decentralization in order to satisfy donor pressure—there is a danger that the widening of involvement, especially among politicians and political activists, will lead to increased competition for patronage and party funding and thus extend and replicate the existing political environment. Indeed, "certain characteristics that are often thought of as increasing representatives, such as multi-party systems that reflect a wide spectrum of interests and open list of proportional representation, may paradoxically cause elected officials to be less responsive to the public interest" (Geddes 1991, p. 389).

Conversely, and equally likely, is an inclination among political leaderships and their client groups (and, on occasion, donors) to resist any expansion of political participation because of the implications for the stability of the state and the potential for social or political turbulence:

> The masses, once aroused, are unwilling to limit their demands to the reforms prescribed by the government. They will tend to broaden out their programme to include demands for far-reaching changes to do-

mestic policies, such as greater political freedom, radical measures to reduce inequalities in income distribution and effective agrarian reform. In many Latin American countries . . . the ruling elite seem well aware of the dangers they would face in the wake of wide-spread popular mobilisation. Indeed, almost all factions of Latin America's bourgeoisie appear to prefer to see their countries slip back into underdevelopment and dependency rather than run the risk of being forced into radical social and economic reforms. (Branford and Kucinski 1988, p. 134)

The Focus of Good Government: Dealing with Corruption

Given political sensitivities, aid donors have tended to soften their demands for good government practices in the political systems (and to a lesser extent in the legal and judicial systems) of recipient countries, advocating good practices more as a preferred condition than a necessary requirement. A much more realizable building block of good governance—and a step that countries receiving foreign aid find hard to dispute—is improving the delivery of public sector services:

> The public sector in many developing countries has been characterised by uneven revenue collection, poor expenditure control and management, a bloated and underpaid civil service, a large parastatal sector that provides poor return on the scarce public funds invested in it and weaknesses in the capacity of core economic agencies to design and implement policies that would address these problems. Not only does this state of affairs contribute to large fiscal deficits requiring adjustment measures, but it also progressively erodes the capacity of the state to provide economic and social services. (World Bank 1992, p. 12)

To make public sector organizations more responsive, effective, and economical, donors routinely require the rationalization of organizational structure, the realignment of activities, and the reduction of staffing levels. This is generally achieved through reliance on markets rather than governments to allocate resources; involvement of end-users in implementing resources; fewer but better-paid public officials; reasonable and clear rules for conduct and more punishment for transgressions; better investment and budget programming; better personnel management; cost-containment measures; moves toward privatization, rationalization, and decentralization; clarification of public enterprise–government relations; transparent decisionmaking; competition for contracts; removal of unnecessary controls and regulations; and transfer of resources toward health and primary education (World Bank 1992; Dia 1993).

Few, if any, such reforms, however, would be effective without complementary preventive and investigative measures against corruption. These might include public service training; staff rotation, particularly in the customs, revenue, and contract-awarding agencies; suitable salary levels; codes of ethics and related disciplinary procedures; watchdog units within departments but reporting to senior ministers; effective organization of decisionmaking and work distribution procedures; effective administrative procedures; task forces, including lawyers, accountants, and engineers, to carry out investigations; the use of publicity and educational programs; and the establishment of anticorruption agencies with extensive investigative powers, a high public profile, honest staff, and governmental support (United Nations 1990). The 8th U.N. Congress also argued for defining the type of offenses that should be made illegal; developing systems for receiving and assessing allegations of corruption and prioritizing the seriousness of cases to be investigated; encouraging the reporting of corruption and establishing ways to reward and protect informants; and improving staff training and motivation, intelligence gathering, and the independence of the investigating agency.

These proposals, however, raise two crucial issues. First, investigation and prosecution may be arbitrary and individualized in organizations where corruption is pervasive. Second, punishment, no matter how desirable, satisfies social demand for retribution more than it serves as a deterrent (Hope 1987, p. 143). Yet reliance on prevention, particularly through codes of conduct and other means of inculcating standards, may be ineffectual without complementary means to police behavior and change practices that the code deems unacceptable (Findlay and Stewart 1992). Increasingly governments with varying degrees of commitment to good government are considering the use of an independent anticorruption agency as a suitable and cost-effective mechanism for pursuing the two functions—prevention and investigation. Such a body could encompass wide cross-sector responsibilities, effectively enforcing reforms or sanctions and liaisoning with key departments to help them complement each other's efforts.

A Model for All Reasons? The Role of an Independent Anticorruption Agency

As a model for fighting unethical and dishonest behavior in government, the Independent Commission against Corruption (ICAC) in Hong Kong,

China, has been the focus of much attention among countries as diverse as Australia and Botswana. Interest stems not only from its operational success, its relative freedom from internal corruption and outside interference, and its ability to attract widespread public support, but also from its apparent capacity to fit into a heterogeneous society with several strong cultural imperatives, as well as its ability to work across both public and private sectors. Although organizationally weighted toward operational investigations, the ICAC also comprises preventive and educational departments as well as intelligence, complaint-handling, and advisory functions.

The ICAC was established in 1974, at a time when the government wanted to retain the confidence of foreign investors, but the main reason for its creation was political. The government expected the public to be more persuaded of effectiveness from an agency independent of the police and civil service than from the current system (Clark 1986, p. 61). From the outset, the ICAC saw its role as extending beyond the investigation of specific cases to identifying major structural factors that gave rise to corrupt behavior, including policy weaknesses, inadequate departmental instructions, unnecessary procedures, inadequate supervision, excessive discretion, unnecessary administrative delays, unenforced laws and regulations, public ignorance of an official's powers, and misuse or abuse of position.

The emergence of the ICAC as a model anticorruption agency under consideration in a number of states does, however, raise questions about its transferability. The ICAC is a particular product of a particular environment. Its resources are ample, its higher echelons have been staffed with seconded and expatriate officers, and it has an intensive selection and training program. It operates within a relatively well regulated administrative culture, under a supportive political and legal framework. It has deliberately developed a highly successful public relations profile, exploiting both mass communications and a media-using population at a time of economic growth:

> One of the special features of the Hong Kong experience has been that the government introduced new legal standards at a time of, and under conditions of, rapid modernisation. . . . Some of these changes might never have occurred were it not for the government's overall policy of promoting Hong Kong as an international business centre. In any event the authorities were singularly fortunate that opposition to the new laws were muted and that the shift to universalistic legal standards occurred when the society and the economy were moving in the same direction. This is not a case of a govern-

ment presiding over a disintegrating economic and social system, or a society verging on collapse. The administrative machine was strong and efficient and able to secure idealistic and talented personnel. Hong Kong also enjoyed an advanced level of economic development that cumulatively permitted successful implementation of the policy. (Clark 1987, pp. 250–51)

For many developing countries, an ICAC may appear to offer not just another layer of expensive control but one whose efforts may be undermined by corrupt or political influence unless it has the necessary political and judicial support. Nevertheless, some countries have already introduced independent agencies, albeit for limited purposes or as a result of specific circumstances. In Zambia a special investigation agency has dealt with malpractice under exchange control and banking legislation. Zimbabwe established an investigation unit within the Ministry of Finance to deal with exchange control, banking, and import/export and trading offenses. In Mexico continuing public concern about corruption, until the government used the issue to deflect criticism from itself (Morris 1991, pp. 122–23), led the government to set up a department responsible for receiving allegations about corrupt officials; adjudicating in allegations of corruption involving contracts; monitoring the possibility of corruption in the National Solidarity Programme (designed to develop infrastructure, services, and agriculture at the community level) through locally elected "control and vigilance officers" on locally elected Solidarity Committees; and promoting improvements in public service with a complaints procedure and free telephone services (Vazquez Nava 1992).

While the ICAC model may be too expensive and too politically threatening for many countries, and other examples of independent agencies may be too limited or too constrained by departmental control, an anticorruption agency provides an immediate building block for good government, as long as its agenda and focus are determined from the outset after internal and external consultation. Setting up such an agency is probably less costly, time-consuming, and prone to substantial slippage than other administrative reforms needed to redraft and update legislation and the judicial infrastructure, as well as to train, organize, and increase the accountability of a reduced number of public sector departments. Still, creating a semi-autonomous, externally led and funded agency is a short-term solution that may well raise resentment among other departments, spark political interference, and possibly cause the loss of experienced personnel to other organizations (Demongeot 1994; Dia 1993).

An independent anticorruption agency should be located centrally within the public sector, preferably close to the treasury or the director of public prosecutions, have clear guidelines on the selection and tenure of senior personnel as well as on operational responsibilities and reporting procedures, and be provided a dedicated budget. Being part of a limited "'cross-executive corps' of senior policy and programme managers" promoted on merit from within the civil service (Demongeot 1994, p. 481) would help create "islands of competence within the bureaucracy and [concentrate] advocates of further reform strategically inside government. Though [these advocates] lose many battles, they rarely disappear from the scene completely" (Geddes 1991, p. 387).

Experienced personnel should be drawn from key departments such as the treasury, the central bank, the central audit office, and the foreign office. A posting to the agency should be part of the career progression of such personnel, or a secondment designed to bring in and later transmit expertise and help develop networks outward. Agency training should be underpinned both by cascade training from outside consultants and by regularly arranging regional or overseas training for senior management, preferably with professional organizations, to maintain morale and professionalism.

An independent corruption-fighting agency should also agree to regular formal relations with other agencies, such as the police and prosecuting authorities, to be able to draw on competent staff as needed and to reinforce its networking and information-gathering activities. Its choice and rotation of such staff should enable the agency to balance its activities, keeping a flexible approach to staffing levels and avoiding a tendency to become overly committed to policing and investigative functions. Not only does this tendency make an agency heavily dependent on the integrity of the judicial system for its results and on the tolerance of the political leadership for its continued independence, but it can lead the agency to focus its financial and human resources on the costly pursuit of cases. With the inevitability of fraud and corruption, such a focus on investigation, while essential to demonstrating robust competence in deterring and potentially prosecuting corruption, is of less long-term value than structural reform—focusing on procedures, control systems, accountability, and the exercise of discretionary authority. (For a fuller description of Hong Kong, China's, ICAC, see chapter 3; for a review of Singapore's experience with its Corrupt Practices Investigation Bureau, see chapter 4.)

A more effective approach would, depending on country-specific issues, be to balance features of an ICAC with those of the inspector generals (IGs) in the state and federal governments of the United States. As internal rather than external units, and without the political or legal framework of an ICAC, IGs seek to bridge preventive and investigative functions within the departments whose activities they monitor. They were established to combine and coordinate investigative, auditing, and sanctioning powers that do not replace established lines of operational authority, but rather allow for independent intervention and evaluation in a number of areas, including auditing; promoting economy, efficiency, and effectiveness in reaching departmental goals; enforcing rules and laws; and preventing fraud and waste.

IGs usually formally report their findings to their department and to external agencies at the same time. IGs tend to concentrate on the more interesting and quantifiable investigative work, but they also perform an evaluation and preventive function that could be much more effective in battling corruption in the long-term. "Instead of participating in programme reviews on a *post-hoc* basis, after the damage already has been done, capacity building would require a more active role for the IGs at the beginning of the legislative and regulatory process," with the emphasis on anticipating and preventing the circumstances that gave rise to corruption and fraud (Light 1993, p. 194; see also Mckinney and Johnston 1986). (For a review of the role of Uganda's Inspector General of Government, see chapter 12.)

Conclusion

Anticorruption agencies will require both donor cooperation and coordination over a number of years to provide effective support, not only to establish the agency but also to sustain its operation. Such support is essential because corruption should not necessarily be associated with political modernization, nor is corruption doomed as a political system matures. According to Werner (cited in Doig 1995), "Corruption alters its character in response to changing socio-economic cultural and political factors. As these factors effect corruption, so does corruption affect them. Significantly, because corruption is in equilibrium, the concept of entropy is not applicable. Simply put, corruption may be controlled through alterations of its character but, most importantly, not destroyed." Thus it may be difficult to perceive a public administration aspiring to, and possibly sustaining, acceptable levels of honesty and efficiency in an environment arising from conditions of excessive indebtedness and inflation, chronic unemployment, abject standards of living, and serious civic strains. However, arguing that corruption is a mere result of underdevelopment risks "embracing a rude evolutionism which envisages a proportionate decline in the volume of abuse with each percentage improvement in GDP [gross domestic product]" (Theobald 1990, p. 164).

Given the issues relating to political and economic change, corruption is unlikely to disappear or diminish. The establishment of properly focused, independent anticorruption agencies may effectively promote probity in government and protection of state income and expenditure, build up a public service ethic and encourage better administrative procedures, offer a means of publicly redressing wrongdoing, and promote good practice across the public sector, thus beginning to make the machinery of government work more productively and efficiently with a concomitant benefit of improving the reputation and performance of the public sector. Such goals will be achieved only gradually and incrementally, but the use of an anticorruption agency may offer a catalyst and a building block with a number of complementary roles that, in the immediate future, may offer donors a sustainable anticorruption strategy to help progress toward good government.

References

Abbott, G. C. 1993. *Debt Relief and Sustainable Development in Sub-Saharan Africa.* Aldershot, U.K.: Edward Elgar.

Alam, M. S. 1995. "A Theory of Limits on Corruption and Some Applications." *Kyklos* 48(3):419–35.

Andreski, Stanislas. 1970. *Parasitism and Subversion: The Case of Latin America.* London: Weidenfeld and Nicolson.

Batley, Richard. 1994. "The Consolidation of Adjustment: Implications for Public Administration." *Public Administration and Development* 14(5):489–505.

Branford, Sue, and Bernardo Kucinski. 1988. *The Debt Squads.* London: Zed Books.

British Council. 1993. *Development Priorities: Good Government.* London.

Clark, David. 1986. "Corruption in Hong Kong—The ICAC Story." *Corruption and Reform* 1(1).

———. 1987. "A Community Relations Approach to Corruption: The Case of Hong Kong." *Corruption and Reform* 2(3):235–57.

Cockcroft, Lawrence. 1990. *Africa's Way.* London: I B Taurus.

Commonwealth Secretariat. 1989. "Reinforcing International Support for African Recovery and Development." In Bade Onimode, ed., *The IMF, the World Bank, and the African Debt.* London: Zed Books.

Cooper, M. N. 1982. *The Transformation of Egypt.* London: Croom Helm.

Demongeot, Patrick. 1994. "Market-Oriented Approaches to Capacity Building in Africa." *Public Administration and Development* 14(5):479–87.

Dia, Mamadou. 1993. *A Governance Approach to Civil Service Reform in Sub-Saharan Africa*. Technical Paper 225. Washington, D.C.: World Bank.

Doig, Alan. 1995. "Good Government and Sustainable Anti-Corruption Strategies: A Role for Independent Anti-Corruption Strategies?" *Public Administration and Development* 15(2):151–65.

Elliott, Kimberly A. 1997. "Corruption as a Global Policy Problem: Overview and Recommendations." In Kimberly A. Elliot, ed., *Corruption and the Global Economy*. Washington, D.C.: Institute for International Economics.

Findlay, M., and A. Stewart. 1992. "Implementing Corruption Prevention Strategies through Codes of Conduct." *Corruption and Reform* 7(1):67–85.

Geddes, Barbara. 1991. "A Game-Theoretical Model of Reform in Latin American Democracies." *American Political Science Review* 85(2):371–92.

Gillespie, K., and G. Okruhlik. 1991. "The Political Dimension of Corruption Cleanups: A Framework for Analysis." *Comparative Politics* 24(1):77–95.

Gong, T. 1993. "Corruption and Reform in China: An Analysis of Unintended Consequences." *Crime, Law and Social Change* 19(4):311–27.

Hope, K. R., Sr. 1987. "Administrative Corruption and Administrative Reform in Developing Countries." *Corruption and Reform* 2(2):127–47.

Huntington, Samuel. 1968. *Political Order in Changing Societies*. New Haven, Conn.: Yale University Press.

Johnston, Michael. 1997a. "Public Officials, Private Interests, and Sustainable Democracy: Connections between Politics and Corruption." In Kimberly A. Elliott, ed., *Corruption and the Global Economy*. Washington, D.C.: Institute for International Economics.

———. 1997b. *What Can Be Done about Entrenched Corruption?* Washington, D.C.: World Bank.

Johnston, Michael, and Yufan Hao. 1995. "China's Surge of Corruption." *Journal of Democracy* 6(4):80–94.

Keefer, Philip. 1996. "Protection against a Capricious State: French Investment and Spanish Railroads, 1845–75." *Journal of Economic History* 56(1):170–92.

Keefer, Philip, and Stephen Knack. 1995. "Institutions and Economic Performance: Cross-Country Tests Using Alternative Institutional Measures." *Economics and Politics* 7(3):207–27.

Kpundeh, Sahr. 1993. "Prospects in Contemporary Sierra Leone." *Corruption and Reform* 7(3):237–47.

Light, P. C. 1993. *Monitoring Government*. Washington, D.C.: Brookings Institution.

Little, Walter. 1992. "Political Corruption in Latin America." *Corruption and Reform* 7(1):41–66.

Mauro, Paolo. 1997. "The Effects of Corruption on Growth, Investment, and Government Expenditure: A Cross-Country Analysis." In Kimberly A. Elliott, ed., *Corruption and the Global Economy.* Washington, D.C.: Institute for International Economics.

McCubbins, Matthew D., and T. Schwartz. 1984. "Congressional Oversight Overlooked: Police Patrols vs. Fire Alarms." *American Journal of Political Science* 28: 165–79.

Mckinney, J. B., and Michael Johnston. 1986. *Fraud, Waste and Abuse in Government.* Philadelphia: ISHA Publications.

Morris, S. D. 1991. *Corruption and Politics in Contemporary Mexico.* Tuscaloosa, Ala.: University of Alabama Press.

Mosley, Paul, Jane Harrigan, and J. F. J. Toye. 1991. *Aid and Power: The World Bank and Policy-Based Lending.* Vol. 1. London: Routledge.

Olowu, Dele. 1987. "Bureaucratic Delay and the Prospects for Regeneration in Nigeria." *Corruption and Reform* 2(3):215–33.

———. 1993. "Governmental Corruption and Africa's Democratization Efforts." *Corruption and Reform* 7(3):227–36.

Overseas Development Institute. 1992. *Briefing Paper: Aid and Political Reform.* London.

Riley, S. 1992. "Political Adjustment? Democratic Politics and Political Choice in Africa." Centre for African Studies seminar, University of Liverpool, U.K.

Schleifer, Andrei, and Robert W. Vishny. 1993. "Corruption." *Quarterly Journal of Economics* 108(3):599–617.

Serageldin, Ismail, and Pierre Landell-Mills. 1991. "Governance and the External Factor." In World Bank, *Proceedings of the World Bank Annual Conference on Development Economics.* Washington, D.C.

Sivalingam, S. 1983. "Bureaucratic Corruption in Malaysia." *Philippine Journal of Public Administration* 27(4):418–35.

Sultan, N. A. 1993. "Bureaucratic Corruption as a Consequence of the Gulf Migration: The Case of North Yemen." *Crime, Law and Social Change* 19(4):379–93.

Tharan, S. 1979. "Systems Corruption and the New Economic Policy." *Philippine Journal of Public Administration* 23(1):39–60.

Theobald, Robin. 1990. *Corruption, Development, and Underdevelopment.* London: Macmillan.

United Nations, Department of Technical Cooperation for Development and Centre for Social Development and Humanitarian Affairs. 1990. *Corruption in Government: Report of an Interregional Seminar, The Hague, The Netherlands, 11–15 December 1989.* New York.

United Nations, Crime Prevention and Criminal Justice Department. 1993. *Crime Prevention and Criminal Justice in the Context of Development: Realities and Perspectives of International Cooperation: Practical Measures against Corruption.* Vienna.

Vazquez Nava, M. E. 1992. "Controlling Corruption as a Social Responsibility." In *Proceedings of the 5th International Anti-Corruption Conference.* Amsterdam: Kluwer Law and Taxation.

Williams, R. 1987. *Political Corruption in Africa.* Aldershot, U.K.: Gower.

World Bank. 1992. "Governance and Development." Washington, D.C.

2

Anticorruption Strategies: Starting Afresh? Unconventional Lessons from Comparative Analysis

Daniel Kaufmann

One of the reasons why governmental corruption has grown to be pervasive in Africa today is primarily because much effort has been spent to remedy the problem rather than to understand it.

— Dele Olowu (1993, p. 227)

Although the insightful remark above refers specifically to Africa, superficial remedies for corruption have abounded in all regions of the world. It is now time to step back and analyze the root causes of corruption. Anticorruption rhetoric appears to be on the rise among governments in the North and South alike, often as a lip-service response to the increasing activism of civil society and the more explicit determination of some in the international community to do something about corrupt behavior. This does not mean that no country has undertaken serious efforts against corruption. But on the bandwagon of pronouncements, decrees, and special governmental anticorruption units are many whose commitment to addressing the problem is seriously in doubt.

Consider the very recent case of Kenya, where prevalent corruption and its negative macroeconomic consequences impelled the International Monetary Fund to suspend its lending in August 1997. In October, on the heels of mounting pressure from civil society and the international community, the president of Kenya issued pronouncements against corruption. As a follow-up to the president's remarks, the Office of the Attorney General released the following statement: "The Government has this morning formed an anticorruption squad to look into the conduct of the anticorruption commission, which has been overseeing the anticorruption task-force, which was earlier set to investigate the affairs of a Government ad hoc committee appointed earlier this year to look into the issue of high-level corruption among corrupt Government Officers" (*The Daily Nation*, October 28, 1997).

This may be an extreme example of how not to address the problem of corruption. Nevertheless, the press has reported many similar statements and decisions in recent years in countries in Asia, Latin America, and the former Soviet Union. Unfortunately, when dressed in more sophisticated clothes, efforts like these may be welcomed by some experts and officials in the international community. After all, the payoff for corrupt politicians to engage in rhetoric about eliminating corruption is now rather high, and the pressure on the donor community to show visible results is also mounting.

One of the challenges at this juncture is distinguishing between a seriously committed program to control corruption, on the one hand, and politically convenient rhetoric, on the other. To do so, it is critical that we understand the fundamental causes of corruption, as well as the preparedness and commitment of a government to tackle these. But hampering the struggle to control corruption are many misconceptions, biases, and ambiguities regarding what constitutes the essential pillars of an anticorruption strategy. This chapter contributes to the debate by analyzing some of these prevailing biases and misconceptions, by providing emerging evidence and results of data analysis on the main determinants of corruption, and by putting forth some principles for designing anticorruption strategies. It attempts to focus squarely on the fundamentals that may determine the prevalence of corruption in a country, moving away from the "quick fixes"—institutional or other—that are currently in vogue.

The Anticorruption Struggle at a Crossroads

First, it is important to place the corruption issue in perspective. Credit is due upfront: the anticorruption advocacy movement has been enormously successful over the past few years. Recognition that corruption is a problem is far more widespread today, as is the involvement of civil society in many places. The international community—and some countries in particular—has been increasingly willing to take action. The role of domestic and international nongovernmental organizations (such as Transparency International) has been key to raising awareness and involving civil society.

The challenge of addressing corruption is now entering a crucial second stage: design and implementation of strategies and concrete actions that are likely to yield durable results. This requires looking at the fundamental causes of corruption in depth and with open minds, avoiding counterproductive biases. These biases are likely to be compounded by the vested interest of some corrupt governments in adopting politically palatable anticorruption platforms in order to appear active in addressing the problem.

The major biases to guard against include:

- *Anti-business bias.* Blaming businesspeople has become a useful rationalization. It stems from the "grease" and "speed money" literature (see next section), as well as from the notion that business interests lobby against the criminalization of bribery abroad. Conventional wisdom is that the whole business sector benefits from its ability to get around excessive regulations (with bribes being the "grease that oils the wheels of development"). Some even argue that business bribery is beneficial to development. This bias works against the logic of collective action to fight corruption and thus against concerted action involving the business sector as an interested party.
- *Tackling-the-symptom bias.* Tackling the symptom, instead of identifying the root cause, involves thinking that the solution is to catch and jail a target number of criminals, for example, or to pass another anticorruption law in the country. Addressing a problem by single-mindedly treating the symptoms is fraught with pitfalls, as governments discovered when they tried to fight inflation by instituting price controls.
- *Quick-fix bias.* Attaining some concrete results promptly is important if civil society is to maintain its momentum in fighting corruption. At the same time, interventions that are insufficiently thought-through ("quick and dirty") run the risk of being counterproductive, as the opening quotation by Olowu attests. The incentive structure for donors and domestic politicians sometimes encourages them to show some quick and visible action, whether or not it produces meaningful, long-lasting results. But are they addressing the real fundamentals?

And if the general public at first does not always clearly see these fundamentals as directly associated with corruption, will a bias emerge against focusing on the less visible, more indirect, yet crucial determinants of corruption?

- *"Injection" bias.* Like the failed Development Finance Corporations' institutional response to the perceived lack of term credit for development in the 1970s, we may face a similar danger today in controlling corruption: injection of resources for stand-alone institutional initiatives, such as watchdog bodies, new charters, and so forth, which may be detrimental to more comprehensive change in the corruption-conducive environment.

- *Anti-counterfactual bias.* Mistaken conclusions often arise from analysis in the absence of proper counterfactuals and controls. One example is ascribing success to anticorruption watchdog bodies in Botswana, Singapore, and other heralded cases by focusing on the details of these watchdogs themselves, without considering the impact of fundamental reforms in the broader environment.

- *Rhetoric bias.* Long proclamations, pronouncements, exhortations, declarations, conferences, and communiqués against corruption abound nowadays. For action, it is imperative to move beyond awareness-raising to in-depth, rational analysis of the evidence at hand and then to appropriate design and implementation of programs. It is a myth that in the sensitive area of corruption, data are virtually impossible to come by.

- *Mechanistic toolkit bias.* Recognition that both the forms of corruption and the relative importance of the various determinants of corruption vary across countries is key to designing programs that are relevant to each particular setting.

- *"Christmas tree" bias.* Instead of identifying the main causes of corruption in a country and prioritizing among them, government leaders may propose too vast an array of reforms. It is a mistake to believe that an ideal program is so fine-tuned, detailed, and comprehensive as to contain many scores of measures and initiatives.

- *Bias against economic reforms.* Some researchers argue that economic reforms accentuate corruption. Others imply that such reforms are a neutral tool in addressing corruption: in the long list of measures suggested to attack the problem, economic reforms are often omitted or included only as an afterthought. This bias is related to the tackling-the-symptom and quick-fix biases in that all ignore the need to address the fundamentals. Opposition to economic reforms has at times also been fueled by insufficient attention to the role of incentives in understanding the prevalence of corruption and possible remedies.

An Empirical Challenge to the "Grease" and "Speed Money" Arguments

[The King] shall protect trade routes from harassment by courtiers, state officials, thieves, and frontier guards . . . [and] frontier officers shall make good what is lost. . . . Just as it is impossible not to taste honey or poison that one may find at the tip of one's tongue, so it is impossible for one dealing with government funds not to taste, at least a little bit, of the King's wealth.

— From the treatise "The Arthashastra" by Kautilya
(chief minister to the king in ancient India),
circa 300 BC to AD 150

The quotation above attests to the existence of corruption in ancient times. Yet it also illustrates that even then corruption was regarded as corrosive to the development of the state and required specific measures in response. The king's adviser perceptively hinted at the link between illiberal trade, bureaucratic harassment at the border, and corruption. And he understood that corruption encompassed far more than bribery: he explicitly addressed the theft of public revenues.

In more recent times a contrasting view has emerged, holding that corruption may not be inconsistent with development and at times may even foster it. Proponents of this contemporary view wrap corruption in a cloud of ambiguity. They suggest, for example, that the definition of corruption varies among cultures, implying that what is perceived as corruption in the West would be interpreted differently within the customs of emerging economies (see box 2.1). Revisionists also characterize corruption's effects on economic growth as ambiguous, drawing on the fact that some of the Asian "tigers" experienced until recently both phenomenal growth and high levels of corruption. Finally, the effects of market reforms on corruption are said to be ambiguous.

A central theme of the "grease-the-wheels" argument is that bribery can be an efficient way of getting around burdensome regulations and ineffec-

Box 2.1 Are Poorer Countries Corrupt and Richer Countries Clean?

"Cultural relativist" rationales that explain away the differences in corruption across countries are being discredited (and seen as paternalistic). Even in traditional settings the cultural norms of gift-giving are distinguishable from what would be regarded as abusive corrupt practices anywhere. The view that corruption can be controlled only when a country is fully industrialized is also being challenged. Although the extent of administrative and bureaucratic corruption is generally inversely correlated to a country's level of development, there are large variations in the incidence of corruption among countries at similar levels. And development does not exempt countries from the problem: in 1997 the Transparency International corruption index ranked Chile, the Czech Republic, Malaysia, Poland, and South Africa as "cleaner" than industrialized countries such as Greece and Italy. It is worth noting that this index focuses on administrative and bureaucratic corruption. It does not incorporate measures of political corruption (where some industrialized countries fare poorly), nor does it measure the propensity of investors from industrialized countries to bribe abroad.

More generally, the determinants of corruption in developing countries are manifold and complex. Our ongoing research suggests that institutions (including the rule of law and protection of property rights), civil liberties, governance (including the degree of professionalization of the civil service), and economic policies, as well as other variables specific to each country (such as size), appear to matter (see Kaufmann and Sachs forthcoming). This chapter gives special emphasis to understanding the effects of economic policy on corruption, yet it underscores that other factors also play an important role. Furthermore, the economic and noneconomic factors are not independent from each other. For instance, the implementation of economic reforms often strengthens those constituencies that spearhead legal and institutional reforms.

tive legal systems. This rationale has not only inspired sophisticated academic models but also legitimized the behavior of private companies that are willing to pay bribes to get business. On closer examination, this argument is full of holes. It ignores the enormous discretion that many politicians and bureaucrats, particularly in corrupt societies, have over the creation, proliferation, and interpretation of counterproductive regulations. Thus instead of corruption greasing the squeaky wheels of a rigid administration, it becomes the fuel for excessive and discretionary regulations. This is one mechanism whereby corruption feeds on itself.

A sophisticated economic variation of the "grease-is-positive" argument is the notion that bribery allows supply and demand to operate. This view maintains that under competitive bidding for a government procurement contract, the highest briber will win—and the firm with the lowest costs will be able to afford the highest bribe. That is theoretically elegant but wrong. First, by focusing solely on bribery, this argument fails to take into account that corruption represents a theft of public resources, impairing macroeconomic stability. Furthermore, the recipients of bribes tend to siphon these funds into overseas accounts. Nigeria, for example, has in this way lost billions from its budget over the past decades. Second, it is wrong to assume that the highest bidding capability stems from cost-efficiency; instead it is often associated with substandard quality. In Ukraine a construction firm that bid US$10 per square meter for tiling a major public building was immediately disqualified because the contractor had dared bid less than the "minimum" cost of US$30 per square meter. The winner of the contract was hardly the most cost-effective firm! Third, politicians rarely subject the object of an illegal payoff to competitive bidding; rather, they seek bribes discreetly from partners they trust to maintain secrecy. Fourth, viewing bribes as a mechanism for equalizing supply and demand misses the fact that many public goods ought not to be allocated to the highest bidder. The aim of antipoverty programs is to allocate resources according to the *needs* of the recipients instead. Finally, the supply-and-demand view of corruption assumes that bribers gets the goods they pay for. This is often not the case, for corrupt transactions cannot be enforced through a court of law.

One school of "corruption apologists" argues that bribery can enhance efficiency by cutting the considerable time needed to process permits and paperwork. The problem with this "speed money" argument lies in the presumption that both sides will actually stick to the deal and not demand further bribes. In India one high-level civil servant who had been bribed could not process an approval any faster because of the multiple bureaucrats involved in the process, yet he willingly offered to slow the approval process for rival companies.

Even in societies where myriad counterproductive regulations have been created in order to extract bribes, there should be a core of laws and regulations that serve productive social objectives. Simple and transparent building codes, sensible environmental regulations, clear regulations to assure the soundness of the banking system, and stringent regulations on the trading of nuclear materials are necessary in any society. The corruption-as-grease argument is particularly insidious in this context, because bribes will serve to override such regulations and harm social aims. For instance, illegal logging in tropical rainforests can be the result of illicit payments to officials.

Another factor that contributes to bribery is politicians' discretion in limiting the access of potential competitors to the market of the briber. Scandals of this sort have occurred in the energy sector in Russia and Ukraine. Unprecedented amounts of "grease" in these cases strengthen gigantic monopolistic structures. The corrupt practices inherent to poorly supervised financial systems and insider lending have contributed to macroeconomic crises in Albania, Bulgaria, and, very recently, some countries in East Asia.

Bribing and rent-seeking also exact a significant economic cost. Talent is misallocated because jobs with the potential to collect lucrative graft attract people who otherwise would accept the more modest financial rewards of truly productive occupations. Corrupt bureaucrats make poor technological decisions by favoring nonstandard, complex, and expensive capital-intensive projects that make it easier to skim significant sums. A large defense or infrastructure contract may thus be favored over the construction of hundreds of primary schools and health clinics. Even more detrimental to development are the many unproductive "white elephant" projects that enrich public officials and suppliers; the recent commission of four incinerators in Lagos, Nigeria, none of which works properly, is one example. Furthermore, entrepreneurs and officials who engage in corrupt activities costs enormous amounts in lost time and productivity. Negotiating deals and illicit payments, ensuring their secrecy, and guarding against the ever-present risk of nondelivery of the promised signatures and permits are time-intensive activities, as is the frequent need to renegotiate or pay an additional bribe to another bureaucrat. All of these activities come at the expense of productively running firms and governments.

Indeed, evidence from various countries indicates a positive relationship between the extent of bribery and the amount of time that an enterprise's manager spends with public officials. A 1996 survey of more than 1,500 enterprises in 49 developing and industrialized countries showed that in Ukraine, for example, firm owners who pay high bribes have to spend almost one-third more time with bureaucrats and politicians than do firm owners who pay little in bribes. Those high-bribing firms also need to spend 75 staff weeks per year of (nonowner) administration time in deal-

Figure 2.1 The Relationship between Business Managers' Time Spent with Bureaucrats and the Frequency of Bribery

Time spent with bureaucrats (percent)

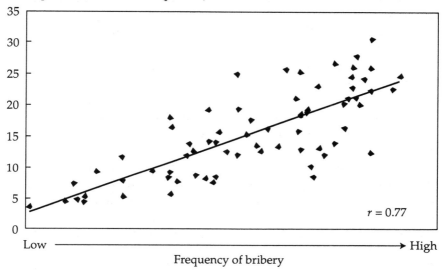

Frequency of bribery

Note: Data points represent country averages, based on a 1996 survey of more than 3,600 firms in 69 developing and industrialized countries. The data do not reflect an institutional endorsement of any particular country or index.
Source: Kaufmann and Wei (forthcoming).

ing with officials, as compared with a yearly average of 22 staff weeks for low-bribing firms. Moreover, cross-country data for more than 3,600 firms in 69 countries indicates that in countries with a higher incidence of bribery, firms tend to spend a higher share of management time with bureaucrats (see figure 2.1). In addition, the 1996 survey provides evidence that where bribing is more prevalent, firms tend to have higher capital and investment costs (see figure 2.2).

The data offer insight into the complex interactions among regulatory interventions, regulatory discretion, and the extent and costs of bribery. Calculations show, for example, that in settings with more regulatory and bureaucratic interference in business, the incidence of corrupt practices is significantly higher (see figure 2.3). Furthermore, the higher the degree of regulatory discretion, the higher the incidence of bribery of officials (see

Figure 2.2 The Relationship between the Cost of Capital and the Frequency of Bribery

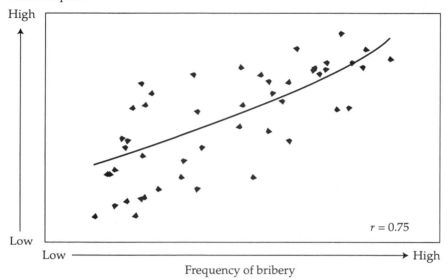

Cost of capital

High

Low

Low ──────────────────────────────→ High

$r = 0.75$

Frequency of bribery

Note: Data points represent country averages, based on a 1996 survey of more than 1,500 firms in 48 developing and industrialized countries. The data do not reflect an institutional endorsement of any particular country or index.
Source: Global Competitiveness Survey conducted by the World Economic Forum, 1996.

figure 2.4). Surveys carried out in some countries of the former Soviet Union show that heavy, discretionary regulations and taxes are associated with the need to pay high bribes to survive. That situation generates a high cost of doing business. Bribery as a strategy, on balance, does not reduce the firms' management time "captured" by local politicians and bureaucrats, nor does it reduce their costs of investing. To the contrary, bribery is fueled by bureaucratic discretion in imposing regulations, fees, licenses, taxes, and tariffs.

The evidence is therefore emerging quite clearly: corruption is negatively associated with developmental objectives everywhere. Opportunistic bureaucrats and politicians who try to maximize their take without regard for the ramifications on the size of the overall "pie" may account for the par-

Figure 2.3 The Relationship between Bribery and State Regulatory Intervention in Business

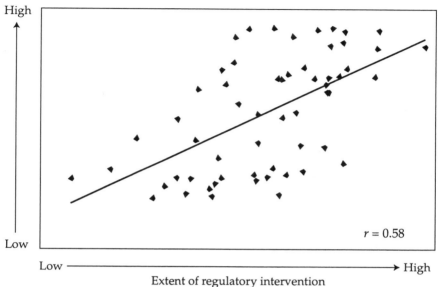

Frequency of bribery

r = 0.58

Low ——————————————————————→ High

Extent of regulatory intervention

Note: Data points represent country averages for 59 developing and industrialized countries in 1997. The data do not reflect an institutional endorsement of any particular country or index.

Source: Global Competitiveness Survey conducted by the World Economic Forum, 1997.

ticularly adverse effect corruption has in some countries of Africa, Asia, and the former Soviet Union. Indeed, a survey of high-level officials from the public sector and civil society in emerging economies offers complementary evidence (see the appendix to this chapter). Respondents rated public sector corruption as the most severe developmental obstacle facing their country, with no significant differences across regions. Everywhere, elite policymakers opined that corruption, far from being a lubricant of development, was development's most formidable impediment.

Data and research showing the deleterious effects of corruption on growth have been mounting. A recent study found that a corrupt country is likely to achieve aggregate investment levels of almost 5 percent less than a rela-

Figure 2.4 The Relationship between Corruption and the Regulatory Discretion of Bureaucrats

Country corruption

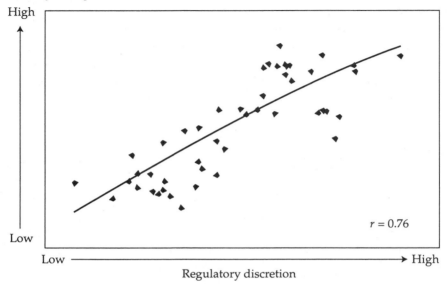

Note: Data points represent country averages for 48 developing and industrialized countries in 1997. The data do not reflect an institutional endorsement of any particular country or index.

Source: Corruption data from Transparency International; regulatory discretion data from the Global Competitiveness Survey conducted by the World Economic Forum.

tively uncorrupt country and to lose about half a percentage point of growth in gross domestic product per year (Mauro 1996). And there is evidence that corruption slows foreign direct investment; investing in a relatively corrupt country, as compared with an uncorrupt one, is equivalent to an additional 20 percent ("private") tax on the investment. The statistical relationship between corruption and lower foreign investment is valid across all regions. Contrary to conventional wisdom, there is no evidence that foreign investors are any less susceptible to corruption in East Asian economies than in other countries in the world.

This finding also challenges the contention that the East Asian experience shows that corruption does not hurt investment and growth. That argument ignores the reality that corruption is only one of a number of factors affecting growth and development. Even the few East Asian countries that are considerably corrupt have developed a credible rule of law, maintained decent macroeconomic management in the past, and prevented corrupt practices from encroaching on their export-oriented policies. Furthermore, although they may have grown fast until recently, the Asian countries where corruption and vested interests permeated lending decisions, or more generally, breached the integrity of their financial sector and their balance of payments position, are now paying a very high macroeconomic cost.

Appendix: What Do Elites in Developing Countries Think about Corruption?

In 1996 the author surveyed 165 elite public and private sector leaders from 63 developing and formerly communist countries (Kaufmann 1997). Almost half of the respondents thought that corruption had increased in their country over the past 10 years, and another third believed that it had stayed roughly the same. Corruption was seen as significantly more prevalent in the public sector than in the private sector. When asked about the severity of possible impediments to development and growth in their country, respondents rated public sector corruption as the greatest obstacle (see figure 2.5).

The survey respondents supported the notion that corruption and lack of economic reform go hand in hand. They were of the view that their country ought to have made more progress implementing economic reforms, and they blamed corrupt interests as one important reason for inaction. At the same time, they believed that economic reforms—particularly deregulation and liberalization, modernization of the budget and the tax regime, and privatization—can play a key role in alleviating corruption (see figure 2.6).

Although the respondents emphasized the domestic causes of corruption, many also regarded the propensity of foreign investors and traders to bribe in their countries as at least as great a problem. A majority believed that member states of the Organisation for Economic Co-operation and Development should implement anticorruption measures targeting their traders and investors abroad, and also that international institutions should make curbing corruption a priority and a precondition of assistance to their countries.

Figure 2.5 How Do Elites View Various Impediments to National Development and Growth?

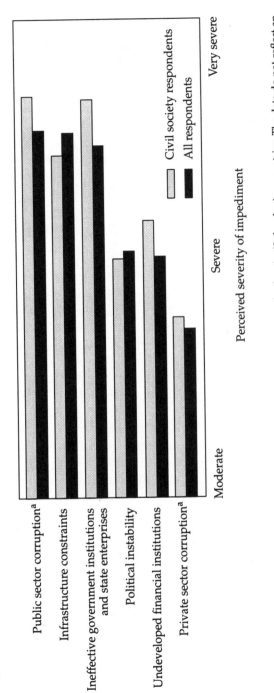

Note: Data are based on a 1996 survey of 165 high-level public and private sector leaders in 63 developing countries. The data do not reflect an institutional endorsement of any particular country or index.
a. Private sector corruption involves only malfeasance within and between private agents; public sector corruption also includes bribery by private firms to public officials and politicians.
Source: Kaufmann (1997).

Figure 2.6 Percentage of Survey Respondents Highly Rating Domestic Solutions to Corruption in Their Country

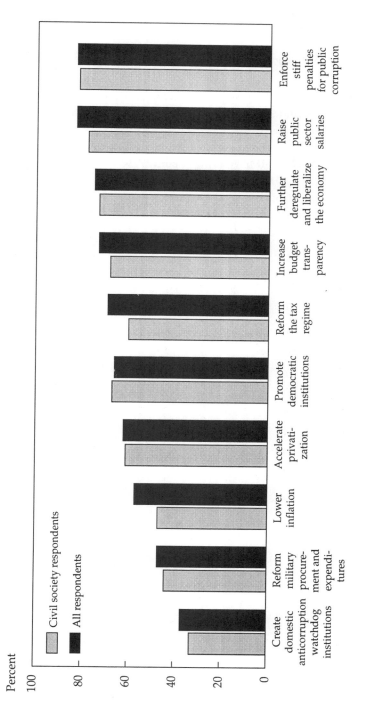

Percent

Create domestic anticorruption watchdog institutions

Reform military procurement and expenditures

Lower inflation

Accelerate privatization

Promote democratic institutions

Reform the tax regime

Increase budget transparency

Further deregulate and liberalize the economy

Raise public sector salaries

Enforce stiff penalties for public corruption

☐ Civil society respondents
■ All respondents

Note: Data are based on a 1996 survey of 165 high-level public and private sector leaders in 63 developing countries. The data do not reflect an institutional endorsement of any particular country or index.
Source: Kaufmann (1997).

References

Kaufmann, Daniel. 1997. "Corruption: The Facts." *Foreign Policy* 107 (summer): 114–31.

Kaufmann, Daniel, and Jeffrey Sachs. Forthcoming. "Determinants of Corruption."

Kaufmann, Daniel, and Shang-Jin Wei. Forthcoming. "Does Grease Money Speed the Wheels of Commerce?"

Mauro, Paolo. 1996. "The Effects of Corruption on Growth, Investment, and Government Expenditure." IMF Working Paper WP/96/98. International Monetary Fund, Washington, D.C.

Olowu, Dele. 1993. "Governmental Corruption and Africa's Democratization Efforts." *Corruption and Reform* 7(3):227–36.

3

The Experience of Hong Kong, China, in Combating Corruption

B. E. D. de Speville

When Hong Kong, China, launched its strategy to fight corruption in the early 1970s, many doubters thought reducing corruption was impossible. Over the past two decades, a fair degree of success has been achieved, however, and the doubters have been proven wrong. Hong Kong, China's, experience offers some pointers of particular value to other countries struggling against corruption.

Succeeding in a Quiet Revolution

Hong Kong, China, established its Independent Commission against Corruption (ICAC) in 1974. Since that time Hong Kong, China, has achieved nothing short of a quiet revolution—a revolution that has changed minds and hearts and yielded sparkling results. But it has not been easy. The community of Hong Kong, China, has come to realize that hard work, business acumen, and risk-taking have produced today's standard of living and material benefits; equally it has come to realize that its achievements could not have accrued without arresting the cancer of corruption.

Consider how far Hong Kong, China, has progressed over the last two decades. First, public service is fundamentally cleaner. In the mid-1970s more than 80 percent of the ICAC's corruption reports related to the public sector; in 1994 less than half (fewer than 1,800 reports) did. In 1974, 45 percent of the corruption reports concerned the police; in 1994 that figure was down to 18 percent. These drastic decreases have been mirrored by a change in the public's perception of government corruption. In the first survey of public opinion conducted in 1977, 38 percent of the respondents thought corruption was widespread in most government departments, while in 1994 only 7.8 percent thought so.

Second, the public's attitude toward corruption has changed remarkably, with the prevailing view being that it is evil and destructive. In the 1994 survey only 2.9 percent of the participants said they would tolerate corruption, and 63 percent said they were willing to report corruption if they encountered it. In addition, people are more willing to openly expose wrongdoing: in 1974 only one-third of those who reported corruption were prepared to identify themselves; in 1994, more than two-thirds did so.

Third, the private (or commercial) sector is not only aware of the dangers of corruption but is prepared to do something about it. The number of private sector organizations seeking the ICAC's guidance in improving their systems to prevent corruption has steadily increased. Furthermore, in 1994, 78 percent of survey respondents agreed that employees should seek their employers' permission to accept advantages related to their work. That happens to be the law governing private sector corruption in Hong Kong, China. But contrast that finding with the 46 percent in 1977 who regarded under-the-table kickbacks as a normal business practice. Clearly people now have a much firmer idea of what constitutes private sector corruption than in the past.

In May 1994 the ICAC began a Business Ethics Campaign. Just 18 months later, more than 1,200 publicly listed or large private companies and trade associations had adopted a corporate code of conduct, while another 670 were actively preparing to. This is certainly a far cry from the early years of the ICAC, when one of the leading chambers of commerce actually petitioned the government to urge that the ICAC be kept away from the business sector!

How could Hong Kong, China, achieve all these changes in just two decades? How did the ICAC obtain the substantial support of the community? What made the public come forward as an active partner in the fight against corruption?

Factors for Success

Recognition of the Problem and Commitment to Solving It

The first component of an effective anticorruption effort is recognition by top government officials of the seriousness of the problem and acknowledgment that it can be overcome only over the medium to long term. This recognition must be backed up by consistent high-level support and the provision of adequate resources to address corruption.

The initiative to set up the ICAC came directly from the governor of Hong Kong, China. By establishing the ICAC as an independent agency solely dedicated to fighting corruption, free from political interference, separate from the police force, and not part of the civil service, the government made credible its opposition to corrupt practices. By consistently supplying adequate resources to fight corruption, the government ensured that the long-term benefits accruing from anticorruption measures would be sustained. This contrasts with other countries, where short-term anticorruption campaigns that are derived from political opportunism and expediency have little chance of success. Anticorruption campaigns that are shallow, superficial, and lacking in sincerity leave the population dejected, disgruntled, and cynical.

An Unimpeachable Anticorruption Agency

The public must also be assured that the fight against corruption is in the hands of a thoroughly reliable agency. The organization charged with this important responsibility must be beyond reproach.

In the case of the ICAC, the staff must have unblemished integrity, quite apart from being dedicated and effective graft fighters. The selection criteria are very strict, and only the most qualified people are recruited. Once hired, they are subject to a strict disciplinary code and to anticorruption checks by an internal monitoring group. For their dedication they are paid well. This results less from Hong Kong, China's, affluence than from the societal recognition that a poorly paid public servant—and particularly a poorly paid corruption fighter—is more vulnerable to the temptation of a bribe than one who is paid generously.

A Well-Planned Long-Term Strategy

A third key to success is the formulation and implementation of a carefully thought-out long-term strategy for the attack on corruption. The battle cannot be won solely by punishing the corrupt and improving the bureaucratic machinery; fundamental changes in public attitudes are also needed.

The strategy in Hong Kong, China, required an integrated fight against corruption on three fronts: investigation, prevention, and education—a three-pronged attack. The first prong is mostly reactive; the ICAC's Operations Department investigates corruption after receiving complaints. The second prong, the responsibility of the Corruption Prevention Department, involves eliminating opportunities for systemic corruption in government and in private sector organizations. The third prong enlists the Community Relations Department to educate the public on the evils of corruption and seek citizens' active support.

The Community Relations Department, with about 200 officers, was created with the recognition that only a change of public attitudes toward corruption could make a lasting difference in the fight against this insidious problem. In broad terms the department's job is to build public support and confidence in the ICAC by explaining antibribery laws, educating the younger generation at school, and encouraging the community to take corruption prevention measures and report any suspicions of corruption offenses.

To harness support, the department segments the community and develops specific involvement programs according to the needs of different groups. Such a community-based strategy builds trust in the ICAC's effectiveness and integrity. It also means that the community itself becomes a driving force against corruption by taking active and sustained action to raise moral standards in the society and improve business management systems to prevent corruption. One measure of the department's success is that businesspeople and the public at large have come to understand that secret commissions mean unfair competition and extra costs, less profitability, and a poisoned free market.

Successful investigation and prosecution encourage the community to report corruption, assist the Community Relations Department in educating people about the dangers of corruption, and assist the Corruption Prevention Department in encouraging both the public and private sectors to think about their systems. In turn, systems that are corruption-proof, as far as practicable, make the detection and prosecution of corruption more likely. The three tactical approaches of the ICAC—the three departments—are interdependent. To achieve maximum efficiency each department depends on the performance of the others. Thus, the whole commission is greater than the sum of its parts.

Attention to All Reports of Corruption

A fourth major factor in effectively fighting corruption again relates to that most precious advantage of obtaining and retaining public confidence. To build trust and encourage people to report their suspicions of wrongdoing, an anticorruption agency must instill confidence that every allegation that is pursuable, no matter how small, will be investigated. This is a cardinal principle of the ICAC and is translated into practice. The person who thinks ICAC officials pay attention and respond to what she or he says is much more likely to report corruption again, perhaps a much more serious incident.

Public appreciation of this aspect of the ICAC's philosophy is illustrated by the marked increase in pursuable corruption reports received since the ICAC began operation. Pursuable reports—those that provide sufficient information to enable an investigation to begin—are usually those filed by people willing to identify themselves. The percentage of such reports has grown from 33 percent in 1974 to 71 percent in 1994. The public also reports on all sorts of problems other than corruption. More than half of the reports made to the ICAC since 1974 have had nothing to do with corruption—a sign of the trust the community has in the commission as a conduit for general grievances against various government departments. The ICAC tries to help by referring these noncorruption complaints to the appropriate departments for action and advising the public that they have done so.

Confidentiality

A fifth major factor for success in controlling corruption is giving the utmost confidentiality to those who report offenses. Exposing corruption usually requires considerable courage. Those who report to the ICAC expect maximum confidentiality, and they are not disappointed. The commission takes the protection of sources very seriously. Its internal computer and filing systems are strictly monitored so that only officers who "need to know" may access information on anyone who has made a report. Files are systematically culled and shredded to dispose of outdated information. Finally, the laws of Hong Kong, China, prohibit the disclosure of the identity of any of the ICAC's sources of information.

Setting in Place the Right Conditions

The ICAC has succeeded because of a combination of factors that collectively produced an advantageous environment in which to counter corruption. Most noteworthy are the independence of the ICAC and the systems in place that ensure external accountability.

The governor of Hong Kong, China, appoints the ICAC's commissioner and deputy; the commissioner reports directly to the governor and appoints all other staff. These provisions effectively prevent any agencies or individuals from interfering in ICAC investigations of alleged corruption within the police. The commission has to negotiate with the government and the legislature for funds, and, for bureaucratic convenience, ICAC staff are generally subject to civil service employment conditions. These matters apart, the ICAC has complete operational independence.

However, although operational independence is key to winning and retaining public confidence, that independence must not be an unrestricted license. The question *"Quis custodiet ipsos custodes?"* or "Who is to keep an eye on the guardians?" is fundamental.

To minimize the possibility of any abuse of power, the ICAC is subject to a stringent system of checks and balances. The commission's work is guided by four advisory committees whose membership is drawn from all sectors of the community and appointed by the governor. A fifth committee, which includes members of Hong Kong, China's, Executive and Legislative Councils, considers complaints made against the ICAC. Each of these committees is chaired not by the ICAC commissioner but by a committee member, with the objective of improving the independence of the supervisory system.

Another important condition is a powerful legislative framework that enables the ICAC to tackle the special problem of corruption. The commissioner is authorized to prevent suspects from disposing of their property; to seek court orders preventing them from leaving Hong Kong, China; to examine their bank accounts and safe deposit boxes; to require them to provide details of their financial situation; and to search their premises. If other offenses connected with corruption are revealed during an investigation, the ICAC is empowered to investigate those related offenses to uncover the underlying corruption.

One of the most potent weapons in the armory of laws comes into play when a civil servant possesses unexplained property or maintains a standard of living in excess of his or her official salary. Unless he or she gives a satisfactory explanation to the court as to how the money or property was acquired, the civil servant is considered guilty of corruption. This has been highly effective in keeping Hong Kong, China's, civil servants honest.

The Changing Scene of Corruption

Immense progress in computer technology and communication systems over the past two decades has led to more sophisticated corruption, particularly in relation to commercial fraud and other crimes that transcend national borders. Those who engage in such crimes have become much more alert and adept at covering their tracks. It is fast becoming apparent that close cooperation between the anticorruption agencies of individual countries and regions, with the impetus that international bodies can provide, is the only means by which the problem can be contained. In Hong Kong, China, the major syndicated public sector corruption of the 1960s and early 1970s has become an evil of the past, but sophisticated private sector corruption is immensely complex, and the demands on resources are a major concern.

Hong Kong, China's, success in this realm cannot be sustained if investigations are fixed only on the domestic scene—they must be broadened to include greater liaison and cooperation with neighboring countries and other partners. China must be involved in the process; in 1997 Hong Kong's sovereignty reverted to China when the former British crown colony became a Special Administrative Region (SAR) of the People's Republic of China. Hong Kong, China, will have as its constitution the Basic Law, which guarantees the ICAC's continued existence after 1997 as an independent organization. The ICAC, by its unrelenting efforts to attack corruption, will continue to play an important role within the SAR government in maintaining a stable and prosperous Hong Kong, China. The cooperation that has developed over the years between the ICAC and the anticorruption authorities of mainland China will likely increase. It is very much in Hong Kong, China's, interest that the struggle against corruption in Guangdong, and indeed all regions of the mainland, should succeed, given economic and cultural proximity.

Conclusion

Each country or region is a unique blend of its own history and culture, each has its own political system and beliefs, and each is at its own stage of economic and social development. What works against corruption in one place may not be valid in another. But sometimes the experience gained in the struggle against this widespread problem can provide guidance elsewhere.

In addressing the social evil of corruption there are two universal truths. First, corruption, however defined, cannot be eradicated in any society. It will persist because it is motivated by two fundamental aspects of human nature—need and greed. But it can be reduced to and contained at a level where it no longer gnaws at the heart of society. Second, within any society corruption can be curbed only if the population at large perceives that the leadership is deadly earnest about attacking the problem, that leaders at the highest levels demonstrate integrity and ethical conduct, and that economic development is filtering down to benefit the lowest levels of society.

To summarize this complex equation in another way, the *need* for corrupt activity in a society can be dissipated. Given the support of the community, and nothing less, the greed can be attacked and constrained. But stop-start, crash-bang, hyperbolic campaigns against corruption will never achieve anything more than temporary, superficial success. Ultimate success can come only in the context of a long-term strategy, flexible shorter-term tactics, and a profound change of attitude in the community.

4

The Experience of Singapore in Combating Corruption

Tan Ah Leak

In October 1951 a gang of robbers in Singapore hijacked a consignment of 1,800 pounds of opium worth about $400,000. Among the thieves were three police detectives. Investigations conducted by the Anti-Corruption Branch of the Criminal Investigation Department revealed that some senior police officers were involved not only with the hijackers but also with the importers of the opium. At the conclusion of the investigation, only an assistant superintendent of police was dismissed, while another officer was pressed into retirement. The colonial government, dissatisfied with the investigation, then formed a special team to inquire into the matter. After the special team concluded its inquiry in September 1952, the government decided to retain the team to replace the Anti-Corruption Branch as an independent organization to look into corruption offenses in Singapore. Thus the Corrupt Practices Investigation Bureau (CPIB) was born.

A Legacy of Widespread Corruption

In 1959, when Singapore attained self-government, corruption was rife throughout all sectors of public service. Syndicated corruption was especially common among law enforcement officials; payment for their services was a "must" and greasing their palms was the norm.

Several problems contributed to this situation. First, the laws to prevent corruption were weak. Offenders were not subject to property seizure, and officers of the CPIB had inadequate enforcement powers to carry out their duties. Second, obtaining evidence was difficult because of the weak anticorruption laws and the fact that many public officials regularly engaged in corrupt activities. Third, the people generally were poorly educated. Most were migrant workers who were accustomed to unfair treatment by public officials. They were submissive to those in authority and dared not report them for fear of reprisal. They did not know their rights, and the only way they knew how to get things done was through bribery. Fourth, public officials were less well paid than workers in the private sector, and integrity suffered as a result. Many civil servants became indebted due to lavish lifestyles, and some resorted to corruption to make ends meet. Finally, CPIB officers were drawn from the Singapore police force on short secondment. Therefore, they were not psychologically prepared to fully commit themselves to combating corruption, especially when it involved their fellow police officers. Furthermore, the short secondments disrupted CPIB activity; before investigations could be completed, most officers were already due for another posting.

Steps to Address Corruption

After attaining self-government, the new political leaders immediately took it upon themselves to act as role models for public officials. They divested themselves of any financial and commercial ties; demonstrated a strong work ethic by coming to work earlier and practicing more meticulous work habits than their subordinates; took no unnecessary official trips at taxpayers' expense or otherwise abused their office; and adopted a policy of zero tolerance for corruption. Thus by personal example, they created a climate of honesty and integrity.

Early Legislative Measures

The new political leaders also took legislative measures to ensure that the anticorruption law (the Prevention of Corruption Act) was adequate and provided sufficient punishment for offenders. The law was revamped in 1960 to give more power to CPIB officers and to enhance punishment for corruption offenses. The law has since been reviewed regularly to ensure that offenders do not escape legal punishment and that corruption does not pay.

For example, the court is required to order any person convicted of accepting a bribe to repay an equivalent penalty amount. CPIB officers, besides having all the powers relating to police investigations, are now given other special powers as well. Under the law the public prosecutor can, among other things, order the controller of income tax to provide information on offenders to the CPIB.

The Anti-Corruption Advisory Committee

In 1973, on the advice of the prime minister on how the CPIB could intensify its efforts to stamp out corruption in the civil service, an Anti-Corruption Advisory Committee (ACAC) was formed. Chaired by the head of the civil service, with permanent secretaries and heads of statutory boards as members, the ACAC served as an advisory body. Its main functions included laying down guidelines for the various government departments and statutory bodies to deal with corruption cases, ensuring that firm and consistent action was taken against both corrupters and the corrupted, monitoring through the CPIB the action taken in all corruption cases by heads of departments and statutory bodies, and helping to speed up departmental or court proceedings against corrupt public officials or the corrupters whenever any delay was encountered. The ACAC was dissolved at the end of 1975 after it had fulfilled its functions.

The Corruption (Confiscation of Benefits) Act 1989

The concept that corruption does not pay was further fortified by the enactment of the Corruption (Confiscation of Benefits) Act 1989. The act gives the court the power to confiscate pecuniary resources when a person convicted of corruption cannot satisfactorily account for those resources. It also provides for the confiscation of benefits derived from corruption if a person under investigation absconds; if the person dies either before proceedings are instituted or before being convicted; or if, six months after investigations have commenced, the person cannot be found or is not amenable to extradition proceedings.

Administrative Measures

Along with legislative action, administrative measures were also taken to reduce the chances of public officials' involvement in corruption and wrongdoing and to make the CPIB more effective. These measures included:

- Replacing seconded police officers with permanent civilian investigators
- Giving the CPIB a free hand to act without fear of or favor toward anyone, irrespective of his or her social status, political affiliation, color, or creed
- Removing opportunities for corruption in government work procedures
- Streamlining cumbersome administrative procedures
- Reviewing civil service salaries regularly to ensure that they are adequate and comparable to those in the private sector
- When contracts are signed, reminding government contractors that trying to bribe public officials administering contracts may cost them the contract (a clause to this effect forms part of the contract).

The government instruction manuals (section L of manual 2) also laid down strict instructions to prevent civil servants from getting involved in corruption or wrongdoing. For example, civil servants cannot borrow money from or in any way financially obligate themselves to any person with whom they have official dealings. Civil servants cannot at any time have unsecured debts and liabilities that exceed more than three months' pay. They cannot use official information for private gain, and they are required to declare their assets when first appointed to the civil service and annually thereafter. In addition, public officials cannot engage in trade or business or undertake any part-time employment without approval; they cannot receive entertainment from members of the public; and they cannot accept any privately offered shares in a company without the approval of the permanent secretaries of finance and public service.

As another preventive measure, CPIB officers give regular talks to civil servants—especially those in the enforcement agencies—on the pitfalls of corruption. Civil servants also get advice on how to avoid involvement in corruption, and they are made aware of the Prevention of Corruption Act through the incorporation of relevant provisions into the government instruction manuals.

Constitutional Safeguards

Singapore's constitution also provides safeguards to ensure absolute integrity in the civil service. The president of the Republic of Singapore, who appoints the director of the CPIB on the advice and recommendation of the Cabinet or a minister acting under the general authority of the Cabinet, can, if he does not concur with the recommendation, refuse or revoke the director's appointment. The director, for his part, can, with the concurrence of the president, make inquiries or investigations into any information, allegation, or complaint against any person, even if the prime minister refuses to consent.

Action against Corrupt Public Officials

Corrupt public officials are dealt with in one of two ways. They are charged in court if there is sufficient evidence for court prosecution; otherwise they are charged departmentally.

COURT PUNISHMENT FOR CORRUPTION. In Singapore both the giver and the receiver of a bribe are guilty of corruption and subject to the same punishment. Any person convicted of a corruption offense can be fined up to $100,000, sentenced to as many as five years in prison, or both. If the offense relates to a government contract or involves a member of Parliament or a member of a public body, the term of imprisonment can be increased to seven years. Besides risking a fine and imprisonment, a person convicted of corruption will be ordered by the court to return the amount of the bribe he or she accepted. In addition, as noted earlier, the Corruption (Confiscation of Benefits) Act 1989 allows the court to confiscate any pecuniary resources and property in the person's possession for which he or she cannot satisfactorily account.

Furthermore, civil servants who are convicted in court of a corruption offense will also lose their jobs and, if they are pensionable officials, their pensions and other benefits. They will also be barred from any future public appointment.

DEPARTMENTAL PUNISHMENT FOR CORRUPTION. Civil servants who are convicted of a departmental charge, depending on the severity of the charge, receive one or more of the following punishments: dismissal from the service, reduction in rank, stoppage or deferment of pay raises, a fine, or a reprimand.

The Success of the CPIB in Combating Corruption

The role of the Corrupt Practices Investigation Bureau today includes corruption prevention in addition to its original task of investigation. As part of its prevention activities, the CPIB researches the administrative and operating procedures of corruption-prone departments and recommends measures that would reduce opportunities for misconduct. It also screens to ensure that those with blemished records are not appointed to key positions.

The bureau has earned the public's confidence and support in its fight against corruption. It is generally regarded as an effective agency and reputed for its single-minded efficiency. Its success can be attributed to a number of factors. One is the cultural climate in Singapore, which is strongly opposed to corruption. A second is a well-paid civil service, which effectively lessens any compulsion for public officials to get involved in corruption. Third, external agencies support CPIB activities with effective administrative measures, including disciplinary proceedings by the Public Service Commission, close scrutiny of government expenditures by the Auditor-General's Department and the Public Accounts Committee of Parliament, and control of public spending by the Ministry of Finance.

In addition, a highly literate and sophisticated society, which is no longer submissive to authority, readily reports corrupt behavior with no fear of reprisal. Members of the public perceive the CPIB as an effective and credible organization and are prepared to come forward to assist. Moreover, CPIB officers are easily accessible to members of the public who seek to give information or complain about corruption. Reports of wrongdoing are attended to speedily, and offenders are brought to book.

Because the prime minister's office directly supervises the CPIB, the bureau has the freedom to investigate even prominent persons. It has enhanced its credibility by pursuing allegations of corruption at the highest levels of government:

- Wee Toon Boon, a minister of state, was investigated in 1975 for accepting bribes from a property developer. He was sentenced to four years and six months' imprisonment, which on appeal was reduced to one year and six months.
- Phey Yew Kok, a member of Parliament and a prominent trade union leader, was investigated in 1979 and charged in court for criminal breach of trust and other offenses. He jumped bail and is now a fugitive.
- The Cheang Wan, a minister, was investigated in 1986 for accepting bribes from two property developers. He committed suicide before he could be charged in court.
- Glen Jeyasingam, a knight, a senior state counsel, and the director of the Commercial Affairs Department, was investigated in 1991 and charged in court for corruption and cheating. He was jailed and fined.

- Yeo Seng Teck, the chief executive officer of the Trade Development Board, Singapore, was investigated in 1993 and charged in court for corruption, cheating, and forgery. He was sentenced to four years' imprisonment.
- Choy Hon Tim, the deputy chief executive of the Public Utilities Board (PUB), was investigated in 1995 and charged for accepting bribes from PUB contractors. He was sentenced to 14 years' imprisonment.

The Role of External Agencies in Combating Corruption

Responsibility for combating corruption does not lie with the CPIB alone. Although the bureau has been entrusted with investigating cases of corruption, the primary responsibility for preventing corruption lies with the respective government departments. A permanent secretary of a ministry is charged with ensuring that each department under him or her has a committee to review anticorruption measures.

The government instruction manuals spell out the secretary's additional responsibilities for ensuring that reasonable and adequate measures are taken to prevent corrupt practices. These measure include improving cumbersome work methods and procedures to avoid delay in granting permits, licenses, and similar documents; making supervision more effective; devising a control system to ensure that junior officials with decisionmaking power do not abuse such power; giving supervisors enough time to check and control the work of staff; requiring senior officials to systematically carry out surprise checks as well as routine ones; ensuring that supervisors and administrative staff take anticorruption measures seriously and are not lax in checking or reporting their subordinates; rotating staff so that no individual or group remains too long in an operations unit; and ensuring that measures set up to prevent corrupt practices are reviewed once every three to five years.

Conclusion

Today Singapore's public sector is reputed to be one of the most efficient and cleanest in the world. Syndicated corruption is rare, and corruption in the civil service is generally petty in nature and confined to junior officials. The change from a corruption-infested civil service to one that is nearly corruption-free is due largely to a combination of factors: the commitment of political and civic leaders to fighting corruption; adequate anticorruption laws that provide sufficient punishment to deter corruption; an efficient agency that is effective in investigating the corrupt, irrespective of their social status, political affiliation, color, or creed; and finally, the support of the public as well as senior public officials.

5

In Pursuit of Public Accountability in Bolivia

Antonio Sanchez de Lozada

New democracies generally inherit disorder bordering on chaos, counterproductive policies, and a legacy of ill-fated government intervention. This situation leads to corruption, which is exacerbated by the lack of managerial tools, ineffective internal and external controls, and profound deficiencies in the reporting and quality of information about government that make financial auditing—much less performance auditing—futile.

The four administrations that have governed in Bolivia since 1982, when democracy was initiated, all faced the same problem—the difficulty, if not impossibility, of adequately implementing policies and decisions. Even the best decisions have often been unsuccessful, or only partially successful, because of the lack of management feedback in their implementation. Good management information systems permit the timely adjustment of decisions and their implementation, so that even policies that were originally deficient can ultimately be quite successful.

Bolivia's experience regarding public accountability is perhaps unique, at least in Latin America. This chapter begins by reviewing the transition to democracy in Bolivia, noting the disorder inherited by the new democratic regime, the ineffectiveness of governmental controls, and the dilution of responsibility to the point where no one in a position of public authority could be held accountable for his or her actions. Next the chapter recapitulates the major reforms undertaken and their effect on corruption; the gestation of the Integrated Governmental Financial Management and Control System (SAFCO); accountability as a fundamental requirement to consolidate new democracies; and the effort to incorporate accountability into Bolivia's public service. After a detailed discussion of Law 1178, which created SAFCO, followed by some observations about problems in its implementation, the chapter concludes with suggestions for further action.

The Evolution of Democracy in Bolivia

Bolivia has been progressing since 1982 in improving and consolidating both representative and participatory democracy. The many previous efforts failed, at least in part, because of the exclusion of the great majority of the population and the top-down approach to building democracy.

Representative Democracy

Until 1952 the short periods of democracy in Bolivia involved limited enfranchisement. From 1952 to 1964 there was in essence a one-party democracy in which previously disenfranchised people now voted. The period from November 1964 to October 1982 was dominated by a series of military governments, punctuated by a couple of short-lived attempts to establish a representative democracy. As the economic situation deteriorated and the probability of violent confrontation with the military increased, a center-left alliance, initially elected in 1980, finally took office in 1982.

The coalition government, which held only a precarious plurality in Congress, attempted to pass a series of nationalist and populist policies that led to a political impasse. The fiscal and monetary disorder, inherited from the de facto governments, became uncontrollable. The crisis was aggravated by the unavoidable burden of long-postponed economic adjustments generated by a less exclusive system of government. Notwithstanding the hyperinflation, a pluralistic political system was consolidated between 1982 and 1985, thanks to the coalition's respect for civil liberties and human rights in spite of the massive demonstrations fomented by pent-up demands for better wages and standards of living.

As was the case in 1980, none of the parties or coalitions won (or has subsequently enjoyed) the absolute majority required for direct election of the president. In 1985 Congress elected the candidate who attained second place by a couple of percentage points less than the winner of the plurality. In 1989 the candidate who came in third, with less than 20 percent of the vote, was elected president with the support of the congressional allies of the second-place candidate. In 1993 the candidate who won the plurality by more than 15 percentage points was elected president. It should be noted that in each election the incumbent party lost. Furthermore, the only significant electoral scandals (in 1989) led to a rapid reform of the process, including the establishment of a truly independent electoral court. Since then, national and local elections have achieved a high level of credibility.

Participatory Democracy

Because of the multicultural and multilingual nature of Bolivia and its limited socioeconomic development, most of the population identifies only with local geographic and political subdivisions. In contrast, the broadening scope of government responsibilities tended to centralize more and more economic activity and public functions in four cities. At the national level, social and political pressure often became diffuse, and the demand for accountability was neutralized. In practice, little effort was dedicated to strengthening local governments, which permits close monitoring by the beneficiaries of public services. Direct participation in determining a community's destiny would later prove essential to breaching the pervasive fatalism of this society.

After almost 40 years, municipal elections were held in 1985. However, the scope of municipal government was constrained by limited resources. In effect, fewer than a dozen municipalities had a tax base, which allowed basic but very deficient services and some public works. Since 1994, when the Law of Popular Participation was enacted, the nation has been divided into 308 territorial municipalities with jurisdiction over not only urban concentrations but all of the surrounding rural areas. Each municipality participates on a per capita basis in the distribution of 20 percent of the national government's tax revenue. Moreover, special funding institutions have been created to help municipal governments finance public investments. This new income base has been accompanied by the transfer of responsibility to local governments for the building and maintenance of schools, health centers, local roads, and minor irrigation, water, and sewerage works, and for the supply of all materials required by public services. Central government continues to cover the personnel costs of education and health services. With the creation of vigilance committees elected by the communities of a municipality, social control is beginning to be effective.

Dysfunctional Government

Between the end of the Chaco War with Paraguay in 1935 and the hyper-inflation of 1985, the social and economic responsibilities of the Bolivian government grew uncontrollably. Government direct intervention and en-trepreneurship, state capitalism, and ever-expanding social services were the dominant dogma, although increasingly divorced from economic re-ality. Furthermore, management capabilities did not grow along with the rapidly enlarging scope of government responsibility and operations. Making and implementing decisions became a process of improvisation under conflicting regulations and procedures, resulting in erratic govern-ment performance.

The 1982–85 economic crisis was precipitated by increasing government control over foreign exchange, prices, international trade, interest rates, employment, salaries, the supply of consumer staples, and other matters. This intervention was aimed at solving the inheritance of a contracting tax base, a growing fiscal and trade deficit, an unserviceable public debt, and the resulting disinvestment. Systematic policymaking and implementation were impossible in the context of limited fiscal maneuverability, which in-cluded chaotic public management; lack of timely, reliable, and relevant information; and counterproductive government controls, which were im-provised, distorted, and not updated in more than 30 years.

Reporting obligations were unclear, contradictory, or simply nonexis-tent. There was seldom any compliance. No real government accounting standards existed. Bolivian government agencies, with one or two excep-tions, produced no regular and complete financial statements. At best, they presented an unauditable so-called balance sheet 6 to 24 months after the end of each fiscal year. Without any timely, reliable, and relevant manage-ment information systems, policy formulation and implementation were inconsistent and unpredictable.

Under the pretext of preventive control, the main function of internal auditing and of the Office of Comptroller General (Contraloria) was the prereview and authorization of contracts, payment orders, and checks. "Precontrol" was the paradigm of governmental control—to comanage with veto power and without responsibility. The precontroller could paralyze the flow of government activity. In view of the enormous diversity of spe-cialties required in modern government, rarely was the exercise of precontrol an effective preventive measure against error or corruption. Because of the scarcity of experienced professionals and executives, if the precontrollers were actually qualified (which almost never occurred), it made more sense that they be reassigned to operational and management responsibilities. Thus, in practice, it was impossible to make precontrols effective, and because they fully or partially released the executives from responsibility for their actions, omissions, and results, they were totally incompatible with the notion of accountability. On the other hand, this created an enormous incentive to obtain employment as a precontroller, in spite of the low official remuneration.

The duties of precontrol occupied two-thirds of the almost 1,200 employees of the Office of Comptroller General. The Audit Department was only 1 of 22 units reporting directly to the comptroller general, and it reviewed a small proportion of the government's operations. Since the Office of Comptroller General had already participated in precontrol, the resulting conflict of interest invalidated the audits. Furthermore, the poor professional quality of the audits is evident from the few working papers produced. The success of audits was measured by the number of deviations from formal procedure the auditors could identify. However, because regulations and standards—issued by continually changing de facto governments—were abundant and conflicting, it was quite easy to produce a "successful" audit—or to challenge one.

Once the audit report, together with a legal opinion, was approved by the comptroller general, it became a mandatory payment order (similar to a bill of exchange or a promissory note). The accused was obligated to prove, to the satisfaction of the accuser, that he or she did not owe the sum contained in the "payment demand" issued by the deputy comptroller or regional comptroller, who acted as both prosecutor and judge. The roots of this "evolution" in administrative capacity can be traced back to the mid-1930s; however, its result was that by the 1980s, government had become highly dysfunctional.

Corruption and the Focus of Reform

Lack of relevant, reliable, and timely information on what was happening in government, as well as limited access and disclosure, made it very difficult for the press and the public to analyze the real situation in government. This in turn facilitated demagoguery and corruption. Although transparency has been improved as a result of democracy, it is still difficult to investigate successfully whether incompetence, irresponsibility, and corruption exist. Thus only limited evidence can be obtained to substantiate the prosecution of administrative malfeasance. Political intervention, ineptitude, and the absence of integrity in the institutions with investigative, prosecutorial, and judicial powers lead to manifest violations and de facto impunity for many perpetrators, testing the social and political viability of the new democracy.

First-Generation Reforms

After September 1985 the rampant corruption generated by direct government controls was eliminated by establishing daily public auctions of foreign exchange and terminating price, trade, and other controls. The number of taxes was reduced from almost 200 (many of which generated a net negative revenue) to fewer than a dozen easily collectible ones. The banking system now processes tax payments so as to avoid extortion and indifference. However, some banks expect flexibility in complying with their contracts. As a bridging operation, inspection companies were contracted to verify declared values of imports and exports. These measures increased tax revenue from about 1 percent of gross domestic product at the height of hyperinflation to about 10 percent after three years. Nonetheless, stagnation at this unacceptable level indicates that tax evasion or noncompliance continues to be one of the most significant forms of corruption.

Public sector purchasing and contracting have always been a significant source of corruption. Although contracting agencies have been employed for almost 10 years to monitor projects, cost overruns are still sizable. There are worrisome indicators that mechanical procedures do not guarantee quality, especially in consultant bidding. Neither contracting agencies nor import/export–verifying companies make updated information available about standard costs. Apparently, they apply broad price ranges and report only the results of the services, without disclosing fully the procedures, grading systems, and calculations, so as to avoid conflict, loss of clients, or even civil liability. These arrangements are flagrant violations of the fundamental principles of transparency and accountability.

In 1990 Bolivia promulgated Law 1178, which created the Integrated Governmental Financial Management and Control System (SAFCO). Two and a half years later the Public Prosecution Law was enacted, making the Attorney General Service independent of the executive branch of government. Both of these laws were characterized as anticorruption measures. Actually, the SAFCO law seeks to improve public sector management information and control systems, and particularly to introduce accountability. Achieving these objectives, however, will make acts of corruption more difficult and facilitate their identification and substantiation.

It is clear that the public sector reforms begun in 1985 were motivated by the need for profound structural adjustment. Bolivia has been successful in stabilizing its economy (8 to 10 percent inflation since 1989, except in 1995), subjecting factor and product pricing to the market, and integrating into the world economy. However, the hyperinflation of the mid-1980s was highly regressive in the distribution of national wealth. Only 30 percent of the population, at most, is participating in the modest rates of growth obtained subsequently (approximately 3 to 4 percent per year), accentuating the socioeconomic polarization of Bolivia.

Second-Generation Reforms

In pursuit of social and political viability, a second generation of reforms was initiated in 1993. These reforms sought to incorporate the great majority of the population into Bolivia's political and economic process. Through popular participation and decentralization, the central government hoped to strengthen its presence in the nine departments in order to deliver public services more effectively.

The public investment program is now implemented with local participation, and the regional control councils are made up of representatives elected by the municipalities. Popular participation and decentralization are essential for implementing the national educational reform program. The latter incorporates multilingual education, respect for cultural diversity, community participation, and a system of qualified, independent evaluation and accreditation of teaching institutions.

Major government corporations are being recapitalized by selling new equity representing 50 percent of each company. After competitive bidding by potential partners with a proven record of management and technological leadership, the sale is awarded to the individual or firm offering the largest investment. None of the capitalized company's original equity is sold; instead it is distributed into pension funds, the beneficiaries of which include all adult Bolivians. In this manner, the citizens are obtaining an equity stake in their country's recapitalized major productive assets.

All these reforms contribute to controlling corruption by activating the capacity of communities for social censure, promoting the economic potential of new generations as an alternative to corruption, and eliminating the opportunities for corruption inherent in an overextended and entrepreneurial government. Notwithstanding these benefits, transparency and accessibility to information continue to be the most fundamental requirements that are lacking for effective and honest government dedicated to public service.

Genesis of the SAFCO Project

Thanks to the national determination to consolidate democracy, Bolivia began to pursue accountability between December 1982 and March 1983. This process, initiated by the U.S. ambassador (who was mobilizing support for the transition to democracy), was facilitated by a president committed to integrity in government and by the rapid and unequivocally positive response of a World Bank/General Accounting Office (GAO) specialist in governmental financial management.

As a result, the evaluation of Bolivian management and control systems began in 1983 with the assistance of experts assigned by the World Bank, the United Nations Development Programme, the U.S. Agency for International Development (USAID), and GAO. Precontrols were phased out, initially by replacing them with a monitoring system. Specialization courses were undertaken. In March 1984 a nine-day interagency meeting was held in La Paz. It was agreed that efforts to introduce accountability into public sector management should begin with the development of expeditious and effective supply and contracting procedures, together with government accounting and auditing.

The $3 million proposal rapidly lost momentum as precontrol employees of the Office of Comptroller General, with the backing of the deputy comptroller, resorted to confrontation. They took over the executive offices, immobilizing senior professional staff and the comptroller general, whose immediate resignation they demanded.

At the beginning of 1985 the Central Bank managers and their union, in contrast to the chairman and board, refused to allow an external audit by the Office of Comptroller General. They requested instead an injunction against the comptroller general and took the case to a full hearing of the Supreme Court. In spite of a unanimous decision in favor of the Office of Comptroller General, twice the Audit Commission was refused entry to the bank. On the third try, led by the comptroller general, the Audit Commission was stopped between the twelfth and thirteenth floors of the bank. After climbing out of the elevator, the audit team was cornered by union leaders in an office suite. The managers disappeared, but after the release of the comptroller general, an arrest warrant was executed against them.

Beginning in 1986, as the stabilization process began to take effect and the Office of Comptroller General was able to lay off about 700 precontrol and inept employees, a new project was formulated with the World Bank and USAID. The Financial Management Strengthening Operation (FMSO) not only covered the SAFCO project but also provided support for the reorganization of the Central Bank, strengthening tax administration and initiating an emergency program to collect and monitor financial information in the 60 largest government entities, which collectively managed over 80 percent of public expenditure. What came to be called FMSO I began in late 1987 and was essentially completed by late 1989.

The SAFCO law was enacted in mid-1990, and the need to implement it justified FMSO II. However, considerable controversy surfaced during the formulation of the second project. The main implementation issues were the nature and technical requirements of each SAFCO system, the scope and magnitude of the training component, the simplistic quantifiable criteria used to mechanically evaluate the attainment of project goals, and poor project management.

Accountability and the Scope of the SAFCO Project

Public accountability is an essential element of the democratic process. Without accountability, no one in the public sector is obligated to assume responsibility for the allocation of public resources, their management, and their effects on the community. In the absence of transparency, publicity, and accessibility, it becomes difficult for voters to evaluate electoral alternatives. Furthermore, accountability and transparency are effective restraints on the abuse of power and its undue concentration.

For accountability to function properly, 10 conditions are required:

(1) A commitment to public service and accountability as the rule and not the exception, along with clear, reasonable principles and procedures for evaluating the behavior and responsibilities of public servants

(2) Open government, especially transparent and consultative policy formulation and implementation

(3) Systematic, integrated, and comprehensive management procedures and norms, with effective internal controls and a clear allocation of responsibilities

(4) A continually upgraded civil service that recruits competitively; periodically trains and evaluates employees; relates remuneration, promotion, and other incentives to performance; and terminates employees who stagnate

(5) Relevant, reliable, timely, accessible, and broadly disseminated information

(6) Independent external controls exercised by qualified parties, particularly regarding the evaluation of management information and internal control systems and the verification of operating results

(7) Well-developed investigative and prosecutorial capabilities that respect due process and civil and human rights

(8) An involved community that demands public sector information and its critical evaluation and is mobilized to exert social control and censure

(9) The support services that permit the careful exercise of oversight functions by Congress and other representative levels of government

(10) An independent, qualified, expeditious, and trusted judicial system based on updated legal concepts.

In spite of the cleanup within the Office of Comptroller General, the traumatic experience left limited professional and operating capability. Because this would have to be built up systematically, it was decided to restrict the scope of the SAFCO project to the tools required for policy, program, and project implementation—accountability requirements 1, 3, 5, and 6 above. This seemed reasonable, as it was expected that the Ministry of Finance would assume responsibility for the management and information systems, thus avoiding jurisdictional conflicts.

As originally designed and financed, the SAFCO project consisted of the following elements:

- Design of government management information and control systems, including the standards and norms required, and their implementation
- Formulation of the principles for public servant responsibilities and accountability
- Drafting of the required legislation
- Development and initiation of a training program for professional staff and middle management
- Transformation of the Office of Comptroller General into the senior authority for governmental internal control, external auditing, and independent evaluation of accountability in public service
- Project management.

Law 1178 on Government Management and Control

Managing and controlling government through regulatory legislation is a formidable challenge. Because of the dynamics of public sector management, the need for its continual improvement, and the difficulties of antici-pating the unforeseen, regulations may be inadequate in the long term and even partially obsolete when promulgated. In Bolivia any attempt to de-velop, make compatible, and integrate—even in moderate detail—the nec-essary policy definitions, system designs, technical specifications, and legal issues would have required several hundred legislative articles. Further-more, traditional administrative law in Latin American countries holds that what is not authorized by law (through regulations, technical and adminis-trative manuals, or norms developed from the law) is prohibited.

Framework Legislation

The approach used in Bolivia was to formulate a "framework" law of eight chapters and 54 articles that establish goals, fundamental principles, and terms of reference. Within this context, each public entity or group of similar agencies can develop specific administrative and technical regu-lations, standards, and manuals that respond to its individual mandate and take into consideration the nature of its operations and unique man-agement needs and yet conform to the law and its basic norms. In this manner, the law may be applied to many diverse circumstances and re-main compatible with its fundamental principles. In addition, a frame-work law permits the evolution and continual improvement of integrated management information and control systems without having to amend the law repeatedly.

Objectives and Scope of the SAFCO Law

The SAFCO law attempts to respond to four objectives: (a) effective and efficient management of public resources so as to implement and adjust public policy programs, services, and projects in a timely fashion; (b) gen-eration of useful, timely, and reliable information assuring the reasonable-ness of reports and financial statements; (c) full accountability of all public servants, regardless of rank, for the allocation and proper management of the public resources entrusted to them and for the results obtained; and (d) development of the management capacity needed to identify and substan-tiate the incorrect use of public resources.

The law regulates three types of management systems. First are those for programming and organizing operations. In this category are systems for designing programs to implement government decisions, organizing pro-gram management and support services, and budgeting the resources needed to operate the programs and assure the functioning of support services. Second are management systems for executing the operations programmed. This group includes systems for managing personnel, the supply of goods and services, finances and debt, and integrated accounting. Third, the law covers systems to control the management of public resources through internal controls and external auditing.

The law applies to all such systems in all entities of the public sector, including the administrative units of the legislative and judicial powers. Furthermore, full disclosure is required from all other persons and entities that benefit from public funds or privileges such as subsidies, concessions, and exemptions, as well as from those that supply public services not subject to free competition. Qualified, independent opinions can be required on the effectiveness of any or all management and control systems.

The Ministry of Finance bears responsibility for the management systems related to programming, organizing, and executing operations, while the governmental control systems are the responsibility of the Office of Comptroller General. Both governing agencies have mandates to issue basic standards and regulations for each system; establish deadlines and conditions for developing secondary or specialized standards for each public agency and regulations for their progressive implementation; evaluate such specialized provisions and make them compatible with basic standards and regulations; and monitor the functioning of each system and integrate the information generated by each.

Accountability in Public Service

The chapter of Law 1178 that deals with accountability begins with a statement that "Each public servant must answer for the results of his or her performance of the functions, duties, and authority assigned to his or her position." Given the highly abstract nature of accountability, the novelty of this concept in Latin American administrative law, and the need to make it legally binding, the pursuit of rigorous definitions and principles may be the main contribution of the SAFCO law. According to the law, the following principles are fundamental for establishing accountability:

- The operations and activities undertaken by public servants are considered to be legitimate until proven otherwise. An act is defined as legitimate if it is lawful, ethical, and transparent.
- Transparent performance of public servants—the basis of credibility—involves communication of useful, timely, pertinent, understandable, reliable, and verifiable information to all involved parties and responsible superiors; preservation of and ready access to this information

for consultation and verification; dissemination of information before, during, and after action by public servants, to protect public interests and ensure the public's understanding; and delivery of information upon reasonable request by the public.
- Any limitation or restriction on transparency must be specific and not general nor institutional. Furthermore, it must be expressly established by a law that clearly indicates the independent authority to whom classified acts must be reported.

In addition to outlining the traditional administrative, civil, and penal responsibilities of public servants, Law 1178 establishes the concept of "executive responsibility." This was a response to the failure of chief executives and board members to (a) report in a full and timely fashion on the allocation and management of resources and the results; (b) obtain "reasonable" results because of executive deficiencies or negligence; (c) register contracts within five days of their execution; (d) deliver financial statements with audit reports within three months after the close of the fiscal year, and (e) respect the independence of the internal audit unit.

By requiring the recovery of damages paid by a public entity, through legal action against an executive found to be personally liable for certain decisions, Law 1178 indirectly introduced the concept of civil responsibility by the state. However, administrative, civil, or executive responsibility cannot be invoked when it is proven that the decisions were made in pursuit of greater benefits or in defense of the interest of the government entity, within the limits of reasonable risk corresponding to the nature of the operation and the conditions prevailing at the time, or when force majeure motivated the decisions or affected the final results.

Law 1178 addresses two other principles of accountability. First, professionals are responsible for their reports. Second, lawyers must answer for procedural negligence in representing public entities in litigation.

A Redefined Mandate for the Office of Comptroller General

Law 1178 established, for the first time, operational, technical, and administrative autonomy for the Office of Comptroller General, beginning with the direct submission to Congress of its proposed budget. However, the law narrowed the Office's mandate, eliminating its role in comanaging operations, exercising jurisdiction over administrative matters and appeals, and performing other administrative or policy functions.

The Office of Comptroller General is now restricted to acting as the governing agency for control systems; the analyst of regulations, standards, and the functioning of management, information, and control systems; the senior government auditing institution, verifying and evaluating operational and other results; the evaluator of public servant responsibility; and the trainer of resource managers, systems analysts, auditors, and administrative law specialists. Furthermore, the powers of the Office of Comptroller General have been restricted to those absolutely necessary to fulfill its mandate:

- Access to all public sector records, files, contracts, and other documents and information, including technical, operating, and internal and external audit reports.
- Authority to contract for systems analysis, external audits, or specialized opinions, or to order other public entities and private organizations that benefit from public resources and privileges to contract for such.
- Access to audit programs, working papers, and other documents related to services contracted by public entities or private beneficiaries of public privileges.
- Authority to order a freezing of public sector bank accounts or suspension of disbursements in the case of noncompliance with the rules.
- Authority to recommend the suspension or dismissal of chief executives or directors of public entities in the case of noncompliance with requests for information or assessment of executive responsibility.
- Capacity to initiate court actions to compel authorities to comply with Law 1178 and its regulations. This includes the right to demand that a public prosecutor initiate criminal action and seek a preventive arrest warrant against any authority that refuses full access to and disclosure of information.

With jurisdiction over administrative matters and appeals transferred to the judicial branch, the Office of Comptroller General is no longer simultaneously prosecutor and judge. It must proceed by judicial due process to obtain arrest warrants and recover public resources, and its decisions can be challenged in the courts. In this manner, restrictions on the right of the accused to defense and other arbitrary powers of the office have been eliminated.

Implementation Problems

Pioneering efforts always face unforeseen difficulties. This section outlines the most critical problems affecting the implementation of the SAFCO project. It should be noted that the author actively participated in implementing the project and thus is not a neutral observer.

Difficulties Recruiting Qualified, Experienced Specialists

Although local professionals are preferable, international financing for contracting them is highly restricted, even if they are qualified or experienced in related specialties. Moreover, the remuneration allowed them is often a fraction of that permitted for external personnel.

Foreign consultants, however, are very expensive, difficult to recruit, and highly variable in competence; in addition, they often have problems adapting their ideas to local realities and needs. Therefore, their assignments should be as concrete as possible and undertaken jointly with the best-qualified local professionals.

The difficulty of recruiting effective and productive consultants should not be underestimated. Beautiful curriculum vitae can be misleading, and references are seldom willing to be frank. Recruiting firms often assign the task to persons with no knowledge or experience in the specialties required. The best sources of candidates are probably organizations that perform similar operations and employ staff with the desired qualifications. If at all possible, preselected candidates should be given written and practical tests by independent and highly qualified specialists. SAFCO is one of the few projects to have fired international consultants.

Incompatibility among Participants and the Absence of Independent Evaluation

Divergence between the various participants in the project complicated and delayed implementation. Whatever the merits of each position on the various issues, the confrontations could have been avoided if, periodically, highly qualified experts, independent from all the parties, had been contracted to evaluate project implementation and key personnel. The project, however, did not include financing for this service, nor did the World Bank later authorize it so this task could have been performed in an opportune and adequate manner. Instead the evaluators were World Bank generalists advised by the consultants they hired.

Downsizing of the Training Component and Misguided Reform of the Civil Service

One of the most contentious issues in both FMSO I and especially FMSO II was the scope and magnitude of the training component. At least 70 percent of the success of management development projects depends on the formation of human resources. Experienced management professionals were amazed that a generalist adviser to World Bank senior management, after quickly reviewing the proposed operation once, cut this component by about 40 percent without any justification other than it seemed disproportionate!

Related to the training controversy was the simplistic effort, initiated as part of another World Bank project, to reform Bolivia's civil service, which represented more than 80 percent of current government expenditure. With political support, the civil service facilitated the adoption of measures that enhanced its own job security. Job security by itself only guarantees mediocrity—something a developing country cannot afford. To assure the continuous upgrading of the civil service, job security should depend on competitive recruitment, continued success in graded formal training, periodic performance evaluation by experienced supervisors, incentives for above-average achievement, and competitive promotion or termination if time limits for remaining in a position or grade are reached.

In effect, the principle needed for professional and managerial staff in the civil service should be "promote or out." Therefore, training should have been the most critical element of the SAFCO project. In practice, however, training was neglected, especially with respect to the management systems for which the Ministry of Finance was responsible: the systems related to programming, organizing, and carrying out operations. Furthermore, training in control, accounting, auditing, and accountability was shortened and simplified because of high failure rates.

Weak Political Will

Because of the blatant corruption generated by dysfunctional government and hyperinflation, Congress enacted Law 1178, the Public Prosecution Law, and similar measures. The legislation passed in spite of objections—a few of which were technically correct.

During the same period the comptroller general invoked executive responsibility for the first time—against the chairman of the State Petroleum Company, the largest and most powerful independent government agency. The comptroller general had already rejected an internal audit report several times because of possible corruption: documentation showed that the chief executive, responsible under the new law for internal auditing, permitted repeated evasive action. A concrete response to the comptroller general's recommendation to remove this chairman was delayed, but he eventually took a leave of absence and never returned.

This example notwithstanding, until recently the various ministers of finance and their senior officers addressed corruption only by issuing instructions, memorandums, guidelines, and the like. Some of the official standards and norms enunciated for the management systems overseen by the Ministry of Finance do not respond adequately to the intent of the law or reinstate traditional procedures. Such is the case with the civil service. The problem appears to be fear of diminished flexibility or being held accountable.

Weak political will may also characterize the staff of international agencies. Even eight years after the initiation of the SAFCO project, some of these personnel remain unsure of the essence of accountability (sometimes even confusing it with accounting) or are skeptical of the value of the tremendous effort that has been expended to date.

It may be time to seek an independent evaluation of the project by a highly qualified expert with no relation to the agencies and governments involved. Such an evaluation could lead to at least a partial reformulation of the project. The evaluator must not have an interest in implementing the recommendations, although he or she could assist in monitoring their implementation. In any event, the international agencies and the Bolivian government must be prepared to allocate adequate funds to ensure the success of both the project and its evaluation. Furthermore, hearings and the ultimate publication of the evaluation findings—as should take place under conditions of full transparency—are indispensable.

The Need for Further Action

As mentioned earlier (see "Accountability and the Scope of the SAFCO Project"), only four conditions for accountability were programmed into SAFCO. In retrospect, all 10 should have been.

Several issues now pending would address some of the missing conditions for accountability. One such matter is a constitutional amendment to improve congressional oversight and strengthen its relation to the Public Prosecution Law. Another issue is enhancing transparency in policy formulation and implementation.

Increasing Congressional Oversight

Bolivia is one of the last countries in which the comptroller general, the senior auditor of the executive branch of government, continues to be accountable directly to the president of the republic. Instead, he or she should manage a qualified and independent service of Congress to enhance its responsibility for legislative oversight. A related problem is the lack of a permanent joint public accounts committee with pluralist participation. Transferring the Office of Comptroller General to Congress requires a constitutional amendment, and the creation of the public accounts committee would be much more effective if it was provided for in the Constitution (condition 9 for accountability).

The separation of the Attorney General Service from the executive branch could be a major advance for controlling corruption. However, the selection and appointment process has become highly politicized. This problem might be solved by the proposed constitutional amendment and by reformulating the process for prosecuting public servants (condition 7 for accountability).

Two further adjustments to the Public Prosecution Law could improve substantially the effectiveness of the Attorney General Service. First, each level of justice—from indictment hearing to trial court to appeals tribunal to the Supreme Court—involves a different prosecutor. If the district attorney, who supervises in the first three instances, and the attorney general are added, a case can be prosecuted by more than six different attorneys, each one having to analyze and prepare or review the prosecution. One prosecutor should handle each case at least through the appeal level, under the supervision of the district attorney. Then the prosecuting attorney should participate fully with the deputy attorney general at the Supreme Court level.

Second, the Attorney General Service depends totally on the investigative capabilities and integrity of the police force, even in highly specialized cases. This can lend itself to deficiencies in developing evidence adequately and even to various kinds of corruption. Therefore, the Public Prosecution Law should provide for four specialized, independent investigative units to assist prosecuting attorneys:

- A Common Crime Investigation Unit, which would verify police evidence, undertake further investigation, and support the prosecuting attorney in the preparation of the case. It would also be responsible for investigating police corruption.
- A Financial and Administrative Crime Investigation Unit, which would work with the Comptroller General's Office, the Central Bank, the Bank Inspectorate, the Securities and Exchange Commission, the Internal

Revenue Department, and other partners to prosecute fraud and other types of white collar crime.
- A Civil and Human Rights Investigative Unit, which would investigate violence against women and children, police abuse, corruption in the court system, and similar human rights violations.
- A Special Investigations Unit, charged with investigating drug, gang, and terrorist activity and carrying out other special investigations.

The deputy attorney general would allocate the services of these units and monitor their performance. Integrating the various specialties may offer advantages, but in view of the Federal Bureau of Investigation's experience in the United States, the excessive concentration of investigative power in one unit should be avoided.

Increasing Transparency in Policy Formulation and Implementation

Open government, especially transparent and consultative policy formulation and implementation (condition 2 for accountability) requires obligatory procedures for:

- Disseminating understandable information related to proposed policies, projects, and programs
- Convening public hearings in which all persons who have submitted position papers have an opportunity within reasonable time limits to question the responsible public servants
- Publicizing diverging positions
- Releasing bidding documents, proposals, evaluation reports, contracts, and information about contract compliance
- Announcing professional and managerial openings, promotions, the procedures followed, and other relevant information
- Releasing budget information (especially commitments and contracts) and relevant information on government operations and the results obtained
- Making government documents and information accessible.

Many of these procedures could be included in an administrative regulations law that would cover the rights of the public in its relationship with government agencies and set guidelines for ethical or prohibited public servant behavior.

A Warning

In trying to extract lessons or guidance from this chapter, readers should keep in mind that the Bolivian experience in pursuing public accountability to consolidate its new democracy is unique. It reflects a very particular cultural, social, political, and economic context at a turning point in the country's history, when hyperinflation created social receptivity for very harsh reforms.

Part II

Toward an Anticorruption Strategy

6

Economic Reforms: Necessary but Not Sufficient to Curb Corruption?

Daniel Kaufmann

In recent years some academics and commentators in the mass media have argued that in transition economies (particularly in the former Soviet Union and Eastern Europe, as box 6.1 discusses) and in some emerging economies, market liberalization and privatization have significantly increased corruption. These reforms supposedly serve the vested interests of the corrupt elite. Even highly respected academics are ambivalent on this issue, advising extreme caution in initiating economic reforms when legal institutions are not yet well-developed. And in the winter 1996–97 issue of *Foreign Policy*, Robert Leiken wrote: "Where corruption is systemic, market and administrative reforms . . . may even become counterproductive. . . . Loosening government controls can facilitate illicit . . . economic activity. Moreover, bureaucrats have been known to compensate for lost revenues by exacting new 'fees' in other areas" ("Controlling the Corruption Epidemic," *Foreign Policy*, vol. 105, p. 55).

The problem with such perspectives is that what passes for economic reform often is not. Half-baked, poorly designed, inadequately implemented market reforms may indeed boost corruption. Well-designed and properly executed market reforms do not. A public monopoly that, through obscure insider deals, becomes a private monopoly controlled by few uncontested

Box 6.1 Market Reforms in Central and Eastern Europe and the Former Soviet Union

Market reforms are frequently blamed for increased corruption in the formerly communist countries of Central and Eastern Europe (CEE) and the former Soviet Union (FSU). But empirical investigation of these economies yields a different picture. While most of the CEE economies and the Baltics (Estonia, Latvia, and Lithuania) implemented far-reaching economic reforms (macrostabilization, privatization, liberalization, deregulation, and the development of market institutions) during the first half of the 1990s, many other countries in the former Soviet Union lagged behind.

As a result, the extent of underground activities has diverged markedly. As figure 6.1 illustrates, countries that implemented comprehensive economic and institutional reforms quickly reversed the initial boom in the underground economy when communism began to falter. At the same time in a number of FSU countries, incomplete reforms that either gave government officials opportunities for discretionary decisions or created monopolistic structures further fueled preexisting corruption.

What has driven much of the economy underground in the less-reformist economies? Enterprise surveys shed light on this question. Consider the share of the enterprise owner's (or senior manager's) time that is spent dealing with public officials instead of productively running the firm. In Chile, El Salvador, and Uruguay, that share is 8 to 12 percent; in Lithuania, 15 percent; in Russia and Ukraine, which have the largest unofficial economies among nonwar transition countries, it amounts to 30 to 40 percent. The inordinate amount of time that Russian and Ukrainian business owners spend with officials is the result of the myriad regulations and licenses required for a firm to operate and trade. Considerable bargaining also occurs over highly discretionary and onerous tax regimes. Firms are forced to bribe to cut their tax and regulatory burdens so that they can survive.

---

shareholders (as happened in prereform Argentina) certainly does not represent progress in the fight against corruption. However, a public monopoly that is de-monopolized and then privatized through an international, transparent bidding process will improve matters. Similarly, lowering import tariffs does little to curb corruption if the rules still give customs officials the discretion to decide the amount of import tax on each container or to revoke an import permit. Yet sound deregulation and trade liberalization

Finally, empirical evidence indicates that privatization also can help reduce corruption. Privatization transactions have, on balance, been less corrupt than others, and some privatization methods in particular have been found to result in less corruption over time. Furthermore, most countries that delayed privatization saw their underground economy skyrocket.

Figure 6.1 The Unofficial Economy in Transition Economies

Unofficial economy as a percentage of the total economy

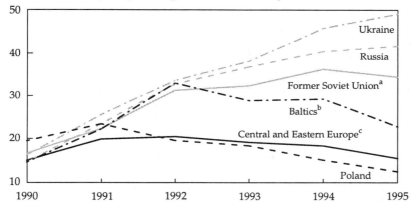

a. Excluding the Baltics.
b. Estonia, Latvia, and Lithuania.
c. Albania, Bosnia and Herzegovina, Bulgaria, Croatia, the Czech Republic, Hungary, FYR Macedonia, Poland, Romania, the Slovak Republic, Slovenia, and the Federal Republic of Yugoslavia.
Source: Kaufmann (1997).

make it more difficult for bureaucrats to extract bribes, and stiff competition will become less a source of corruption.

Furthermore, analysts who see market reforms as fuel for corruption often fail to consider the increased corruption that would occur in the absence of well-implemented reforms. A lack of economic reform can help perpetuate corruption because elite interests become more entrenched as their financial might accumulates through monopolistic structures. In fact, such a "war chest" becomes a major weapon to impede or distort reforms. Through this vicious circle, the costs of delaying reform can increase substantially over time.

By contrast, fewer regulatory and trade interventions, macroeconomic stability, and moderate, simple tax regimes with little discretion will do much to limit the opportunities for corruption. Evidence shows that corruption is reduced by fewer regulations, less regulatory discretion for bureaucrats and politicians, trade openness, product competition, and moderate, single, and uniform tax regimes. Survey responses from the elite in developing economies also refute the notion that economic reform fuels corruption. The vast majority of respondents report that corruption would be alleviated by further deregulation and liberalization, budget and tax reforms, and privatization (see the appendix to chapter 2).

Can Corruption Be Controlled?

Those in the "fatalist" camp often point out the dearth of successes in anticorruption drives. More generally, they stress that few countries have significantly reduced corruption in less than a century. However, Hong Kong (China) and Singapore offer examples of countries that shifted recently—and quickly—from being very corrupt to being relatively "clean." Moreover, other countries have managed to reduce the incidence of corruption relatively quickly, even if they are far from rendering it irrelevant. Botswana, for example, has made improvements over the past dozen years or so, and the Philippines, Poland, and Uganda have also scored some successes recently.

What are the most common features of these successes? Anticorruption bodies, such as the Independent Commission against Corruption in Hong Kong, China, and smaller institutional variations thereof in Botswana, Chile, Malaysia, and Singapore, are usually credited with much of the progress in fighting corruption. By contrast, the broader, complementary economic and institutional reforms that have taken place simultaneously often get insufficient credit. Botswana, for example, probably owes its success to the sound economic and public sector management policies it instituted early on, rather than to the later advent of an anticorruption agency. Uganda, too, may have been relatively successful in curbing corruption because of its broad institutional approach: the Museveni government, which came to power in 1986, implemented economic reforms and deregulation, reformed the civil service, strengthened the auditor general's office, empowered a reputable inspector general to investigate and prosecute corruption, and undertook an anticorruption public information campaign. Recently, however, with

Uganda's institutional and economic reforms tapering off, corruption control appears to have suffered somewhat, in spite of the continuous, valiant efforts of the reputable anticorruption watchdog body. Similarly, in Tanzania the courageous watchdog agency has not been able to ensure concrete progress on its own.

The survey responses of 165 public and private sector leaders in developing economies provide a sobering perspective on the value of anticorruption agencies. Fewer than 40 percent of the respondents thought highly of such bodies. To be credible, they said, such institutions must go hand in hand with honest leadership and be free of political interference. Otherwise anticorruption bodies are easily rendered useless or, worse, misused for political gain. Moreover, respondents emphasized the importance of complementary economic reforms, seeing no point in creating anticorruption agencies where bureaucrats and politicians intervene at will to apply regulatory restrictions. These responses suggest that many countries are long overdue for in-depth analysis of the evidence on anticorruption agencies, taking into consideration the broader institutional, public sector, and economic environment and using counterfactuals.

One illustration of effective institutional reform is the cleanup of the Philippine tax system in the 1970s under the charismatic and squeaky-clean leadership of Judge Efren Plana. Another is the ongoing overhaul of Argentina's bloated social security system (ANSES). In both cases the process included the immediate firing of corrupt personnel, the professionalization of the staff, new control systems, and modern incentive and performance assessment systems. Broader reforms also played an important role. In the Philippines, tax reforms were implemented simultaneously with the institutional revamping of the Bureau of Internal Revenue: tax rates were simplified, and exemptions were significantly reduced. These measures severely curtailed the incentives and discretion to extract bribes. In Argentina, competition is aiding the internal cleanup and reform effort: ANSES is ceasing to be the state monopoly provider of social security, as private pension institutions are being set up instead.

Many of the other successful institutional cleanups—in places such as Botswana, Chile, Hong Kong (China), Malaysia, Poland, Singapore, and Uganda—have also involved economic liberalization and reduced discretionary regulations. In the much-heralded case of Singapore, for instance, the crucial economic liberalization measures of the early to mid-1980s are often underplayed, while analysts of Hong Kong, China's, success in addressing police corruption overlook the impact of legalization of off-track betting.

The evidence emerging from some countries in the former Soviet Union is also telling. The leadership of Ukraine has repeatedly ordered various stand-alone institutional initiatives to address the corruption problem. New decrees have been passed, anticorruption campaigns have been launched, and special units have been created. Yet at the same time economic regulations continue to proliferate. For instance, the Kiev province recently decreed that any firm selling goods within its 14 counties must have a special trading permit for such intra-province transactions. No anticorruption drive can succeed in such a policy framework.

More Reform, Less Corruption

The economic reform agenda in many countries is far from finished, and its anticorruption potential often has been underemphasized and even maligned. Yet the evidence clearly points to promoting economic reform as a way of addressing corruption.

In designing reform programs, it is important to identify the discretionary control rights at the disposal of politicians and bureaucrats. Even when the majority of politicians and officials are honest, civic-minded citizens, a significantly corrupt minority can take a large toll on an economy. Typically, the main activities in need of reform are those that involve discretion. These include:

- Issuing licenses, permits, quantitative import restrictions (quotas), passports, customs and border-crossing documentation, and banking licenses
- Implementing price controls
- Blocking new firms and investors from entry to markets and providing monopoly power
- Awarding public procurement contracts
- Granting subsidies, soft credits, tax exemptions, and inflated pensions and allowing tax evasion
- Imposing foreign-exchange controls resulting in multiple exchange rates, the overinvoicing of imports, and the flight of capital
- Allocating real estate, grain storage facilities, and telecommunications and power infrastructure
- Selectively enforcing socially desirable regulations such as those that apply to public health and the environment
- Maintaining obscure or secret budgetary accounts or otherwise facilitating "leakages" from the budget to private accounts.

The discretionary control rights of officials can be sharply curtailed through a package of economic reforms. Although some regulations ought to stay because of their social desirability, transparent market mechanisms can be used to limit abuses (pollution quotas can be auctioned, for example). Other economic regulations should disappear altogether. Conventional economic reforms can have a significant effect: macroeconomic stabilization removes the discretion to provide subsidies and soft credits; privatization depoliticizes state-owned enterprises; and the building of a constituency that favors competition and broad market liberalization reduces the opportunities for and tolerance of corruption. Yet simply reforming macroeconomic policies is insufficient.

Further emphasis must be placed on fuller liberalization, microeconomic deregulation, tax reform (the creation of a simple, nondiscretionary regime with moderate, uniform tax rates, coupled with determined enforcement and the elimination of exemptions), government and budget reform (the establishment of transparent, financially sound revenue and expenditure mechanisms), and, over the long term, broader institutional reform (the revamping of customs, the elimination of redundant ministries and agencies, and civil service and legal reform). Also critical is setting up an improved civil service pay system, with adequate salary incentives and enforceable penalties for malfeasance. Countries whose system of rewards for civil servants is competitive with the private sector have less corruption. Many countries should also strengthen efforts to develop the financial sector, because market-determined interest rates, improved banking supervision by independent central banks, transparent accounting standards, reserve-requirement compliance (where owners put their own equity at real risk), and effective payment systems all reduce the opportunities for fraud-driven financial crises. In addition, they limit the loopholes that enable money-laundering to grow out of control.

These pillars of government and regulatory reform—the next stage beyond macroeconomic reform—have been neglected in many developing and transition economies. The state of the art in these areas is not as advanced as in macro-stabilization or trade liberalization, where experience has proven what to do and how to do it. By recognizing that corruption is a symptom of deep-seated institutional and economic weaknesses, emerging economies and the international community must elevate the priority of these difficult and time-consuming reforms. The payoff will be substantial: Virtually all economic, deregulation, and government reform measures would not only help curb corruption but also help sustain national growth strategies.

7

Elements of a Successful
Anticorruption Strategy

Jeremy Pope

Combating corruption is not an end in itself. Rather, it is instrumental to the broader goal of more effective, fair, and efficient government, which in turn is associated with greater economic development. Anticorruption activists are concerned not solely with corruption but also with its impact on development and society. How does corruption hinder poverty alleviation by distorting developmental decisionmaking? How inefficient is bribery? Who ultimately pays the cost of corruption?

Although corruption itself is costly, attempting to eliminate it entirely would not be worthwhile. Realistically, under many conditions it would simply be too expensive to reduce corruption to zero, and the process would unreasonably and unacceptably infringe upon fundamental human rights and other freedoms. Furthermore, program elimination might be unjustified, bureaucratic discretion might be necessary for effective administration, and stronger enforcement and deterrence might be unaffordable. Thus the aim should not be the complete eradication of corruption, but rather a fundamental increase in the integrity—and so the efficiency and fairness—of government.

Background conditions vary greatly from society to society, but the basic policy responses to corruption are likely to fall into three types: substantive, structural, and moral. Individually and together, these policy responses unite the interests and involvement of government, the private sector, and civil society.

Some Lessons from the Past

An analysis of the (comparatively rare) successes and the (numerous) failures of past anticorruption efforts in various countries identifies several key elements that can block progress:

- *Limits of power* at the top. An incoming administration may wish to tackle corruption effectively, but if it inherits a corrupt bureaucracy, that bureaucracy may impede efforts for change.
- *Lack of leadership.* There has often been an absence of commitment at the top. Overly ambitious promises have led to unrealistic and unachievable expectations and a consequent loss of public confidence.
- *Uncoordinated, piecemeal reforms.* No one "owns" the reforms, commits to them, and is motivated to see them implemented and kept up-to-date.
- *Overreliance on legal remedies.* Changing the law and improving its enforcement is an uncertain strategy for changing the way people behave. And too much reliance on enforcement leads to repression, abuse of enforcement power, and the emergence of further corruption.
- *A focus only on the "small fry,"* with reforms overlooking those at the top. If the law is seen as applied unfairly and unevenly, it soon ceases to be heeded at all.
- *Lack of a specific and achievable focus.* Reforms that fail to deliver any "quick wins" have quickly lost public support. Even when reforms have been focused and changes real, they have not endured when institutional mechanisms have not outlived the leaders of the reforms.
- *Failure to engage partners outside the government.* Above all, an attempt by the government alone to achieve reforms without drawing in the actors best able to assist it from civil society and the private sector have met with minimal successes.

Toward an Overall Strategy

The development of a coherent, overall, holistic strategy involves a clear commitment by political leaders to combating corruption wherever it occurs. This means leaders will have to submit themselves to scrutiny. Experience shows that primary attention should be given to preventing future corruption and changing systems rather than indulging in witch hunts.

Comprehensive anticorruption legislation needs to be adopted and implemented by agencies of manifest integrity (including investigators, prosecutors, and adjudicators). Areas of government activity most prone to corruption need to be identified, and relevant procedures reviewed as a matter of priority. Salaries of civil servants and political leaders should adequately reflect the responsibilities of the posts and be as comparable as possible with those in the private sector, both to reduce the "need" for corruption and to ensure that the best people are available to serve the state. Legal and administrative corruption "remedies" should provide adequate deterrence (for example, corruption-induced contracts rendered void and unenforceable, large transactions closely monitored, random intensive audits instituted, and licenses and permits obtained through corruption voided). Most important, a creative partnership needs to be forged between government and civil society, including the private sector, professions, religious organizations, and so on.

Reforms may be conceptualized under the four headings of prevention, enforcement, public awareness, and institution building. In each case, the goal is to make corruption a high-risk, low-profit undertaking.

Prevention

Simplifying government programs and procedures will help reduce the opportunities for corruption. The more efficient the design of a program, the less prone to corruption it will be. One reform is to eliminate those "gatekeepers" who are in a position to exact tolls from users. Another is to reduce the number of steps required to gain government approvals and payment for goods supplied. In addition, simplifying and enforcing government regulations will not only diminish the need for people to resort to bribery but will also ease the transaction of business in general. Finally, payrolls should be cleaned up to eliminate "ghost workers" and render their reappearance more difficult.

Areas of discretion should be minimized or, where possible, eliminated. Where retained, clear written guidelines for exercising such discretion should be published. Staff manuals and similar materials should likewise be published and made accessible to department users and others. Opportunities for corruption will also be reduced by demystifying the role of government, because corruption thrives when the public is unaware of its rights.

Fewer opportunities for corruption will exist if face-to-face contact is minimized, thereby depersonalizing government. Random elements can be introduced so that those doing business with the government cannot predict the officials with whom they may be dealing. Another strategy to consider is the regular rotation of key staff, which will lessen the risk of unhealthy relationships developing between individual staff and the public they serve, as well as within groups of government workers.

Available mechanisms that offer speedy and effective reviews of contentious decisions should be examined. Managers at all levels should be responsible for the activities of subordinates. The effectiveness of supervision can be increased by empowering superior officers to review and control the work of their staff through routine and impromptu checks. Also, managers should regularly certify their subordinates' compliance with civil service regulations and the law. Complaint channels should be organized to enable junior officials to complain about their superiors' corruption, and the press should be free to expose malfeasance.

Civil service workers should be paid a living wage in line with reasonable needs and expectations. Rewards for achievement should be implemented, with good performance recognized and rewarded, and role models acclaimed. Mechanisms for involving civil society should be established and should feed into a continuous process of review. The public should be polled periodically for its perception of what has changed. In addition, the income, assets, and liabilities of officials with decisionmaking powers should be monitored effectively to ensure consistency with known earnings and reasonable expectations. Appropriate bans on post–public employment by the private sector should also be made.

It is important to create an open, genuinely competitive, and transparent system of public procurement. To reinforce anticorruption efforts, professional associations of accountants, auditors, and lawyers should denounce participation in corrupt activities (including money-laundering) and make such behavior cause for being professionally barred. The reporting of all gifts and hospitality received by government officials should be required, as well as the reporting and recording of all political donations.

It is desirable, too, to review and enforce appropriate conflict-of-interest regulations. This might involve introducing ethics programs and periodically holding group discussions of real-life ethical dilemmas drawn from civil servants' own experiences. In some cases it might be desirable to remove certain activities from the mainstream of the public service (for example, constituting a separate revenue authority) so that, among other things, workers in sensitive jobs could be paid better salaries without distorting civil service relativities. The removal of "monopolies" within the bureaucracy is also important in order to provide rival sources of services (the issuing of drivers' licenses, for example), thereby ending unofficial "charges" or at least driving the price down.

Finally, coalitions of interests in support of corruption prevention should be built. Such coalitions should draw in both the private sector and civil society and in certain cases undertake public awareness campaigns to decrease tolerance of corruption.

Enforcement

Independent enforcement mechanisms should be implemented to increase the likelihood of corruption being detected and punished. Investigators, prosecutors, and adjudicators must be able to perform their professional duties in a transparently independent fashion and enforce the rule of law against all who breach it, whatever their positions (thus depoliticizing law enforcement). Adequate powers of investigation and prosecution, consistent with international human rights norms, will be necessary. For example, investigators should have access to all government documentation and records held by lawyers and financial advisers. Sound arrangements for international mutual legal assistance should be developed with relevant countries. And wealthy persons should bear the onus of proving that their wealth has been acquired legitimately.

Provisions should be made for transparent mechanisms lifting any immunities that high-level public officials enjoy by reason of their office. Effective channels for complaints should also be established for both whistle-blowers within government and members of the public, because it is essential that neither feels unnecessarily exposed to reprisals. Examples of such channels include telephone hotlines and counseling services (preferably independent of the civil service). In addition, when necessary, physical protection for key informants should be provided, whether inside or outside the country. Furthermore, private parties who lose money and contracts because of corruption should be able to sue for damages in ordinary civil courts.

Mechanisms for punishing those outside a country's jurisdiction should be developed. The use of civil penalties should be considered (as judgments of the ordinary courts, civil penalties may be enforced abroad, whereas criminal sanctions generally cannot). Another option is blacklisting corrupt firms and sales staff (and publishing their names as a way of ensuring that other countries and competitors are aware of the corrupt activities). Extradition arrangements should be made so that corrupt officials who flee will be returned by court order from the most attractive countries of refuge. Legal measures should be taken to enable the assets of the corrupt to be seized and forfeited, whether these are inside or outside the country.

Public Awareness

Public understanding should be engendered regarding the harm done by corruption and the fact that the corrupt are stealing the public's money. It is equally important to educate citizens about their rights to services—at a given price or no cost at all—as well as their duty to complain and procedures for doing so when officials behave corruptly in specific cases. In addition, public perceptions should be ascertained about how much corruption is taking place and where, to provide a baseline against which progress can be measured.

To keep the public informed, the legal and administrative environment must provide for a free press. There should be no censorship, nor should the government discriminate against media outlets by withdrawing advertising, denying access to newsprint, or using other means. Freedom-of-information laws should be enacted, and defamation and "insult" laws reviewed to ensure that they cannot be used to unreasonably fetter the press. (Indeed, public figures, as legitimate objects of public interest, should enjoy less protection than ordinary private citizens.) Efforts should also be made to raise professional standards and ensure that state-owned media employees can maintain independence and exercise professional responsibility.

The environment in which civil society operates must be appropriate for a free and democratic society. For instance, voter registration should be a right, not a privilege, and simple, inexpensive registration procedures should exist.

Institution Building

First, all relevant institutions must have adequate staff and other resources. Clear ethical guidelines and rules of conduct should be formulated and disseminated. In-service training should be provided for civil servants at all levels, and the training needs of all relevant departments and agencies should be assessed.

Internal financial management systems must be reviewed to ensure their adequacy and effectiveness. The supreme audit institution must be independent, professional, and equipped with a mechanism for thoroughly screening and appointing staff, the ability to generate widespread publicity for its reports, and the authority to implement its recommendations. The ombudsman or equivalent office should likewise have adequate powers, including the ability to publicize its existence and its reports and ensure response to its recommendations.

The contractor general must establish the need for independent oversight of government contracting and public reporting of public contract activity. Procurement must be professionalized by examining present practices against "best practice" and the most transparent systems. Choice must not be captive to departmental advice and interests; "outsiders" should be integral participants. Decisionmakers should be pooled with no predictability as to who will be involved in any particular exercise. Speedy decisionmaking should be enforced to eliminate delays during which corruption can take place. Departmental procedures should be scrutinized regularly, as well as when complaints are made.

The elections commission should be ensured independence and impartiality to sustain public and political-party confidence, and it should maintain transparency in all aspects of the elections system (except, of course, the ballot). The commission should foster public participation in the monitoring process to build public confidence while familiarizing its staff and party officials with the system and training them to monitor it professionally.

Legislative mechanisms for accountability, including a public accounts committee, should be reviewed periodically and revised if needed. Public access to legislative proceedings should be maximized. A capacity for regular polling of public opinions and concerns should be developed.

When corruption is alleged, investigations and prosecutions must be conducted independently. Certain questions must be answered, including:

- Is there a need for an independent commission against corruption?
- Are the laws of evidence appropriate to a modern era?
- Are existing penalties too low (no deterrent value) or too high (deterring prosecutions)?

Finally, access to the courts for purposes of remedying complaints should be simplified, and adequate judicial review of administrative action should be ensured.

Conclusion

Anticorruption reform is a long-term process in which appropriate attitudes and conduct must be taught and reinforced at all levels. Initially, reforms should tackle only those issues where they can be most effective or add the most value. The process of reform must be visibly "owned" by and supported from the top. In the end, tackling corruption is not just about tackling corruption; it is about strengthening the public's confidence in, and loyalty to, the state—and strengthening the state's financial and policy abilities to serve citizens.

8

Enhancing Accountability and Ethics in the Public Sector

Jeremy Pope

Structural corruption in a public service is a litmus test of the service's ethics and accountability. Of course, every public service should aspire to the highest standards, but in the real world, governments need sticks as well as carrots, because public servants motivated by private greed are virtually inevitable. Consequently, this chapter focuses on the realistic containment of corruption in the public sector, rather than on the unattainable ideal of eliminating it.

It is important to appreciate from the outset that if the political will is lacking—both for change and for rigorous implementation at all levels of government—no legislation can ever be effective in containing corruption. One of the greatest obstacles to reform lies at the very heart of government—with the politicians and political interests in power. These will almost invariably see moves toward greater transparency and greater accountability as an erosion of their power, as indeed they are. Perversely, the officeholders with the greatest conflicts of interest are often those in the most powerful positions to frustrate reforms.[1]

---

1. For example, consider the resistance among British parliamentarians to suggestions that they curtail their outside interests and that an independent element

It is important to bear in mind two other truisms. First, legislation is unlikely to be effective unless it is accompanied by measures to ensure implementation—measures that maximize accountability and transparency and minimize vulnerability in the areas where corruption is most likely to flourish. Second, the ultimate goal must be to change the perception of corruption from a low-risk, high-profit activity to one with high risks and low profits.

It is a sobering reflection on the effectiveness of the law that even though most countries in the world provide for criminal sanctions against those involved in corruption, the laws are widely flouted and sanctions are rarely imposed. Even when they are, they tend to be directed against the small fry rather than the big fish. Successful reform therefore depends on the political willingness and ability to provide a legal framework and appropriate administrative measures that can and will be implemented fairly and consistently.

Given that corruption is a universal phenomenon and that there will always be individuals and groups in a society who attempt to enrich themselves unjustly, how should corruption be attacked? Solutions are difficult to design partly because corruption is difficult to expose. Unlike the situation in many other types of crime, corruption benefits people on both sides of the equation—those paying bribes to gain favors, for example, and those receiving bribes—giving both an interest in secrecy. Also, the victims—for example, taxpayers who are overcharged for public services, or honest businesspeople who lose contracts because of corrupt procurement practices—do not usually know what has happened. Nevertheless, experience shows that corruption can be curbed by reducing the opportunities for and benefits of wrongdoing by making all participants more vulnerable to detection and sanction. The government needs a well-coordinated, well-understood overall strategy that limits opportunities for abuse of public office, increases the likelihood of corruption being detected, and reduces the likelihood that individuals will be able to profit from corrupt acts, whether they are giving or receiving bribes.

---

be introduced into the policing of their conduct. Such suggestions are portrayed as an attack on the sovereignty of Parliament and on the integrity of parliamentarians. Contrast this negative attitude with the positive approaches being adopted in South Africa by the African National Congress, including the opening up of parliamentary processes to public scrutiny and the imposition of a code of conduct on all political parties.

To repeat, the aim of an effective anticorruption policy is simple: corruption must be seen by the community at large as a high-risk, low-return activity. It is also important that the measures taken are cost-effective and do not damage public service morale and efficiency.

No single line of attack is likely to be effective. Rather, a holistic approach is required:

- Political leaders must make a clean commitment to combating corruption, no matter who practices it.
- Comprehensive anticorruption legislation must be adopted and implemented by a strong, independent agency of manifest integrity.
- The areas of government activity most prone to corruption must be identified, and relevant procedures reviewed.
- Salaries of civil servants and political leaders should adequately reflect the responsibilities of their posts and be as comparable as conditions allow with corresponding salaries in the private sector. Fair salaries both reduce the need for corruption and help attract the best people available to serve the state.
- Legal procedures and remedies must provide an effective deterrent. For example, if contracts induced by corruption are legally void and unenforceable, self-interest would compel export guarantee organizations to monitor much more closely the nature of the international transactions they are underwriting.
- All licenses and permits obtained through corruption should be made void. This gives the general public a powerful incentive to protect itself by reporting corrupt demands.

Singapore was so deeply riddled with corruption at the time of independence that its very prospects for survival as a nation were at risk. Yet the problem was tackled in a determined and comprehensive way by a government whose ethics were transparent and above reproach. The experience of Singapore (and other economies such as Hong Kong, China) shows very clearly what can be achieved, given the political will, the appropriate infrastructure, and the determined implementation of an anticorruption policy. It also shows that a cleanup can be launched even before the adoption of remuneration policies that effectively reduce temptation for key officials.

There is a clear and constructive role for the private sector to play in strengthening ethics in the public sector, particularly in the context of business transactions between the two sectors. A free press (to educate the public about the evils of corruption and the measures taken to contain it) and open political debate and accountability are also important.

Conditions for Successfully Implementing Reform

To bring more integrity to government, appropriate attitudes and conduct must be taught and reinforced at all levels. Reform is a long-term process, involving a series of building blocks that must be put in place gradually. Initially, reformers should tackle only those issues where they can be most effective or where there is the most added value.

To make a real change in the ethical environment, certain conditions have to be fulfilled. First, leaders must not promise what they cannot deliver. Even if the government is good and honest, promises that are broken simply reinforce public cynicism about politics. Second, the rules must apply to lawmakers as well as to lawbreakers; they must apply to the grand corruption of senior politicians and officials as well as to the routine, petty corruption of local clerks. Third, whatever is implemented must be "owned" by someone—that is, someone has to be responsible for it, police it, and keep it up to date.

Reforms must address core political and administrative goals that are not only integral to management functions but also realizable. Clear, long-term objectives should be set, and regular reports made and evaluated (progress confirms promise). Reforms must focus on strategic areas (such as the police or treasury) where wider gains are achievable in a visible way and relatively quickly. The public's respect for the rule of law and confidence in the state's machinery may be enhanced if the police—who are directly responsible for enforcing the law on a daily basis and who are the government representatives with whom the public most frequently comes into contact—are seen as honest. The state can also reap public relations benefits, as well as financial rewards, from honest and regular collection of taxes and effective scrutiny of public expenditure.

Reforms at a low level should focus on activities where one individual has too much power or authority. Special attention must be paid to conflict-of-interest situations, where the potential for corruption is especially acute. In these cases, decisions should be made jointly rather than by individuals. Furthermore, decisions must be transparent and reported, or at least available, to an independent source of confirmation and verification.

In addition, reforms must be horizontally integrated to share information and best practice, and vertically integrated to demonstrate commitment. Recruitment, training, and recognition of good performance are as important as the threat of investigations and possible sanctions.

Four Types of Strategies to Reduce Corruption

Anticorruption strategies can be divided into four broad categories. The first are those that take the underlying structure of government programs as given and focus on improving government integrity, enforcing the existing law, designing effective penalties for bribers and bribe-takers, and developing international support mechanisms.

Strategies in the second category reform the procedural basis of government to increase transparency and discourage corruption. This involves reforming bureaucratic procedures and public procurement practices, reforming political campaign financing and electoral laws, and creating an independent judiciary.

Strategies in the third category address government programs that may give rise to corruption because they are poorly designed or unnecessary. Regulatory statutes might be reviewed to determine if they are necessary and whether they can be streamlined. Public procurement specifications might be redesigned to emphasize standardized, off-the-shelf products to reduce manipulation of tailor-made specifications. Government benefits traditionally allocated at the discretion of officials might instead be allocated in accordance with clear and readily verifiable criteria. The scope for restructuring will, of course, vary from program to program. Many types of permits and licenses could be eliminated altogether; others could be allocated to the highest bidder; still others could be assigned on the basis of clearly defined public-interest criteria.

The fourth and final group of strategies relate to public attitudes and the role of self-regulation in the private sector. Public attitudes (and attitudes within the corporate sector) can be changed so that corruption is no longer viewed with cynicism, resignation, and acceptance. This change can only be achieved if it goes hand in hand with credible efforts to reform the public sphere. If people have good grounds for cynicism about their government, their attitudes are not likely to change.

Category 1: Working within the System

Enhancing Civil Service Ethics

Corruption often grows in the absence of a public service work ethic or an understanding of the concepts of public accountability and responsibility. This is particularly evident in societies where public servants owe their posts not to the public they serve but to the relatives who appointed them. Nepotism results in apathy toward the public as "customers" and a disinclination to accord them service.

Integrity in public life and public service develops when legislation, regulations, and codes of conduct spell out proper and improper behavior; when religious, political, and social values create expectations of honesty from politicians and officials; when there is professionalism among officials and a sense of elitism among senior civil servants; and when the political leadership takes both public and private morality seriously. Together these conditions establish and foster a tradition of ethical public life and an atmosphere in which most politicians and officials are assumed to be honest. In such an environment, it is also assumed that the laws and means of law enforcement are sufficient to deal with the few who break the rules, accept bribes, and commit fraud.

It is, however, important to bear in mind several crucial points:

- The ethical environment must be owned, policed, adapted, and updated throughout the public sector.
- The purpose and intentions of legislation, codes of conduct, and rules of behavior apply equally throughout the public service.
- The ethical environment is akin to an ecosystem, in that its elements can be mutually self-sustaining and integrated. Potential weaknesses may include a decline in political participation or lack of control over important factors (such as effective investigative media). The environment must be reviewed periodically, with new means of accountability being introduced or existing means upgraded and reinforced.
- Sustaining the ethical environment requires political commitment and leadership to inspire confidence and trust, but politicians should not be the only ones to carry this responsibility.
- The ethical environment should be determined at the macro level, from which micro-level changes—the details of reform—must develop.

The consequences of degradation of the ethical environment in public organizations and departments will be weak guidance on standards of conduct, poor compliance with procedures, management indifference or ignorance, inadequate financial and management information systems, lax working practices, poor staff relations, too much suborganizational autonomy, poor recruitment and training policies, and, crucially, little or no attempt by senior officials to control, monitor, or police the contact with private sector values, practices, personnel, and procedures.

Strengthening Existing Mechanisms

The best deterrent to corruption (or any other kind of crime) is a high expectation of detection, prosecution, and punishment. It is essential, therefore, to have efficient investigatory agencies whose laws and procedures—including prescribed penalties—deter not only government officials but also companies and top executives from corrupt practices.

Existing investigatory and prosecutorial agencies should be reviewed to ensure that their powers, procedures, and resources are adequate for their task and to determine whether existing penalties for offenses will deter would-be corrupters and corruptees. The government of Uganda has taken a promising initiative in this respect; it has established an official interdepartmental coordinating group that brings together the various actors involved in combating corruption. This ensures a holistic approach and maximum cooperation among all the agencies involved.

Scrutiny should also be given to existing mechanisms for the independent judicial review of administrative decisions, to ensure they are lawful and made in good faith in accordance with established procedures. Legal procedures and remedies should be reviewed, too, to see that they provide an effective deterrent.

Singapore's comprehensive approach to improving public sector integrity began in July 1973, with a circular from the Ministry of Finance. The circular instructed public officials to review and improve the measures taken to prevent corruption by minimizing the opportunities for unethical practices. Among other things, the permanent secretaries (heads of ministries) were asked "to make their officers aware of the government's serious efforts to eradicate corruption and to advise them to report any cases of corruption" (Quah 1989, p. 845). They were also requested to take appropriate anticorruption measures in those departments where wrongdoing was most likely to occur. Such measures included improving work methods and procedures to reduce delays; increasing the effectiveness of supervision by enabling superior officers to check and control the work of their staff; rotating officers to ensure that no individual or group remained too long in a single operational unit; carrying out surprise checks on the work of officers; making the necessary security arrangements to prevent unauthorized access to department premises; and reviewing anticorruption measures every three to five years, with the aim of introducing further improvements.

Improving Public Sector Pay

There is little doubt that inadequate pay for public officials contributes to corruption, at least at the petty level if not throughout a system. Of course, many developing countries are simply not in a financial position to pay high salaries to public officials. They are caught in a vicious, self-perpetuating spiral: low pay leads some officials to appropriate government funds, and the misuse of official funds leaves the government with insufficient resources to increase compensation. Combating corruption is one way of addressing low pay, because it may create the additional wealth required to pay higher salaries.

For this reason the adequacy of salaries in the public sector should be kept constantly under review. Singapore has been conspicuously successful in developing a vibrant economy based on little more than its human resources, despite starting from a low economic base and high, endemic corruption. The salaries Singapore pays its civil servants are among the highest in the world, but this was not always so. As the economy has grown, the government has become able to offer civil servants top compensation. But Singapore's anticorruption strategy started before the country was in a position to pay well, and its anticorruption efforts were reinforced through the salary structure only when this was economically possible.

The government of Uganda has taken an even more ambitious approach: wholesale reform of the civil service, a halving of staff numbers, and a trebling of salaries. Reformers realize that if a job is underpaid, it will not be valued by the jobholder, who will have little to lose if he or she is dismissed. (For a description of the process, see Langseth 1995).

Category 2: Reforming the Procedural Basis of Government

To be effective, a program to reform the procedural basis of government to increase transparency and discourage corruption should include:

- An open, genuinely competitive, and transparent system of public procurement
- A radical simplification of regulations, not only to diminish the need to resort to bribery, but to ease the transaction of business of all sorts and facilitate access to public services generally
- An adequate salary structure that will eliminate the need for civil servants to supplement their incomes through bribery, although this component may not necessarily be a priority
- Strict limitation and regular supervision of the discretionary authority of officials (minor officials in particular, but no level should be exempted)
- Frequent transfers of officials, to prevent long-term relationships with suppliers and customers from developing
- Effective and well-understood laws and procedures preventing improper association between officials and suppliers, covering such matters as the receipt of gifts and hospitality

- Published and publicly available guidelines for decisionmaking
- Speedy and effective reviews of decisions allegedly made without following published guidelines
- Efficient investigatory agencies
- Appropriate channels for subordinate officials to use when reporting corruption by their superiors.

Corruption generally originates in the monopoly of power enjoyed by public officials (including, of course, politicians). It is a universal phenomenon found in all states, rich or poor, and at all stages of development. It is, however, particularly prevalent in two different types of states.

On the one hand, corruption can be a way around the rigidities of an overcentralized and planned society. Individuals in "gatekeeper" positions can demand payoffs in return for providing key services or access to scarce commodities. On the other hand, corruption can also be a way to overcome the uncertainties of a weak state and a poorly developed open economy. In this case, the incentives to make and receive payoffs can arise from too few rules rather than too many.

If the state has not established clear, well-enforced guidelines for economic activity and the exercise of administrative discretion, private individuals may play it safe by paying officials to give them the needed permits or protection. It is only one step further for these same officials to prevent the entry of competitors for government business, or to divert public funds for private purposes.

Efforts to reduce corruption by decentralizing decisionmaking can, however, backfire badly. Unless a strong team is appointed to oversee and audit public procurement, corruption can—and most probably will—flourish. Once entrenched, corruption is difficult to root out, because, among other reasons, too many of those influential within the political process have a stake in maintaining the status quo.

Although subsidiarity—decisionmaking at the lowest possible level— has its enthusiasts, others maintain just as firmly that a properly overseen centralized system can function less corruptly than one that is widely dispersed. The arguments for and against subsidiarity cut both ways. The French experience has been that where there is too much subsidiarity with too little control, things degenerate into a situation of endemic corruption. The political parties that control the various local governments receive virtually automatic percentage payoffs for public contracts—a situation that was not known to exist before control of local government was decentralized.

It is clear that subsidiarity is not in itself an antidote to corruption. The delegation of decisionmaking power must be accompanied by strategies for policing the exercise of that power and ensuring that new decisionmakers fully understand their accountability.

Category 3: Concentrating on Government Activities Particularly Susceptible to Corruption

Corruption is most widely found in certain activities of government. These are public procurement, customs, taxation, police work (especially traffic control), immigration, provision of services where there is a state-owned monopoly, issuance of construction permits and land zoning decisions, issuance of other licenses and permits (including drivers' licenses), and government appointments.

Public procurement in particular is notorious for the levels of corruption attained by dishonest politicians and officials. Throughout the world, procurement procedures that foster bribery and corruption have been allowed to develop. Nonetheless, there are approaches that may reduce corruption in this traditionally very difficult area. One is the "no-bribery pledge" now being introduced in Ecuador for major public procurement exercises. Tendering chief executive officers are required to personally warrant that no bribery has taken place and to personally certify returns of all commissions and other payments made to or for the benefit of third parties in connection with particular transactions.[2] Another approach is the introduction of specific mechanisms for monitoring the awarding and execution of public contracts, such as the ones now instituted in Jamaica and, more recently, Belize.

An important area in which the state may need protection is that of the post–public service employment of senior officials and decisionmakers. Not only are these people likely to possess valuable confidential information when they leave public service (such as knowledge of tenders and plans not yet in the public domain), but they may also have a network of personal contacts in the sector they worked with. More importantly, for decisionmakers still in public office, the prospect of well-paid, private sector employment after retirement can, of itself, be a highly corrupting influence. Corruption can occur without payment of money; an official

---

2. The government of Ecuador has developed these procedures in association with Transparency International (TI), and details are available from TI's Berlin office. If the corruption leakage is of the order of 10 to 15 percent, then on a single contract worth US$600 million, even a 50 percent success rate through the new system could save the public purse about US$40 million.

might, for example, give a private firm special treatment in exchange for a lucrative job with the firm later. Such quid pro quos can be dealt with through legislation on public sector ethics. For example, civil servants could be prohibited from accepting work related to their official duties for several years after leaving public office.

Category 4: Enlisting the Public in the Fight against Corruption

It is essential for the public to understand fully the rationale behind any major public sector pay increase and to appreciate that with the "carrot" of higher pay comes the "stick" of accountability and the likelihood of corrupt officials being weeded out. However, the role of the public in curbing corruption is a much broader one than this. Certain segments of civil society—private business, professional organizations, teaching institutions, and spiritual leaders—are particularly valuable in building a more ethical society. But a successful assault on corruption calls for widespread public support. It is significant that the Italian prime minister's July 1994 attempt to reform procedures for investigating corruption cases collapsed in the face of public hostility. This happened mainly because the public had not been consulted, and, according to a British Broadcasting Corporation report on August 16, it felt its "ownership" of the process was being threatened.

Most importantly, public participation must be reinforced through mechanisms that give appropriate protection to those who "blow the whistle" on corrupt practices and thereby expose themselves to retribution and endanger their careers. At the same time, the positive aspects of ethical behavior should be stressed. People should be encouraged to be honest, not out of fear of the consequences otherwise, but for reasons of personal integrity and the enhanced self-image this engenders. Those who may have become rich through corruption should be seen as figures of contempt and pity, rather than role models.

Leadership and Public Confidence: The Ultimate Determinants of Clean Government

At the end of the day, all anticorruption efforts will be in vain if leaders are not committed and the public does not have confidence in the reformers' sincerity and ability to effect change. Leaders must lead from the front and openly encourage those charged with monitoring, investigating, and disciplining wrongdoers to perform those duties without fear or favor. In particular, the police and the courts must know that they are not just permitted to prosecute anyone who has fallen from grace, but that they are actually encouraged to do so.

The example of President Benjamin Mkapa of Tanzania is inspiring (see chapter 11). After coming to power in 1995, Mkapa publicly disclosed his assets and income and explained how he came to own what he does, and he made a similar declaration about his wife. This is the most outstanding demonstration of personal commitment that the African continent has witnessed yet. Mkapa also declared himself committed to wholesale reform and established an independent President's Commission of Inquiry against Corruption, with wide powers and a mandate to report by the end of October 1996. Public opinion surveys on corruption levels have been conducted and baselines established, against which the success or failure of individual reforms can be measured.

A governance and reform unit has been developed within the Office of the President, which will be able to monitor closely the implementation of reforms by a wide variety of actors. It will ensure that the president is kept well informed and is able to make strategic personal interventions when these are called for. A whole calendar of events has been planned to ensure that the reform effort remains very much in the public eye.

The whole enterprise will succeed or fail on the strength of President Mkapa's leadership. As we have seen elsewhere (the Philippines under President Ferdinand Marcos, for example), some reforms last only as long as the individuals who achieve them hold power. They are personal to the reformers, not structural. And they do not endure.

Once there is leadership at the highest level, as in Hong Kong (China) and Singapore, meaningful reform can follow. The public can be won over, however, only if it believes that the leadership is serious. In a corrupt environment, convincing the masses will never be easy. But principled leaders can win over the doubters and set a country on the path to sustainable reform.

References

Langseth, Petter. 1995. *Civil Service Reform in Uganda: Lessons Learned.* EDI Working Paper 95-05. Washington, D.C.: World Bank.

Quah, John S. T. 1989. "Singapore's Experience in Curbing Corruption." In Arnold J. Heidenheimer, Michael Johnston, and Victor T. Levine, eds., *Political Corruption: A Handbook.* New Brunswick, N.J.: Transaction Publishers.

9

Involving Civil Society in the Fight against Corruption

Mohammad M. Kisubi

History is littered with postures at reform—with grandiose promises and conspicuous lack of delivery by governments. In some cases the intentions are genuine: newly elected leaders come determined to clean out the stables but are quickly overwhelmed by the mess with which they are confronted. A corrupt bureaucracy is hardly one that embraces reform and follows the letter of the new laws. Other leaders simply grandstand, making speeches and signing laws in the absence of any expectation that meaningful change will follow. Indeed, not infrequently, these leaders or those close to them are themselves deeply involved in corruption.

Where the attempts have been genuine but nevertheless failed, invariably one ingredient is missing—the involvement of civil society. Where anticorruption efforts have succeeded—usually in the wake of a revolution—reform measures have been backed by a public whose expectations have been high and whose leaders have been empowered to tackle the problem. The status quo has been swept away; there have been no stakeholders in the old corruption process. If new leaders can move quickly enough, then meaningful reform can take place before self-interest takes hold and motivates those within the system to obstruct change.

In the fight against corruption, passing laws is no answer by itself, because public attitudes can overshadow legal definitions, and public cooperation in reporting and investigating offenses is needed. Fighting corruption demands that the general public be informed and enlightened as to what constitutes corruption, particularly in countries with a long history of corrupt practices and a populace that may be resigned to at least certain low-level corrupt practices as a way of getting things done.

Yet in any government, whatever its reputation, there are men and women of integrity. In the most corrupt countries they may be a very small minority, but they exist and may be biding their time before reform can be achieved. They will be empowered not by agents within the system (who may wittingly or unwittingly have effectively marginalized them) but by the public.

Amongst the general public, too, are similar people of integrity who are anxious to see the corruption issue tackled and who realize that unless public attitudes (often a resigned acceptance) are reversed, little will take place. Yet almost invariably, civil society's response to the problem is fragmented at best. The lawyers may be policed (with greater or lesser effectiveness) by their codes and societies and bar associations; the accountants by their professional bodies; and so on. Few in civil society have positioned themselves to take an overall view, contemplate what the integral parts of a national integrity system can and should look like, and press for relevant reform under a holistic blueprint.

Furthermore, we cannot—and should not—ignore the role of civil society in the corruption process in the first place. The notion that state activities can take place in a vacuum simply does not stand up to experience. Every individual builds a unique store of "social capital" through personal relationships and networks—family ties, school friendships, workplace connections, and the like. And the acquisition and expenditure of social capital means that individuals do not, and to some extent cannot, act independently, nor do they act wholly selfishly.

Of course, favors exchanged under an honor system can defy monitoring and eradication. A favor done may add to an individual's social capital but perhaps not be repaid or reciprocated until months or years later, without any direct linkage being established. A generous wedding present for a daughter or a good job offer for a graduating son may follow well after the event and not be viewed as a bribe or even a form of undue enrichment. Obviously there will always be some questionable activities that evade the best-designed net. But this reinforces why each society has to define for itself the levels of acceptable conduct and what can—and cannot—be tolerated.

There is, therefore, a constructive role for the civil sector to play in developing and strengthening ethics and practices in the public sector, particularly in the context of business transactions between the public and the private sectors. A free press (to expose corruption, educate the public about its harmful consequences, and inform them of measures taken to contain the problem) and open political debate and accountability are also important. The real objective, however, must be for civil society to claim and defend its own values and not leave this integral function to those in power.

Some of the solutions to corruption lie within civil society—reducing public tolerance of corruption, making the unaccountably rich into figures of contempt rather than role models, and encouraging citizens to actively report and provide evidence of corruption wherever it occurs. Civil society can not only address the problem on a nonpartisan basis, but it can draw on the talents of accountants and lawyers in private practice, academics, other leading figures in the private sector, and, perhaps most significantly, opinion makers and religious leaders.

But just as some of the solutions lie within civil society, so too does a part of the problem. Corrupt public officials are a product of—and participants in—that society. In addition, it is often members of the general public who are paying bribes, sometimes with resentment but sometimes to actively court corrupt consequences. It is, too, in the interface between the private and public sectors that grand corruption flourishes and the largest bribes are paid.

All too often the business community has become inured to bribing public officials to gain business. Some would describe it as extortion—if they do not pay, they cannot get contracts. Others simply see it as a fact of life and oppose any change in the ground rules that might result in their losing business. The challenge is to achieve a scenario in which the rules change for all at the same time, so no one profits or suffers. The only "winner" would be society as a whole, which would benefit from a cleaned-up process by getting better value for its money, and the only "losers" would be the unethical firms and individuals who should not be getting the business in any event.

Any attempt to develop an anticorruption strategy that neglects fully to involve civil society is neglecting one of the most potentially useful tools available. Of course, in many countries plagued by corruption, civil society is weak or only in the early stages of mobilization and organization. These are not reasons to neglect its role, however. Indeed, the very involvement of an emerging civil society can provide strength and stimulus for further efforts for the good of all.

This is not a wholly novel notion. Over the past decades, distinguished citizens from outside government have been appointed to review boards, oversight committees, and formal investigatory commissions to conduct public inquiries. All of this tends to be ad hoc and spasmodic—a response to crisis rather than part of a well-planned strategy for addressing corruption.

Where to Begin?

Many people in civil society have a fundamental interest in achieving an effective integrity system for their country. These include principled people in business and the professions, religious leaders, the press, and, above all, ordinary citizens who may have to bear the brunt of corruption on a daily basis. There is thus a constituency waiting to be galvanized into an effective coalition. Yet in most countries a feeling of impotence, of not knowing where to begin, prevails.

A number of countries take advantage of some of what civil society has to offer by tapping individuals outside the system to serve on ad hoc oversight boards. A classic example occurred in New Zealand, where, after a massive nationwide protest campaign to save Lake Manapouri from inappropriate power development, the New Zealand Parliament established by law a "Guardian of the Lake" committee, empowered to independently monitor developments and consult on undertakings. Other examples include the appointment of respected independent citizens to commissions and committees of inquiry (such as the recent Nolan Committee on sleaze in British public life).

In addition, certain segments of civil society have endeavored, but again in an ad hoc manner, to stave off government interference in sensitive areas. Most notably, the press has established press councils and created professional codes of conduct, not so much to raise standards but to act as a buffer to government interference and prescription (for example, by heading off calls for legislation creating rights of privacy or codes of conduct drafted and imposed by politicians). Prominent, too, has been the legal profession's use of "lay observers" to handle complaints about lawyers, reassuring the public that their grievances will be handled by someone other than the lawyer's colleagues.

Another example is the Independent Commission against Corruption in Hong Kong, China, which devotes an entire department to community relations and has advisory committees that incorporate significant involvement by the private sector and other elements of civil society. Neighborhood Watch schemes are now established features in many countries, with citizens harnessed to support policing efforts. In Australia workers participate in industry safety inspections, and New South Wales is tapping consumer movements to identify hazardous products on sale in the state.

Some countries allow private prosecutions by citizens. In Kenya, however, a citizens' group (the country's law society) has been blocked in its efforts to prosecute the wrongdoers in a fictitious gold and diamond export operation that recently came to light. The United States goes further in empowering citizens to bring lawsuits against public officials who take bribes. However, when citizens abuse this procedure and file frivolous suits, independent and transparently ethical law officers can intervene. Such interventions invariably give rise to allegations of bias from one quarter or another, rendering the device of a "special prosecutor" a particularly useful one.

If the government does not take advantage of what civil society has to offer—and even if it does—civil society can, and will, still organize to defend its essential interests. For example, tired of abuses of power by privatized monopolies in New Zealand, a loose-knit group of largely commercial interests has come together to seek legislation to rein in monopolies, as well as more accountability for companies controlling crucial sectors of business. The group, known as Major Users of Monopoly Services (MUMS), covers interests from international airlines and telecommunications to pulp-and-paper producers, film production companies, and the Consumers Association. Its aim is to put teeth into the watchdog established by the Commerce Act.

Leadership

Leadership at the top within the body politic will always be the greatest single factor in achieving fundamental change. Enforcers of laws, rules, and codes of conduct must know they are expected to perform their functions without fear or favor, and they must be confident of support at the highest level even if leading political figures should fall into their nets.

Leadership within civil society is vital too. Civil society is the ultimate victim of corruption, but if the public remains apathetic, it cannot expect change. By contrast, if the corrupt are treated with contempt rather than indifference or envy, and if honesty is accorded respect, then the key building block is in place for enduring reform. In a nutshell, what is needed is for the resources of civil society to be tapped in a much more coherent fashion. As an example, whenever a board is being set up to investigate corruption, those creating it should, as a matter of course, consider inviting outside, independent parties to participate, and they should try to provide a window of transparency to assure the public of the board's integrity. Of course, participants must be not only impartial but focused, professional, and dedicated.

Decentralization as a Means of Empowering Civil Society: The Case of Uganda

Uganda has enhanced its national integrity system by empowering people and making them responsible for their governance and service delivery through decentralization. There is evidence of increased public service coverage, with special attention to rural areas and to women, children, and the poor; greater citizen satisfaction; more cost-consciousness; and improved resource mobilization.

Decentralization seems to have opened the doors to responsible and innovative local leadership that, in turn, has become a driving force for building capacity. Community participation—people voicing demands, making choices, and being involved in the implementation of programs and projects—is increasing, providing the basis for sustained local government capacity and for the development of a local integrity system in which people not only know their rights and duties but demand what is due to them.

If decentralization is properly steered, the capacity of local government can be enhanced through skillful innovations even under difficult circumstances, given the right political incentives and the determination of the community and its leadership. Sustainable development of capacity at the local level is possible only when there is effective demand by communities. Therefore, there is a need to promote innovative and responsible leadership as well as civic involvement. Governmental and nongovernmental organizations can play a role if they respond to, and are guided by, local demands.

The diffusion of institutional change and hence the development of an integrity system will depend on how much and how quickly information is made available regarding the best practices and solutions for fighting corruption. Again, this is where the media play a central role.

In a decentralization approach, the many civil society actors—public and private, national, regional, and local—become the agents of change. The main way forward is to enhance the incentives for local governments to innovate, to improve the information that district officials and voters or citizens need to make thoughtful decisions, and to let voter taxpayers voice their approval or disapproval of local government performance through opinion polls or other means.

Decentralizing without Increasing Opportunities for Corruption

Since the beginning of Uganda's decentralization process, districts have experienced a sharp increase in available resources. They now have the impetus to raise more local resources because they retain most of what they collect and have access to additional resources from the national level, either as block grants or equalization grants, as well as access to credit for the first time. Under the new system, districts assume key responsibilities for the provision of basic water and sanitation services, for feeder roads, for extension services and the promotion of rural development, and for maintaining law and order at the local level.

A question is whether political leaders and the new district administrators and managers will squander the resources and be corrupted by the system. To prevent this, a mass campaign is needed to educate citizens on how to detect, expose, and report corrupt practices. Because localizing services will improve transparency and accountability, decentralization could be a way of combating corruption. But this requires that the general public be involved in decisionmaking and in demanding accountability and transparency.

Reversing Public Perceptions of the Corrupt

Historically Ugandans have considered people successful if they have many material possessions, irrespective of how those possessions were acquired. This admiration for aggrandizement helped destroy Uganda's previous national integrity system and threatens the development of a new one. It is incumbent upon civil society and the media to deglamorize the corrupt and increase respect for good citizens with less property by contrasting them with those who have embezzled government funds and stolen from the public.

The public must also be educated to question how people in their midst are getting rich overnight. Citizens should learn to expose, challenge, and demand accountability from those suspected of being corrupt. It is only through such deliberate acts that Ugandans will be able to transform their country into one with an enviable national integrity system.

Implementing Political Reforms

Setting up the political environment within which local governments operate is also an important step in enhancing national integrity. If leaders are corrupt and untrustworthy, then one can anticipate that the entire system will be corrupted. It is not surprising that during Uganda's years of turmoil and uncertainty, people resorted to taking what was possible as fast as possible, for they did not know what would happen tomorrow. This has now changed. The district leaders and councilors at various levels have been popularly elected—a process that is more transparent and fair. Citizens' participation has been increased to the extent that they can now question the performance of their leaders and even recall them.

Ensuring Citizens' Satisfaction

Building a national integrity system will not succeed if citizens remain dissatisfied with the services rendered by their local administrations. Thus a key element in assessing a national integrity system's effectiveness should be assessing the views of citizens. Service delivery surveys and mechanisms for monitoring citizen satisfaction could assist in this regard while helping to meet needs and ensure quality.

A Key Question: How to Increase and Sustain Momentum?

Overall, the evidence suggests a positive record of development of a national integrity system in Uganda. Experience so far suggests that Ugandans are increasingly confident in their leaders and more aware of their own responsibilities to pay taxes, demand transparency in government, and hold public officials accountable. However, the key question is how the momentum can be increased and sustained.

The answer seems to lie in the emergence of popular power—giving people a voice on issues of local and national importance by developing local leadership, fostering community participation, and setting up responsive, transparent, and accountable governments. Experience in local districts indicates that competition for political office has, in many cases, led to responsible, more transparent, more accountable, and more innovative local leadership. This, in turn, has become the driving force behind the efforts to build a national integrity system. More widespread community participation and growing civic involvement have expanded the range of possibilities open to citizens.

Participation by the community individually or collectively—voicing demands, making choices, and being involved in projects and programs—through formal and informal channels, is as important in sustaining capacity as leadership is in launching it. The presence of an active community increases demands for effective, transparent, and accountable local governments, generating incentives for building a national integrity system. The challenge for local governments is therefore to open their administration and encourage community participation.

Direct community involvement—in constructing and maintaining programs and buildings as well as operating services—is a strong factor in the success stories arising in districts. The practice of involving communities in deciding the priorities and contributing labor and materials for public programs and projects is increasing not only the available resources but also cost-effectiveness and user satisfaction.

The consistent expression of community demands and preferences has been an important factor enhancing a national integrity system. The voice of citizens has made local authorities more accountable and more responsive to the public, increasing the political costs of inefficient and inadequate decisions. As a result, it has made local governments more interested in changing their administrations and personnel to make them more effective. In several cases, protests and civic mobilizations have forced the local government to make decisions and act in favor of the citizens.

The Challenge for Civil Society

While signs of the establishment of a sound national integrity system are beginning to appear in Uganda, the process may be impeded by doubt, uncertainty, and strained relations among the different players in the civil society. A legacy of antagonism, indifference, irresponsibility, unaccountability, and lack of transparency may creep in to derail the process. The evidence, however, suggests that many Ugandans are fed up with living with corruption and, for once, feel their efforts at reform are being viewed with admiration and respect by outsiders. It is high time that Ugandans resolved not to go back to the patently corrupt climate of the 1970s and early 1980s but strived instead to strengthen public ethics.

The political and social systems are now opening opportunities for competition in the selection of local leaders and for civil society's involvement in local affairs. Efforts should be made to foster these fundamental qualities of civic life. Stimulating the development of local leadership and encouraging civic involvement would have the double effect of increasing demand for local capacity development and increasing capacity itself in the form of better district chairpersons, council members, and local participants. Promoting leadership and community participation should thus become an integral part of any effort to revitalize a national integrity system.

10

National Integrity Systems

Petter Langseth, Rick Stapenhurst, and Jeremy Pope

Corruption reports unfold in the news media daily, demonstrating that abuse of office is not exclusively, or even primarily, a problem of developing countries. Recent events in Europe and North America have shown all too clearly that corruption is not a topic on which the industrialized countries have any moral high ground.

Corruption is a complex issue, grounded in a country's social and cultural history, its political and economic development, and its bureaucratic traditions and policies. To generalize, corruption tends to flourish when institutions are weak and economic policies distort the marketplace (World Bank 1997b). It distorts economic and social development by engendering wrong choices and by encouraging competition in bribery rather than in the quality and price of goods and services. Nowhere does corruption cause greater damage than in developing countries (Langseth, Stapenhurst, and Pope 1997). Too often, the world's poorest must pay for the corruption of their own officials and that of the foreign companies their country does business with, although they are least able to afford its costs. Moreover, available evidence shows that if corruption is not contained, it will grow. Once a pattern of successful bribes is institutionalized, corrupt officials have an incentive to demand larger bribes, begetting a culture of illegality that breeds market inefficiency (Rose-Ackerman 1996).

The argument is not simply a moral or culturally specific one. Corruption has been described as a cancer. It violates public confidence in the state and endangers social cohesion. Grand corruption—where millions of dollars change hands—is reported with increasing frequency in rich and poor countries alike. Petty corruption is less reported but can be equally damaging. A small bribe to a public servant for a government service may seem only a minor transgression, but when such bribes are multiplied a million times, their combined impact can be enormous. If left unchecked, the accumulation of seemingly minor transgressions can erode the legitimacy of public institutions to the extent that even noncorrupt officials and members of the public see little point in remaining honest (World Bank 1997a).

Forms of corruption need to be contained for practical reasons. Faced with the challenge of maintaining or improving standards of public service delivery, no country can afford the inefficiency that accompanies corruption. While apologists for corruption may argue that it can help grease the wheels of a slow-moving and overregulated economy, evidence indicates that corruption increases the costs of goods and services, promotes unproductive investments, and leads to a decline in the quality of public services (Gould and Amaro-Reyes 1983). Indeed, recent evidence suggests that rather than expediting public service, corruption may be more like "sand in the wheels": in Tanzania a recent corruption survey showed that people paying bribes to public officials actually received slower service than those who did not (Government of Tanzania 1996).

As noted in the introduction to this volume, corruption can be defined as the abuse of public power for personal gain or for the benefit of a group to which one owes allegiance. Governmental corruption occurs at the intersection of the public and private sectors, when public office is abused by an official accepting, soliciting, or extorting a bribe (corruption in the private sector is outside the scope of this chapter). Individual corrupt acts take place when opportunity and inclination meet.

Klitgaard (1996) has developed a simple model to explain the dynamics of corruption:

$$C \text{ (corruption)} = M \text{ (monopoly power)} + D \text{ (discretion)} - A \text{ (accountability)}$$

In other words, the extent of corruption depends on the amount of monopoly power and discretionary power that officials exercise and the degree to which they are held accountable for their actions. Monopoly power can be large in highly regulated economies. Discretionary power is often large in developing countries and transition economies where administrative rules and regulations are often poorly defined. And accountability may be weak, as a result of poorly defined ethical standards of public service, weak administrative and financial systems, or ineffective watchdog agencies.

Such a taxonomy is important, as it points to interventions that can curb corruption in these settings. Successful anticorruption strategies simultaneously seek to reduce officials' monopoly power (for example, by market-oriented reforms), reduce discretionary power (for example, by administrative reform), and enhance accountability (for example, through watchdog agencies).

Such mechanisms, when designed as part of a national effort to reduce corruption in the public sector, constitute an integrity system. Put another way, an integrity system creates a system of checks and balances that limit situations in which conflicts of interest arise or have a negative impact on the common good. This involves both prevention and penalty. An integrity system embodies a comprehensive view of reform, addressing corruption in the public sector through government processes (leadership codes, organizational change) and through civil society participation (the democratic process, private sector activity, media activity). Thus reform is initiated and supported not only by politicians and policymakers but also by members of civil society.

National Integrity Systems

Appropriate economic policies that reduce the opportunity for corruption (M in the above model—the monopoly power of officials) may be considered a precondition for successfully curbing corruption.[1] With regard to institution strengthening, country strategies vary a great deal, but worldwide the policy responses to corruption typically involve one or more of the following eight "pillars": political will, administrative reforms, watchdog agencies, parliaments, the judiciary, public awareness and involvement, the media, and the private sector.

Ibrahim Seushi, president of Transparency International–Tanzania, developed the notion of a national integrity system built on these pillars. The concept is straightforward: the eight factors identified above are interdependent and together support the superstructure of national integrity that underlies sustainable development, much as pillars might support the roof of a house (see figure 10.1). In this model, the pillars are embedded in ap-

---

1. This section develops some of the concepts in Langseth, Stapenhurst, and Pope (1997).

Figure 10.1 Pillars of a National Integrity System

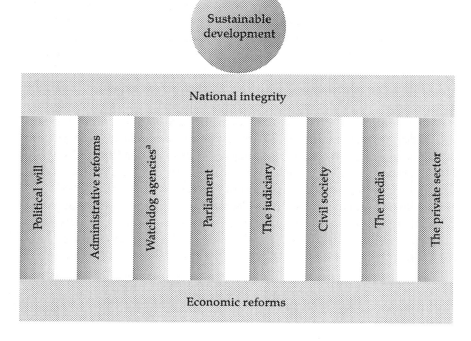

a. Anticorruption agencies, supreme audit institutions, and ombudsman's office.

propriate economic reforms. If any one of the pillars weakens, an increased load is thrown on the others. If several weaken, their load will tilt and the round ball of sustainable development will roll off (Langseth, Stapenhurst, and Pope 1997). The general equilibrium of the pillars is therefore important, and the government has an incentive to keep all eight in balance.

Political Will

Successful anticorruption initiatives require a visionary leader, or "champion," who recognizes the high costs of a venal bureaucracy. In Uganda, for example, as Sedigh and Ruzindana note in chapter 12, one key to relative success has been a leadership that has brought political stability and peace. The leadership has initiated and implemented a series of policies and programs in the economy, politics, and governance that have made democracy and a constitutional order possible. A single person often leads the country to an equilibrium wherein corruption is considered criminal and even unpatriotic.

Fundamentally, a leader's commitment is key to successful anticorruption policies. Those who have instituted effective anticorruption reforms and who share a commitment to reducing the incidence of bribery include presidents Masire of Botswana, Mkapa of Tanzania, and Museveni of Uganda. Among African leaders, these three are remarkable for the drives against corrupt practices in their respective governments.

In addition to political commitment at the highest level, sustainable anti-corruption efforts must include commitment from other agents of the state as well. Creating popular opposition to corruption is a function of the political leadership's willingness to make corruption an issue. Consider Ronald MacLean-Abaroa, who in 1985 became the first democratically elected mayor of La Paz, Bolivia, since 1948. During his three terms in office, MacLean-Abaroa's commitment to decreasing corruption in La Paz was a critical factor in the strategies employed. However, his observation that the problems of corruption resurface in the absence of a committed leader demonstrates that the responsibility must be deeper than a single individual. Hence reforms must address the need for broad-based commitment to controlling corruption.

Administrative Reforms

The responsibility for maintaining standards and minimizing corruption within the public service falls on the public administrator. If properly conceived, regulations governing conflict of interest in the public service are directed toward erecting and maintaining an administrative and management system to protect the public decisionmaking process. Rather than detecting and punishing the wrongdoer after the fact, such a system reduces the risk of corruption occurring in the first place. In a well-managed administrative system, the incidence of corrupt practices would be minimized, and where they did occur, swift disciplinary action would be the norm. Focus should be placed, therefore, on reforming public service procedures and systems to make them more accountable to the public interest.

In other words, in an environment of systemic corruption, significant civil service reform will prove elusive if corruption is ignored. In fact, the result could be a reformed but more efficiently corrupt system. Corruption must be faced at the outset of the reform process and dealt with as an integral part of the process.

Codes of Ethics

Curbing corruption requires a clear ethical commitment by political leaders to controlling corruption wherever it occurs. One promising extension of this principle in some countries is the establishment of a public sector code of ethics. Such a code sets out the ethos that should guide those in managerial or leadership positions; it reminds them of their responsibilities to the public and requires declarations of assets and income. Yet these codes have not met with great success, due mainly to lack of enforcement. An exception is in Papua New Guinea, where the code is central to the activities of, and enforced by, the ombudsman's office. Political figures at all levels have felt the weight of the ombudsman's authority, and in a number of cases senior political careers have come to an abrupt end.

Establishing and maintaining ethics codes depends on several critical conditions. The ethical environment must be backed by political commitment and leadership, accepted by a broad segment of the public sector, and broadly supported by civil society. Furthermore, violations must be dealt with equally and consistently across the public sector.

Improved Remuneration

The inadequacy of public sector salaries contributes greatly to petty corruption driven by need. Ensuring living wages is crucial to public sector efficiency and effectiveness. Singapore has been conspicuously successful in this endeavor. The country's anticorruption strategy included gradual pay raises and fair salary structures. Now Singapore's civil servants are among the best-paid in the world, and their productivity and effectiveness are widely recognized. As in other countries, there is an occasional Singaporean official who succumbs to the temptations of grand corruption, but the problem of corruption is fairly well under control.

Uganda has undertaken the challenge of civil service reform with support from the World Bank and substantial bilateral assistance (Government of Uganda 1995). In the course of this reform, all civil servants' benefits have been assigned a monetary value. Civil servants are now allowed to decide whether they wish to receive actual benefits or their monetary equivalent. It is hoped that this freedom to create discretionary spending with their benefits package will enhance the value they attach to their posts, decrease the temptation to accept bribes, and lead to higher standards of service delivery to the public.

It is essential, of course, for public servants and the public at large to understand fully the rationale behind any major public sector pay raises, and for them to appreciate that together with the benefit of higher pay comes the responsibility of enhanced accountability. Raising pay without increasing oversight could simply result in prospective job candidates paying for the privilege of obtaining a government job.

Better Administrative Practices

Organizational change within the civil service can help minimize the opportunities for corrupt practices. Such measures include (Langseth 1995, p. 10):

- Improving work methods and procedures to reduce delays
- Increasing the effectiveness of supervision by enabling superior officers to check and control the work of their staff
- Carrying out surprise checks on the work of officers
- Formulating and disseminating clearly defined ethical guidelines and rules of conduct and instituting in-service training for civil servants at all levels
- Developing internal financial management systems that ensure adequate and effective controls over the use of resources
- Providing channels for junior officials to complain about their superiors' corruption
- Rewarding achievement, recognizing good behavior, and acclaiming role models
- Making the necessary security arrangements to prevent unauthorized access to a department's premises
- Reviewing anticorruption measures every three to five years, with the aim of introducing further improvements.

A discretionary element in decisionmaking contains the potential for abuse. Eliminating discretionary decisions altogether would be impossible and impractical. Instead, in those areas where discretion must be maintained, it would be more realistic to reduce the monopoly power of bureaucrats by providing rival sources of supply. For example, citizens could be allowed to apply for a driver's license at any motor vehicle office, and businesses could be permitted to obtain operating licenses from any of several officials or offices. In addition, police forces could operate in overlapping jurisdictions so that no official could guarantee a lawbreaker protection from arrest. Such reforms might not end unofficial "charges" but they will at least drive the price down. If the level of bribes is low enough, even a modest effort at law enforcement may discourage corrupt officials (Government of Uganda 1995).

It is possible to limit the scope for abuse more systematically by narrowly defining the areas of discretion and by providing clear, public guidelines for the exercise of this discretion. A good example of the guiding principles of administrative law can be found in Zambia's Lusaka Statement on Government under the Law (1992) endorsed by commonwealth law ministers in 1993 and by successive meetings of senior judges in various regions.

Disclosure of Income, Assets, and Gifts

One of the key instruments for maintaining integrity in the public service is requiring all persons in positions of influence to periodically complete forms stating their income, assets, and liabilities. Those taking bribes will certainly not report this, but forcing them to record their financial position may lay an important building block for subsequent prosecution. However, evidence points to the inadequacy of voluntary and informal disclosure systems. Corruption can be reduced only if it is made a high-risk, low-return undertaking.

To whom should politicians give a financial accounting? Appropriate candidates include the speaker of parliament, the ombudsman, or the people at large, depending on the country. Likewise, the matters to be disclosed will differ from country to country. Clearly, disclosure should cover all significant assets and liabilities. A few countries insist that officials also include a copy of their latest income tax return. Some countries extend these requirements to close blood relatives; others limit disclosure to officials and their spouses (although even this practice is contested on the grounds that a spouse should be entitled to privacy from his or her partner). In any case, disclosure laws must embody what a society regards as fair and reasonable. If not, enforcement will be impossible, thereby undermining the integrity system.

There is also the matter of gifts received by those in public office. Gifts can take many forms—a lunch, a ticket to a sports event, an expensive watch, shares in a company, a trip abroad, perhaps school fees for a child. Some are acceptable; others are not. Excessive hospitality, such as an all-expense-paid vacation for a purchasing officer and spouse, is clearly unacceptable. More difficult to classify are such things as lunches or festive presents, although accepting even seemingly trivial gifts and hospitality can, over time, lead officials to become unwittingly ensnared by "donors." The dividing line usually rests at the point where the gift places the recipient under some obligation to the gift-giver. The acceptable limit will differ from one society to another, but it can be set in monetary terms so that gifts exceeding it must be declared.

Most governments have written rules clarifying what a minister may and may not accept as a personal benefit. For example, Malawi recently adopted the following guidelines (Corrupt Practices Act, section 3):

A "casual gift" means any conventional hospitality on a modest scale or an unsolicited gift of modest value offered to a person in recognition or appreciation of his services, or as a gesture of goodwill towards him, and includes any inexpensive seasonal gift offered to staff or associates by public and private bodies or private individuals on festive or other special occasions, which is not in any way connected with the performance of a person's official duty so as to constitute an offense under Part IV [which governs corrupt use of official powers].

Policy and Program Rationalization

Public programs riddled with corruption can sometimes be reformed through redesign and rationalization efforts. The preferred option, however, is program elimination. Many countries have rules and regulations that, even if honestly administered, serve no broad public purpose. They can and should be discontinued. Other programs might serve a valid function but are not effective where corruption is endemic.

Alternatively, if the basic purpose is worth retaining, the program could be redesigned to make it simpler and easier to monitor. For example, if economic efficiency is a program goal, then reforms could introduce legal, market-based schemes. But simplification will not always reduce corruption if the rules are very rigid. Bureaucratic rigidity frequently breeds illicit behavior on the part of both public servants and suppliers. Thus simplicity will work only if it is not excessively arbitrary and if senior officials or independent enforcement officials aggressively pursue anticorruption measures.

Finally, privatization of state-run enterprises and services can curb corruption, mainly because private sector accounting methods and competitive market pressures reduce the opportunities for wrongdoing and make it more difficult to hide. These benefits however, must be weighed against the possible adverse effects of privatization: unemployment of civil servants and the risk of private sector monopolies.

Substantive policy reform, involving reform of the regulatory and tax systems and the elimination of unnecessary programs, is a difficult and time-consuming task. It is also an undertaking that must be geared to the needs and problems of a particular country. Identifying the sources of corruption in programs and reducing or eliminating them requires detailed, country-specific knowledge.

Improved Procurement Procedures

Kpundeh and Heilman (1996) have outlined a number of criteria for improving public service procurement procedures. First, procurement should be economical. It should result in the best quality of goods and services for the price paid, or the lowest price for the stipulated or acceptable quality. This does not necessarily mean procurement of the least costly or highest quality goods available, but the best combination of these factors to meet the particular needs.

Second, contract award decisions should be fair and impartial. Public funds should not be used to provide favors; standards and specifications must be nondiscriminatory; suppliers and contractors should be selected on the basis of their qualifications and the merit of their offers; and all bidders should receive equal treatment in terms of deadlines and confidentiality.

Third, the process should be transparent. Procurement requirements, rules, and decisionmaking criteria should be readily accessible to all potential suppliers and contractors, preferably announced as part of the invitation to bid. The opening of bids should be public, and all decisions should be fully recorded.

Fourth, the procurement process should be efficient, with the rules reflecting the value and complexity of the items to be procured. Procedures for purchases of small value should be simple and fast; for more valuable and complicated items, more time and more complex rules are required to ensure that principles are observed. Decisionmaking for larger contracts may require committees or a review process, but bureaucratic intervention should be kept to a minimum.

Fifth, accountability is essential. Procedures should be systematic and dependable, and records should be maintained that can explain and justify all decisions and actions. Competence and integrity in procurement encourages suppliers and contractors to make their best offers, in turn leading to improved procurement performance. Purchasers that fail to meet high standards of accountability and fairness should be identified quickly as poor partners with which to do business.

Finally, a sound and consistent framework is required to establish the basic principles and practices to be observed in public procurement. This can take many forms, but there is increasing awareness of the advantages of a uniform procurement code setting out the fundamentals for all government agencies, supplemented by more detailed rules and regulations for the implementing agencies. A number of countries are reviewing existing laws that may have developed in haphazard fashion over many years and consolidating them into such a code.

Watchdog Agencies

A nation serious about fighting corruption may need to establish new institutions to help guard against bribery, theft, and other abuses of public power. Anticorruption agencies, the office of the ombudsman, and supreme audit institutions might all assume such a watchdog role.

Anticorruption Agencies

In recent years governments have sought to bolster detection efforts by introducing independent anticorruption agencies or commissions that typically step in after corruption is alleged. Given that prevention is more efficient and effective than prosecution, a small investigative and monitoring unit with appropriate authority—perhaps reporting directly to the legislative body—may be much better placed to ensure that effective preventive steps are identified and taken. To operate successfully, an anticorruption agency must possess committed political backing at the highest levels of government, the political and operational independence to investigate even the most senior officials, adequate access to documentation and power to question witnesses, and leadership that is publicly perceived as being of the highest integrity (Pope 1996, p. 103). It is also important that any special powers conferred on an anticorruption agency conform to international human rights norms and that the agency itself operate under the law and be accountable to the courts.

From the outset, the shape and independence of a commission may well be determined by how commissioners are appointed and removed. If the appointing mechanism ensures consensus support for an appointee through the parliament, rather than government, and an accountability mechanism exists outside government (for example, a parliamentary select committee on which all major parties are represented), the room for abuse can be minimized.

It is important that the anticorruption agency have the power to freeze those assets it reasonably suspects may be held on behalf of people under investigation. This presupposes the need for a vital tool—a well thought-out and effective system for monitoring the assets, income, liabilities, and lifestyles of decisionmakers and public service officials. When speed is of the essence, it may be desirable for the agency to be able to freeze a suspect's holdings prior to getting a court order. Without this power, funds can be transferred electronically in a matter of minutes.

It is usual for an anticorruption agency to have the power to seize and impound travel documents to prevent a person from fleeing the country, particularly if its power of arrest arises only when there is reasonable cause to believe that an offense has been committed. It is also customary that the agency be empowered to protect informants. In some cases, informants may be junior government officials who complain about the corrupt activities of their supervisors.

If an extravagant lifestyle is the only evidence corroborating a charge of corruption, it will not be of much use. Where a civil servant in a position to profit personally is enjoying a lifestyle wholly out of line with his or her known income, some countries do not consider it unreasonable to require the civil servant to provide an acceptable explanation for his or her wealth (Kpundeh and Heilman 1996).

The Ombudsman

The office of the ombudsman independently receives and investigates allegations of maladministration. The primary function of the ombudsman is to examine two kinds of matters. The first are decisions, processes, recommendations, and acts of omission or commission that are contrary to law, rules, or regulations; that depart from established practice or procedure; or that are perverse, arbitrary, unjust, biased, oppressive, discriminatory, or motivated by bribery, jobbery, favoritism, nepotism, or administrative excesses. The second are cases of neglect, inattention, delay, incompetence, inefficiency, and ineptitude in the administration or discharge of duties and responsibilities.

As a high-profile, constitutional institution, the office of the ombudsman is potentially better able to resist improper pressure from the chief executive than are other bodies. It can perform an auditing function to stimulate information flows that reveal the extent of corruption in government. The confidentiality of its procedures gives the office an added advantage in shielding informants and complainants from possible intimidation (Government of Tanzania 1995, p. 49). The office of the ombudsman also acts to prevent corruption and maladministration. It can recommend improvements to procedures and practices and give public officials an incentive to keep their files in order at all times.

The office of the ombudsman should be responsible for its own budget and not be subordinate for funding to another, larger department. With a lack of resources to fulfill the mandate of the post, it is often only personal will that sustains the ombudsman in the job. This undesirable situation should be addressed when reforming a country's integrity system.

Supreme Audit Institutions

Responsible internal financial management is crucial to national integrity, but supreme audit institutions are in many ways the linchpin of a country's integrity system. As the agency responsible for auditing government income and expenditure, the supreme audit institution acts as a watchdog over financial integrity and the credibility of reported information (as well as auditing performance or "value for money"). Although supreme audit institutions are known by different names from country to country—for example, in Anglo-Saxon countries this institution is the auditor general, while in many French-speaking countries it is the Cours de Comptes—the functions of the office are similar (House of Commons 1981):

> The [supreme auditor] audits the Appropriation Accounts on behalf of the House of Commons. He is the external auditor of Government, acting on behalf of the taxpayer, through Parliament, and it is on his investigations that Parliament has to rely for assurances about the accuracy and regularity of Government accounts.

The auditor general is also responsible for ensuring that the executive complies with the will of the legislature as expressed through parliamentary appropriations. Other responsibilities include promoting the efficiency and cost-effectiveness of government programs and preventing corruption through the development of financial and auditing procedures designed to reduce the incidence of corruption and increase the likelihood of its detection.

The supreme audit institution is of such significance that it warrants special appointment and removal procedures for staff, as well as protection from the interference of the governing party, politicians, and senior civil servants. Ideally, the issues of staff selection, accountability, and authority can be incorporated into a country's constitution.

To be effective, any external auditor must be neither accountable to nor susceptible to pressures from its clients (the parliament or a like body) or its subjects (the officials entrusted with public expenditure). Being part of or managed by a government department it audits would create a systemic conflict of interest and open the door to manipulation. Unfortunately, this office can be particularly vulnerable to pressure from its clients and, in the majority of cases, from the executive. To assure independence, the office should have relative freedom to manage the department's budget and to hire and assign competent professional staff. The latter is important if it is to maintain its ability to match the capability of senior officials in government.

Parliament

One of the principal functions of a parliament is to oversee the executive branch of government, including government finances. By helping ensure accountability and transparency in public sector finances, the parliament can contribute to curbing corruption.

South Africa's recent experience shows how reforming parliamentary practices and procedures can prepare a path toward accountability and transparency, thereby restricting corruption in the democratic process. Reforms in South Africa center on rendering the parliamentary process as open to the public and press as possible and empowering select committees, particularly the Public Accounts Committee, to hold the chief executive accountable. All select committees meet in public, and if they wish to go into a closed session, they must publicly debate the reasons for doing so. Parliamentarians have been empowered to call civil servants to account and to participate in the detailed scrutiny of budgetary estimates. Not only does the South African constitution guarantee open, fair, and transparent government procurement, but it also ensures access to information and other rights of due process.

Accountability of the Judiciary

In the common law system of a number of countries, the attorney general is not only a member of the executive branch but also the chief law officer of the state.[2] As the latter, the attorney general acts as the "guardian of the public interest" (Langseth 1995) and has extensive powers and discretion with respect to the initiation, continuance, and termination of criminal proceedings. The attorney general also has primary responsibility to provide legal advice in matters of public administration and government. The proper performance of these functions depends on impartiality and freedom from party political influences; this can be threatened if the attorney general is subject to cabinet control and if the parliament is effectively dominated by the executive.

One of the most blatant abuses by the executive is the practice of appointing supporters to the courts. The judicial appointment process is a critical one, therefore, although some governments have found that their own supporters develop a remarkable independence of mind once appointed to high office. To combat this independence, the executive may manipulate the assignment of cases, perhaps through a compliant chief justice, to control which judge hears a case of importance to the government. It is essential that the task of assigning cases be given not to government servants but to the judges themselves and that the chief justice enjoy the full confidence of his or her peers.

At the lower level of the court structure, a variety of corrupt means are used to pervert the justice system. These include influencing the investigation and the decision to prosecute before the case reaches the court; inducing court officials to lose files, delay cases, or assign them to corrupt junior judges; corrupting judges themselves (who are often badly paid or who may be susceptible to promises of likely promotion); and bribing opposing lawyers to act against the interests of their clients.

Clearly, these corrupt practices call for action on several fronts. Those responsible for the investigation and prosecution of cases must impose high standards on their subordinates. Court officials should be accountable to the judges for their conduct and subject to sanction by the judges when, for example, files are "lost." And the judiciary itself must insist on high ethical standards within its own ranks, dealing with complaints carefully and, where necessary, dispatching inspection teams to ensure that the lower courts are functioning properly.

The ways in which judges are appointed and subsequently promoted are crucial to their independence. Appointments and promotions must not be seen as politically motivated but based solely on competence and political neutrality. The public must be confident that judges are chosen on merit and for their individual integrity and ability, not as a reward for party ser-

---

2. This section is based on Government of Tanzania (1996).

vice or as a precaution by the executive branch to ensure a friendly face on the bench if the rule of law is violated.

It is implicit in the concept of judicial independence that provision be made for adequate remuneration of the judiciary and that a judge's right to the remuneration not be altered to his or her disadvantage (Government of Uganda 1994). If judges are not confident that their tenure of office or their compensation is secure, they may be more susceptible to corruption.

It is axiomatic that judges must enjoy personal immunity from civil damage claims for improper acts or omissions in the exercise of judicial functions. This is not to deny the aggrieved person a remedy but to say that the remedy is against the state, not the judge. Judges should be subject to removal or suspension only for reasons of incapacity or behavior that renders them unfit to discharge their duties. Situations involving widespread corruption and judicial tampering can be dealt with by establishing commissions of inquiry or appointing a "special prosecutor"—a public office used with conspicuous success in the United States (to investigate the Watergate scandal, for example).

There are several good reasons for having strong recovery mechanisms against corruption in the civil (as opposed to the criminal) law. Civil courts provide a less onerous atmosphere than the criminal courts for dealing with the consequences of corruption. In civil court, the burden of proof is not as demanding, and in appropriate cases the burden of disproving assertions can be more effectively and fairly placed on the suspect. Evidence obtained through civil law need only establish guilt via a "balance of probabilities" rather than "beyond a reasonable doubt."

There are several reasons, too, why private citizens should be able to sue in cases of corruption. One involves the state's potential liability for the losses sustained by a citizen or group because of the actions of a corrupt official. For example, if the state can be shown to have been negligent in its administration, then those who suffer a loss as a result of a corrupt public procurement exercise may well have a substantial claim for compensation.

Public Awareness and the Role of Civil Society

Anticorruption campaigns cannot succeed without public support. If ordinary people and businesses at all levels of society expect to pay bribes and are accustomed to dealing with the state through payoffs, even as a "necessary evil," then a change in attitude is essential before fundamental, systemic change can occur.

Several complementary strategies can have an impact. Some countries have engendered public understanding through public awareness programs focused on the harm done by corruption, the fact that the corrupt are stealing the public's money, citizens' rights to services, and the public duty to complain when officials behave corruptly. As part of such a program, Tanzania studied public perceptions of existing levels of corruption and where it was taking place, to obtain a baseline against which progress in reducing corruption could be measured (Heilbrunn 1997). These studies also give insight into what behaviors civil servants regard as corrupt, what they are prepared to report or discipline, and what prevents them from doing so.

The role of civil society is integral to a national integrity system; the notion that state activities can take place in a vacuum simply does not stand up to experience. Civil society encompasses the expertise and networks needed to address issues of common concern, including corruption. And it has a vested interest in doing so: most corruption involves two principal actors, the government and the private sector, with civil society as the major victim.

The ability of civil organizations to monitor, detect, and reverse the activities of the public officials in their midst is enhanced by their proximity to and familiarity with local issues. Indeed, this may be the training ground needed to gain the experience and confidence for action at the national level. Of course, in many countries where corruption is rife, civil associations are weak. However, the very involvement of an emerging civil society can, of itself, strengthen and stimulate its further development.

Civil society can address issues of corruption by drawing on the expertise of accountants, lawyers, academics, nongovernmental organizations, the private sector, religious leaders, and, perhaps most importantly, ordinary citizens. In Australia, workers in some occupations are involved in industry safety inspections, and consumer groups in the state of New South Wales help to identify hazardous products on sale. In New Zealand a loose-knit group of largely commercial interests has come together to fight abuses of power by private and government monopolies. The group acts as a watchdog on businesses ranging from international airlines and telecommunications concerns to pulp-and-paper producers and film production companies.

There are also examples of joint citizen-state action. For example, Neighborhood Watch schemes are now an established feature of many countries, strengthening links between citizens and police. Hong Kong, China, has set up its Independent Commission against Corruption, with an entire department devoted to community relations and advisory committees.

The Media

There is a close correlation between freedom of the press and the existence of corruption. The right to know is linked inextricably to accountability.

Informed appraisal of government by the public, press, and parliament is a difficult, even impossible, task if government activities and decisionmaking processes are obscured from public scrutiny.

Legislation, including freedom-of-information (FOI) laws, is often required to ensure an unfettered press. Not only can FOI legislation establish a right of review (by the ombudsman, for example), it also can establish disclosure practices that must be observed, even by those least willing to do so. In short, it can help reverse the presumption of secrecy. Citizens are given the legal right of access to official documents without having to first prove special interest, and the burden of justifying nondisclosure falls on the government administration. Naturally, documents whose release might actually harm the public interest (such as reports of criminal investigations, budget proposals, and sensitive economic information) are exempted.

Freedom of information is also enhanced through a free press, which ranks alongside an independent judiciary as one of the twin powers that can serve as a powerful counterforce to corruption in public life. Unlike judges, public prosecutors, and attorneys general, the privately owned media are not appointed by politicians but rather sustained by the public. Regardless of ownership, the media should be, and can be, free of the political patronage system.

The degree to which the media are independent is the degree to which they can be effective public watchdogs over the conduct of public officials. Just as the legislature should keep the executive under day-to day scrutiny, the media should diligently monitor both the legislature and the executive for corruption. Politicians and civil servants may be more tempted to abuse their positions for private gain when they are confident they run no risk of public exposure and humiliation through the media. Even today, many countries censor the press and jail journalists.

Laws declaring freedom of expression require support and enforcement from the courts. An independent judiciary is the handmaiden of a free press. A prerequisite for building a free press, therefore, is a legal system that is independent of political influence and gives firm constitutional support to a free press.

Through the responsible judgments of editors and journalists, a culture of freedom of the press develops. This culture is an important guarantor of the ability of the press to operate as a watchdog on public officeholders.

Independence of the media is a complex concept. In general terms, it focuses on the notion that journalists should be able to responsibly practice their profession free of interference from authorities. In reality, the owners of the media intervene daily in the operations of the journalists under their employ. In many countries the government itself is the largest media owner, which can undermine the independence of the media. Where this happens, efforts should be undertaken to strengthen the independence of the media, possibly through the privatization of state-controlled media. Diversifying media ownership could ensure that competition stimulates a wider range of perspectives on public policy issues and provides a check on the political power of media magnates.

In numerous countries, laws uphold the notion of a free press but also include constraints in the form of "reasonable limits" to protect national security or individual privacy. There may be times when national security demands temporary limits on the media (to limit hate literature or curb racial and ethnic tensions, for example). The danger is that governments can abuse such discretion.

The Private Sector

The most compelling reason for companies to review their ethical behavior is likely to be that of self-interest. As noted above, a growing body of evidence suggests that companies tolerating corruption by their employees abroad are placing themselves at risk. "Off the books" accounts, secret bank accounts, payments to staff while they serve prison terms, and the use of former senior staff as "middlemen" all cultivate an atmosphere in which the bottom line justifies criminal activity. This is inherently dangerous, and it may be only a matter of time before the company finds that it is the victim of similar conduct on the part of its employees.

There appears to be considerable scope for international professional associations and federations of private companies to include a mandatory anticorruption clause in their ethics codes, with expulsion from membership as the sanction for nonobservance. When such an association has strong worldwide membership, its members have relatively little to fear from nonmembers gaining an unfair advantage from bribery.

Conclusions

In practically every country some combination of strategies has been used in combating corruption. The Economic Development Institute (EDI) of the World Bank has recognized that successful anticorruption programs combine different strategies, as demonstrated at workshops for parliamentarians (Ethiopia, April 1996; Tanzania, August 1996; Uganda, March 1997), for private sector actors (Jordan, September 1996), for civil servants (South Africa, April 1995), and for journalists (Uganda, April 1996; Tanzania, April–May 1996; Benin, May 1996). Targeted groups then share the lessons they receive with others in their societies, thereby raising public awareness of corruption and its costs. However, the initiatives from EDI are effective only if the government remains committed to reducing bribery.

Indicators of commitment are present in the variety of programs that a government enacts to control corruption. Legislation, government reports, media coverage of scandals, and watchdog agencies are an effective mix to reduce corruption. In some countries, however, reform initiatives tend to be concentrated in the president's office. When the president is demonstrably a reform-minded champion, this structure of responsibility poses no obstacles. However, when an anticorruption agency is close to the president, it loses considerable credibility as an autonomous and nonpartisan office. Hence, other initiatives need to complement executive actions.

Watchdog agencies investigate allegations of bribery, prosecute corrupt practices, and educate the public about the costs of corruption. In Botswana, Hong Kong (China), Singapore, and Uganda, anticorruption agencies have fulfilled these three goals with relatively high degrees of success. Benin, Bolivia, Malawi, Peru, and Tanzania are among the countries that have implemented legislation and watchdog agencies with less clear results. All these countries are noteworthy for their president's expressed commitment to reducing corruption. However, their programs are still in the early stages and their achievements are yet to be demonstrated.

The national media are partners with anticorruption agencies in controlling corruption. The publicity over a corrupt act—political leaders taking public funds for personal use, for example—can cause a scandal. And when public outrage assumes the proportions of scandal, it is "a sign that a country recognizes the difference between the public and the private" (Rose-Ackerman 1996, p. 365). Raising public awareness about corruption is a task for the media as much as for the educational branch of a watchdog agency. Together, the two pillars are critical in reducing the incidence of corruption in a given country.

Some governments face fiscal and political limitations on their capacity to engage anticorruption agencies to reduce the incidence of bribery. The reasons for their limitations are financial. It is perhaps no coincidence that the countries with an unambiguous record of anticorruption restraint possess sufficient resources to fund an agency. In Hong Kong, China, for example, "there has been recognition from the very top of the Government of the seriousness of the problem of corruption. This recognition has been backed up by the provision of adequate resources" (de Speville 1996, p. 160). In effect, Botswana, Hong Kong (China), and Singapore have been able to combat corruption effectively partly because of the availability of funds and the government's willingness to consecrate them to that cause. The financial constraint demonstrates the necessity for broad-based efforts that involve all the "pillars of integrity" if a government is seriously committed to reducing corruption.

References

de Speville, B. E. D. 1996. "The Experience of Hong Kong in Combating Corruption." In Petter Langseth and Fiona Simpkins, eds., *Uganda International Conference on Good Governance in Africa: Empowering Civil Society in the Fight against Corruption.* Berlin: Transparency International.

Gould, David, and José Amaro-Reyes. 1983. *The Effects of Corruption on Administrative Performance: Illustrations from Developing Countries.* Staff Working Paper 580. Washington, D.C.: World Bank.

Government of Tanzania. 1995. *The National Integrity System in Tanzania.* Dar es Salaam.

———. 1996. *Report on the State of Corruption in the Country.* Dar es Salaam.

Government of Uganda. 1994. *National Integrity System in Uganda.* Kampala.

———. 1995. *National Integrity System in Uganda II.* Kampala.

Heilbrunn, John R. 1997. "Corruption, Democracy, and Reform in Africa." Paper presented at the Third Vienna Dialogue on Democracy, "Institutionalizing Horizontal Accountability: How Democracies Can Fight Corruption and the Abuse of Power," Vienna, June 26–29.

House of Commons. 1981. "First Special Report from the Committee of Public Accounts, Session 1980–81." In *The Role of the Comptroller and Auditor General,* vol. 1: Report. London: HMSO.

Klitgaard, Robert. 1996. "Bolivia: Healing Sick Institutions in La Paz." In Patrick Meagher, ed., *Governance and the Economy in Africa: Tools for Analysis and Reform of Corruption.* College Park, Md.: Center for Institutional Reform and the Informal Sector.

Kpundeh, Sahr J., and Bruce Heilman. 1996. "'Rushwa:' An Examination of Corruption in Tanzania." Unpublished manuscript.

Langseth, Petter. 1995. *Civil Service Reform in Uganda: Lessons Learned.* EDI Working Paper 95-05. Washington, D.C.: World Bank.

Langseth, Petter, Rick Stapenhurst, and Jeremy Pope. 1997. *The Role of a National Integrity System in Fighting Corruption.* EDI Working Paper. Washington, D.C.: World Bank.

Pope, Jeremy, ed. 1996. *Transparency International Source Book.* Berlin: Transparency International.

Rose-Ackerman, Susan. 1996. "Democracy and 'Grand' Corruption." *International Social Science Journal,* Special Issue on Corruption in Western Democracies, 48(3):365.

World Bank. 1997a. *Helping Countries Combat Corruption.* Washington, D.C.

———. 1997b. *World Development Report 1997: The State in a Changing World.* New York: Oxford University Press.

Part III

Three Case Studies

11

The Fight against Corruption in Tanzania

Shahrzad Sedigh and Alex Muganda

Soccer clubs are popular and powerful institutions in Tanzania.[1] Tanzanians are avid fans of the game, and at times the sport appears to approach the status of a religion—albeit a secular one. So it was a measure of the extent of corruption in the country when the 1993 soccer season was marred by persistent, convincing complaints of bribery and thrown matches.

Two of the top clubs—Simba and Yanga—traded accusations throughout the year that each had bribed other teams to obtain favorable results in crucial league matches. In one instance, five Simba players were arrested after an important match that club leaders had paid the opposing team to lose. Bribery was not restricted to players and club officials. It was common knowledge that soccer fans regularly bribed police to gain entry to matches at prices well below ticket cost. The response of the Football Association of Tanzania to accusations—and, in some cases, public admissions of bribery—was telling: no measures were taken against the offending teams.

The 1993 soccer season is a striking example of the pervasiveness of corruption in Tanzania. It also demonstrates the widespread acceptance of corruption among large sections of the population, as well as Tanzanians'

---

1. This chapter relies heavily on an unpublished paper by Sahr J. Kpundeh and Bruce Heilman entitled "Rushwa: An Examination of Corruption in Tanzania."

seeming inability to deal effectively with a phenomenon that has exacted tremendous costs on their country's development and future prospects.

The soccer improprieties were only one example of the dishonorable practices that had become commonplace in Tanzania by the 1990s. Each day the media was rife with stories of wrongdoing, from the grand corruption of rich businesspeople subverting the legal system and purchasing government favors to the petty corruption of traffic cops seeking to augment their meager incomes. However, events reached a crisis point in 1994, when the international donor community jointly suspended aid to Tanzania, largely in response to massive irregularities in the tax system. Donor countries, whose assistance underwrote a substantial part of the Tanzanian budget, accused government officials of deliberately allowing wealthy businesspeople to cheat on their taxes. Donors vowed not to resume assistance until the government took steps to collect evaded tax, recover exempted tax, and initiate legal proceedings against corrupt tax officials.

The following year Tanzanians received another shock. Former President Julius Nyerere scathingly denounced the corruption and mismanagement of public affairs by the ruling party, which he had helped found many years before.

The Evolution of Corruption in Tanzania

The story of how Tanzania reached this state of affairs is a long one. Corruption did not begin with independence from colonial rule, nor, as is sometimes alleged, does it reflect an African propensity for wrongdoing. In fact, corruption and the absence of transparency in government were marked features of colonial rule in Tanzania, as they often were throughout Africa. Accountability to the local people was, almost by definition, absent during the colonial period. Colonial governments were accountable to imperial capitals and their courts, and the state apparatus existed not to do justice or serve local populations but to reinforce colonial rule and repatriate whatever profits could be earned in overseas holdings. Government was repressive and derived its authority from the imposition of foreign control rather than from the consent of the governed.

It was this administrative legacy that was handed down to national governments upon independence. Indeed, the patterns of corruption that typified colonial regimes in Tanzania and other parts of East Africa find a close echo in the practices that have become so prevalent today. Portuguese rule in East Africa from the fifteenth to the seventeenth centuries is full of examples of illegality and corruption. Other powers, including African, Arab, and Indian traders, also engaged in corrupt practices along Africa's east coast. Together with the colonial regimes established by Britain and Germany, these forces ensured that corruption long outlived the gradual demise of most of Portugal's empire. Customs evasion remained commonplace, taxes often went unpaid, and local governments and administrators regularly demanded special commissions or payments to perform the duties entrusted to them.

Tanzanian independence in 1964 did not signal a marked increase in corrupt practices. In the years immediately following independence, corruption tended to be restricted to low-level officials who demanded and received negligible sums of money. Corruption had not yet spread upward into the higher ranks of public servants, and its impact was still slight enough not to undermine the efficiency of the civil service as a whole. The existence of a socialist leadership code and President Nyerere's firm commitment to fighting corruption, combined with high pay for public officials and sound rates of economic growth, helped discourage excessive corruption and keep more egregious practices in check.

The cost of living in 1960s Tanzania was relatively low, and public servants earned a decent income. High-ranking civil servants could afford their own automobiles and houses, while those further down the pay scale were able to support families on their salaries without having to resort to second jobs and part-time work. Moreover, Tanzanian public servants were respected figures in a country that had just won its independence from foreign administrators, and the challenges and promises that independence offered gave these public officials a strong sense of integrity, commitment, and service to the nation.

However, the late 1960s and mid-1970s brought the beginnings of a dramatic and costly decline in the efficiency, professionalism, and integrity of Tanzania's public service. A number of factors came together to create an environment ripe for the development and spread of corruption on a massive scale.

The Growth of Corruption in the 1970s

It has been argued that one of the most important causes of the spread of corruption in the 1970s was the program of socialist construction enshrined in the Arusha Declaration of February 1967 and the resulting massive expansion of the state into virtually every sector of Tanzanian life. In the years following the Arusha Declaration, the Tanzanian public sector grew at a rapid rate, forcing a corresponding decline in the role of the private sector in the economy. Between 1966 and 1979 the number of parastatals in Tanzania increased from 43 to 380.

Indeed, the 1967 nationalization of private corporations made the government the single largest employer in the country, involved in everything from retailing to import-export trade and even baking. As the scope of government authority grew, so too did the ranks of the public service and the opportunities for individual public servants to exploit their newfound power for private gain.

The atmosphere for private enterprise grew decidedly unfriendly. Thirteen years after independence, Tanzania enacted the Leadership Code Act No. 6. Its initial intent was to promote a socialist morality throughout the country and to ensure that Tanzanian leaders acted in a manner consistent with this new morality. Civil servants, politicians, and managers of parastatals were prohibited from having more than one income, owning shares in a company, renting out houses, or engaging in other acquisitive activities. However, the leadership code, like the Arusha Declaration, was seen as antagonistic to the free market and private enterprise.

The reaction of the private sector was to search for ways around bureaucratic procedures and regulations. The business community began to evade taxes, bypass controls on foreign exchange, and circumvent regulations on exports and imports by paying off public officials or shifting operations into the underground economy.

The multiplication of cumbersome bureaucratic procedures for virtually every transaction with government introduced unnecessary delays and frustrations for those on the receiving end of public services such as the granting of travel documents, foreign exchange, business licenses, and import/export certificates. Time-consuming and frustrating paperwork abounded, and as a result, the door was opened wide for those who sought to avoid delays by bribing all-too-willing government employees. Public officials who headed trade corporations became especially highly prized contacts, and businesspeople soon grew accustomed to using bribery as a means of getting business done.

In this sense, the Arusha Declaration and efforts to instill a new socialist morality in the country had the unintended result of encouraging the spread of corruption. Business became governed by the individual morality of those undertaking a transaction, rather than a matter governed by law. In effect, the rule of law was replaced by the rule of the black market, and new entrepreneurs entering the marketplace were molded in an environment that encouraged secrecy, graft, and bribery. Success in such an environment became dependent on networks of personal contacts with other corrupt businesspeople and with corrupt civil servants. Those who did not participate found their opportunities for advancement considerably restricted.

The spread of corruption was greatly aided by the steady decline in Tanzania's economic growth and prosperity in the 1970s. Various factors contributed to Tanzania's economic woes, including the 1973 increase in prices for petroleum products, the 1974 drought that destabilized a mainly agricultural economy, the 1977 collapse of the East African Community, and the 1978–79 war with Uganda that consumed much of Tanzania's already meager foreign exchange reserves.

Internal mismanagement of the economy was partly to blame as well. Often, government policies stifled economic growth. For example, excessive taxation of locally produced goods stunted the growth of local factories. The "villagization" campaign demoralized small farmers and led to low agricultural production. The shilling was devalued and the supply of consumer goods shrank. The government established monopolistic public enterprises, such as the regional trading companies, and abolished local cooperatives. Massive amounts of public funds were misappropriated and put to unproductive use. Tanzania's high rate of taxation was also a major inducement to corruption, for businesspeople preferred paying the smaller stipend demanded by the tax collector, rather than the charge assessed by the tax system.

The growing economic crisis, and the government's response to it, inevitably affected the livelihood of Tanzania's public servants. As the cost of living rose at an unprecedented rate and essential commodities grew in short supply, a culture of survival emerged within the the public service. Corruption set in to offset the decline in purchasing power. Civil servants began to look for any means—legal or illegal—to supplement their incomes. For perhaps the first time, public servants became more concerned with their secondary than their primary sources of income, regardless of the implications for their official duties. At the same time, the government introduced a system of permits (*vibali*) that allowed public officials in strategic positions to amass huge sums of money in exchange for the *vibali*.

Supervision and accountability of public servants began to weaken, leaving many employees with the mistaken impression that they were accountable to no one and could perform their duties as they saw fit. This greatly increased the opportunities for abuse of power and made the delivery of public services highly dependent on the integrity—or lack thereof—of individual public servants.

Finally, civil service morale and sense of duty plummeted. In the 1960s and 1970s the civil service had been staffed by many dedicated and honest individuals. This began to change in the mid-1970s as the impact of Tanzania's economic decline began to be felt among public servants. They could no longer be assured of a decent wage or a comfortable retirement, and over time the temptation to use public office for private gain became increasingly difficult to resist.

The cumulative effects of these changes were pivotal. A foundation for systematic and pervasive corruption had been laid.

A Massive Problem in the 1980s and Early 1990s

By the mid-1970s corruption reached into virtually every sector of Tanzanian life. In 1979 it escalated into a crisis as the Tanzanian economy collapsed. Social services and the country's physical infrastructure disintegrated. Civil service wages dropped below subsistence level, and corruption among the nation's elite reached epidemic proportions.

Tanzania's ruling party sought to control corruption by moving toward a more orthodox Marxist position and launching a campaign on March 25, 1983, against "economic sabotage" and "economic saboteurs." The targets were black marketers, embezzlers of public funds, and poachers. Hundreds of people were arrested and detained. A month later, Parliament enacted the Economic Sabotage (Special Provisions) Act, which was amended after three months and then repealed and replaced by the Economic and Organized Crimes Control Act. Yet the campaign failed to make a dent in the spread of corruption within the country. If anything, corruption gained even wider acceptance in Tanzania as an essential means of getting things done.

In 1985 Julius Nyerere resigned as president and was replaced by Ali Hassan Mwinyi. Mwinyi moved immediately to liberalize the economy, partly in hopes of reducing the incentive and opportunity for corruption. For example, the government relaxed restrictions on business, including the leadership code.

Liberalization did promote economic growth, but in the absence of any penalties for the dubious conduct of business, it also intensified corruption. For example, businesspeople with funds outside the country were allowed to import goods without ever being asked about the sources of their capital. The areas most susceptible to corruption within the public sector remained the Ministry of Finance (especially the tax department), parastatal banks, customs, traffic police, magistrate courts, immigration, the Ministry of Lands Office, and the Dar es Salaam City Council, which was responsible for land allocation and title deeds.

The government's efforts to contain corruption were largely ineffective. They consisted mainly of tackling individual cases, amid much fanfare, without addressing the overall context that allowed and encouraged the spread of corruption. A large part of the response involved anticorruption squads that were narrowly focused on enforcement and often susceptible both to political pressure and to the very corruption they were intended to eradicate.

Alarmed by the rapid rise in corruption and its inability to curb it, the government issued Presidential Circular No. 1 in 1990. It set out guidelines for strategies to deter corruption and measures to ensure that the policies and procedures of the civil service would reflect the principles of transparency and accountability.

In the early 1990s Minister Augustine Mrema—who was later dismissed for his anticorruption enthusiasm—launched a campaign against corruption that relied extensively on commissions of inquiry to look into accusations of financial mismanagement or inefficiency. These commissions, appointed by the minister, were soon caught up in their own controversies amid charges of financial irresponsibility and laxity in issuing reports. Moreover, critics noted that when reports were issued, the government typically took little action on them.

Stronger Determination to Fight Corruption

As Tanzania shifted from a one-party to a multiparty system in the mid-1990s, both the government and the public focused sharper attention on corruption, particularly as the electoral process itself became imperiled by corrupt practices. In the run-up to the October 1995 elections, the government launched a radio campaign against electoral corruption and warned the public against selling their votes or giving in to intimidation.

Benjamin Mkapa won the presidency in 1995 and immediately set about demonstrating his commitment to ending corruption. He began with a sweeping cabinet shuffle that removed much of the old guard—generally perceived to be implicated in the massive fraud of the preceding years—and he reduced the number of ministries from 29 to 18. Mkapa appointed only individuals with sound reputations as ministers, and both he and his prime minister set an example for other public figures by declaring their assets within days of being sworn into office.

The president also formulated the Public Leadership Code of Ethics Act No. 13 of 1995 to encourage high standards for present and future ministers. The leadership code required new cabinet ministers, as well as top civil servants, to declare their assets and sign a code of ethics. A breach of this code would constitute a violation of Tanzania's constitution and could cost the offender his or her job. The leadership code also stipulated that any property or asset acquired by a public official after the initial declaration of assets and not attributable to income, gift, or loan approved in the code would be deemed to have been acquired in breach of the code unless proved otherwise.

Whether the campaign launched by President Mkapa will succeed is still in question. However, for Tanzanians it is clear that the stakes are substantial and involve nothing less than the development prospects of the country and its people.

The Costs of Corruption for Tanzania

Every society pays a price for corruption, but the costs are especially high for a country like Tanzania, which is already grappling with difficult, sometimes intransigent, development challenges. When corruption becomes widespread, pervasive, and a habitual way of doing business—as it has in Tanzania—its effects are far-reaching and destructive to social, political, and economic life. Corruption betrays civic trust, as well as confidence in government and in the value of public service. It erodes the legitimacy of the state and those who act on its behalf and for the public good.

Corruption has clearly taken a heavy toll on Tanzania. It has contributed to economic stagnation and helped to concentrate power and wealth in the hands of a few. Huge amounts of tax revenue have gone uncollected because of widespread tax evasion and irregularities in assessment and collection. The kickbacks and commissions demanded by the public officials—elected and unelected—who negotiate and award government contracts have drained money from more productive uses and distorted public priorities and decisionmaking. Too often, the end result of dubious contract-awarding in such areas as transportation and communications has been shoddy work that is soon in need of repair and further government investment.

Given the distortions corruption introduces into the economy and into public and private decisionmaking, it is beyond doubt that the losses resulting from corruption greatly exceed the sum of individual profits derived from it. Decisions made for reasons completely unrelated to economic logic or the social good are unlikely to reap much reward for society as a whole. The Chavda episode described later in this chapter and the capital flight that resulted clearly demonstrate how vulnerable Tanzania's economy is to pervasive corruption.

Corruption has also led to a crisis in public administration in Tanzania. It has distorted public decisionmaking and transferred responsibility for government priorities and spending away from vested public authority to individual civil servants or politicians and their corrupt sponsors. Public sector decisionmaking should be subject to, and reflect, the laws and regulations that govern the civil service. When public servants make decisions on the basis of bribery, they surrender responsibility for decisionmaking to those who bribe them. In effect, government priorities and services are purchased and determined by the highest bidder, rather than decided by the public at large and the policies of the state.

As corruption becomes more widespread, the decisions of corrupt public servants, which are made in defiance of official regulations and stated priorities, irrevocably undermine the efficient management of public affairs. Moreover, as corruption spreads, it steadily eats away at the integrity and dedication of the people who make up the civil service. Public office is seen less and less as a way to serve one's country and contribute to the public good, and more and more as a means to acquire wealth and privilege.

Corruption in Tanzania has had another, potentially dangerous effect: it has contributed to political instability and increased ethnic tension. In 1990 a number of wealthy businesspeople, some Asian, began to take part in a series of fund-raising ventures. Some purchased photographs or personal items from prominent Tanzanian politicians; others won opportunities to dine or travel with the country's leaders. Some of these businesspeople began to use the fund-raising schemes for their own purposes. For example, several used photographs of themselves with Tanzanian leaders to bolster their claims of having close ties to the government and the ability to influence its decisionmaking. With the photographs as evidence of their clout, they sought to obtain payoffs from members of their own ethnic communities in return for favorable decisions on a range of public sector matters.

News of these ventures created a backlash against minorities in Tanzania and intensified racial animosity. Many Africans felt that the Asian community had used its wealth to win support and favors from the country's political leaders. An unregistered opposition party, the Democratic Party, quickly capitalized on this resentment for its own political purposes. Its leader, Reverend Mtikila, claimed that 181 wealthy Asian businesspeople, in collaboration with African leaders, were transferring the country's wealth abroad and impoverishing ordinary Tanzanians. The reverend also charged that the government was selling the country to Arabs and Zanzibaris. After one particularly inflammatory speech, angry Africans stoned cars driven by Asians, dragged their occupants into the street, and beat several of them.

Racial tension intensified during the October 1995 elections, and, somewhat predictably, a number of politicians sought to exploit it. As a result, there was an enormous capital flight from Tanzania before the elections, and many Asians were ready to flee to other countries with their belongings if the country erupted in racial conflict. The situation calmed, however, and race relations have since improved somewhat.

Clearly, the pervasive corruption that has beset Tanzania for the past two decades has been felt in virtually all aspects of life. Corruption has had a devastating impact on the effectiveness of nearly every form of government program. It has sabotaged economic development and subverted the rule of law. For ordinary Tanzanians it has meant countless frustrations—and added costs—to obtain services that are rightly theirs. Medical patients find themselves required to pay special commissions for treatment, even though they have paid the requisite consultation fees. Parents are asked to pay illegal stipends simply to enroll their children in schools.

The current government in Tanzania seems determined to bring an end to widespread corruption within the public service and within its own ranks. The country's future prospects depend to a large extent on how successfully it can do so.

Tanzanian Approaches to Curbing Corruption

Three decades after independence, Tanzania was a society in which corruption was rampant. Yet laws and institutions already existed to keep corruption in check and to punish those who committed bribery or fraud. For example, the Civil Service Act No. 16 of 1989, building on earlier legislation, codified standards for the public sector and regulations governing the operations of the civil service. The Prevention of Corruption Ordinance, replaced in 1971 by the even tougher Prevention of Corruption Act, spelled out the penalties for offenses. Standing orders passed by Parliament in 1971 prohibited civil servants from giving or accepting personal benefits or valuable presents, whether in the form of money, goods, or travel. Part II of Tanzania's 1977 Constitution included the provision that public affairs should be conducted for the common good and in ways that prevented corruption.

In spite of these legal strictures, the 1970s were marked by the rapid spread of corruption, as already noted. It is instructive to look at the anticorruption mechanisms and policies in place at the time in order to identify their failings—and their successes—in the hope of applying these lessons to present-day efforts to control corruption.

In Tanzania three key organizations have historically been entrusted with special powers and responsibilities to guard against corruption. They are the Permanent Commission of Inquiry, the Prevention of Corruption Bureau (originally called the Anticorruption Squad), and the Ethics Secretariat (originally called the Commission for the Enforcement of the Leadership Code). In addition to these bodies, an Office of Controller and Auditor General has been in operation since independence.

The Permanent Commission of Inquiry

The Permanent Commission of Inquiry—or, as it is better known, the Office of the Ombudsman—was established in 1966 to safeguard the rights of Tanzanians against the possible abuse of power, maladministration, and arbitrary decisions of public officials. When it was created, President Julius Nyerere explicitly recognized the need for it (Government of Tanzania 1995, p. 49):

> [T]he nature of our economic problems in Tanzania demands that many officers of the government, the party and the law itself, should be entrusted with great powers over other individuals. At the same time, our recent history, and the educational backwardness of the majority of our people means that automatic checks on the abuse of power are nonexistent. To the people in the villages and scattered homesteads of our country, it is the policeman, the magistrate, the TANU official who represent government in their everyday life. And in the district and regional headquarters it is the commissioners who wield direct and effective power in a manner which affects the life of our fellow citizen. This is inevitable and necessary. Only by entrusting real responsibility to such people can our nation be transformed. But we have to recognize that these powers can be—and have been—abused. And the sufferers are the people on whose behalf Government is and should be conducted.

Section 129[1] of the Constitution gives the Permanent Commission of Inquiry the jurisdiction to examine the conduct of any persons in connection with the exercise or abuse of their office or authority. Thus the commission has the power to investigate a wide range of acts, including arbitrary arrest; negligence or omissions in the performance of duties; improper use of discretionary powers; nepotism; decisions made in bad faith, with malicious motives, or with unnecessary or unexplained delays; and decisions that are contrary to law, unjust, or oppressive.

The commission has helped educate citizens about corruption and provided them with a means of voicing complaints. Since its establishment, the commission has been involved in a number of regional tours where it sought to make the peasants and workers aware of their rights, including their right to appeal grievances. Sometimes called the poor man's lawyer, the commission received approximately 3,000 cases each year in the early 1990s. Half of all complainants were referred to other authorities. About 20 percent of the complaints were found to be justified and remedies provided. Another 20 percent were found to be unjustified, and 10 percent were withdrawn or declined for a variety of reasons.

However, the commission has clearly failed to stem the rising tide of corruption throughout the country, and its efficiency and effectiveness have been questioned. Criticism has focused on the following areas:

- *Independence.* The commission's independence has been questioned because it has historically operated at the pleasure of the president. The president appointed its members, had the power to deny it access to certain documents and to stop investigations, and was the only person who could act on the commission's recommendations. These flaws have been recognized, and proposals have been put forward to amend the structure of the commission and make it answerable to Parliament.
- *Confidentiality.* Transparency is vital for combating corruption, yet the commission has conducted proceedings in private, and the public has not been kept informed. However, proposals have been made to offer the public greater access to the deliberations of the commission, provided this does not infringe on the confidentiality of investigations.
- *Awareness and accessibility.* Many Tanzanians remain unaware of the commission's existence, especially those who live outside Tanzania's main cities and towns. Still others have only the vaguest understanding of its functions and mandate. As a result, many who could use the commission's help have failed to avail themselves of its services. The commission has tried to overcome this problem by undertaking tours of the countryside, as noted. However, limited resources and the lack of reliable transportation have made tours infrequent and less wideranging than desirable. The commission is now renewing its efforts to make citizens more aware of its services. It has undertaken a public

outreach campaign that relies on radio, television, newsletters, pamphlets, lectures, and workshops, and it is also hoping to open zone offices to reach people in more remote areas.

- *Delays.* Commission investigations can be lengthy and time-consuming. Some delays are unavoidable because of the complexity of a case, the type of evidence to be gathered and the effort involved (for example, travel), the need to call witnesses or experts, and the extent of cooperation of the authorities concerned. The poor communications system in Tanzania has also contributed to delays. The result has been frustration for many and suspicions of foot-dragging and a lackluster commitment to fighting corruption on the part of the commission.

The Prevention of Corruption Bureau

Tanzania's Anticorruption Squad, now known as the Prevention of Corruption Bureau (PCB), was established in 1975 and entrusted with three key functions:

- Taking necessary measures for preventing corruption in the civil service and parastatals
- Under the direction of the director of public prosecutions, investigating allegations of corruption and prosecuting offenses under the Prevention of Corruption Act, as well as other offenses involving corrupt transactions
- Advising the government and its parastatal organizations on ways and means to prevent corruption.

The squad was created in response to the rapid spread of corruption in Tanzania during the late 1960s and 1970s. Until then, the police had been charged with containing corruption. It was clear, however, that the scope of the problem put it beyond the realm of everyday police work and that the average police officer often lacked the skills to deal with it.

The Prevention of Corruption Bureau is located, institutionally, within the office of the president, and its director general is appointed by the president. Its officers have both police and legal training, and some also have backgrounds in economics and sociology.

The activities of the PCB focus on two broad areas. The first is *policing*. To ensure that the bureau would be able to perform effectively, Parliament granted it the same prosecutorial and investigative powers as those allowed senior police officers. These included the powers to arrest suspects and to search and enter premises.

The PCB's second function, *prevention,* involves awareness and educational activities. For example, the bureau studies public organizations and identifies those areas where corruption—or the temptation for wrongdoing—is likely to arise. It identifies deficiencies in procedures, regulations, and accountability systems and recommends improvements to public organizations. Using radio programs, educational pamphlets, workshops, and seminars, the bureau also tries to raise public awareness of corruption and its costs. The aim is to encourage the public not only to report corruption but also to refuse to participate in it—for example, by refusing to pay commissions for services they are entitled to, such as admission to a hospital.

However, the PCB has suffered from weaknesses similar to those experienced by the Permanent Commission of Inquiry. It has lacked sufficient resources to fulfill its mandate, and its efforts have been hampered by reporting requirements that make the bureau accountable only to the president and not Parliament.

Tanzania's Code of Ethics

As noted earlier, 13 years after independence, Tanzania enacted the Leadership Code Act No. 6 to instill a socialist morality in the country. Twenty-two years later, in 1995, that legislation was replaced by the Public Leadership Code of Ethics Act No. 13. The 1995 act aims at building transparency and integrity in order to restore public confidence and strengthen national ethics. It establishes a statutory basis for the development of standards of ethics for public leadership. The basic principle underlying the act is that public leaders should be of incontestable integrity—honest, untarnished, impartial, and open.

The code covers a wide range of issues and includes the following provisions:

- *Ethical standards:* Public leaders shall, while in office, act with honesty, compassion, sobriety, continence, and temperance and uphold the highest possible ethical standards so that public confidence and trust in the integrity, objectivity, and impartiality of government are conserved and enhanced.
- *Public scrutiny:* Public leaders have an obligation to perform their official duties and arrange their private affairs in a manner that would bear the closest public scrutiny—an obligation that is not fully discharged by simply acting lawfully. All public leaders, whether elected or appointed, are to declare all their property, assets, and liabilities

and those of their spouses and unmarried minor children, without prejudice to the right of wives and husbands of public leaders to own property independently of their spouses.

- *Decisionmaking:* Public leaders shall, in fulfilling their official duties and responsibilities, make decisions in accordance with law, in the public interest, and with regard to the merits of each case.
- *Private interests:* Public leaders shall not have private interests, other than those permitted by the code, that would be affected particularly or significantly by government actions in which they participate.
- *Public interest:* Upon appointment or election to office, and thereafter, public leaders shall arrange their affairs to prevent real, potential, or apparent conflicts from arising between their private interests and their official duties and responsibilities. If such a conflict does arise, it shall be resolved in favor of the public interest.
- *Gifts and benefits:* Public leaders shall not solicit or accept transfers of economic benefit other than incidental gifts, customary hospitality, or other benefits of nominal value, unless the transfer follows from an enforceable contract or property right of the public leader.
- *Preferential treatment:* Public leaders shall not step out of their official roles to assist private entities or persons in their dealings with the government where this would result in preferential treatment of any person.
- *Insider information:* Public leaders shall not knowingly take advantage of, or benefit from, information obtained in the course of their official duties and responsibilities and not generally available to the public.
- *Government property:* Public leaders shall not directly or indirectly use or allow the use of property owned or leased by the government for purposes of according economic benefit to themselves.
- *Later employment:* Public leaders shall not act, after they leave office, in such a manner as to bring the service to ridicule or take improper advantage of their previous position. This provision minimizes the possibilities that public officials will:
  - Allow prospects of outside employment to create a real, potential, or apparent conflict of interest while they are in office
  - Obtain preferential treatment or privileged access to government after leaving office
  - Take personal advantage of information obtained in the course of official duties and responsibilities before it becomes generally available to the public
  - Use public office to unfair advantage in obtaining opportunities for outside employment.

The Public Leadership Code of Ethics Act No. 13 also requires the president to continuously scrutinize and, as necessary, revise the principles and ethical standards for leaders in the country. In addition, the code established an ethics secretariat to inquire into any alleged or suspected breach of the code by public leaders subject to it.

It is still early to determine the effect that this code will have on corruption in Tanzania. It does establish a high standard of ethics for public leaders, and, if observed, it should increase public confidence in the government and reduce public tolerance of corruption.

The Controller and Auditor General

In Tanzania, as in other countries, the Office of Controller and Auditor General is vested with the authority to oversee and report on administrative ethics and financial accountability, and its independence is guaranteed in the Constitution. It is responsible for auditing accounts, appropriations, and spending to ensure their compliance with government rules and regulations and sound accounting practices. Although the office has considerable power to investigate and report on maladministration, it also has a mandate that is too narrow to deal with corruption of the magnitude faced by Tanzania.

For example, the controller and auditor general has been unable to perform a strong role in examining government revenues and the functioning of the taxation system from original assessment through to collection. Yet this has been one of the areas most affected by corruption, and the specific focus of donor concern when aid to Tanzania was suspended in 1994.

The controller and auditor general has been prevented from undertaking more comprehensive audits in large part because of a severe shortage of qualified and trained staff, especially at the senior professional levels. The office has been underfunded and the independence of its operations compromised because its budget has been subject to executive approval rather than approval of the legislature.

These limitations have been reflected in the office's inability to properly investigate the spending and accountability of Tanzania's public enterprises. During the 1970s and 1980s, public enterprises consumed enormous amounts of government revenue and typically did not meet the expectations held of them. But instead of being audited by the controller and auditor general, these enterprises have been audited by the Tanzania Audit Corporation, which is composed mainly of members of the civil service or those serving on an ex officio basis. This is in sharp conflict with the fundamental precept that the audit function must be entrusted to an organization independent of the executive.

As part of its responsibilities, the Office of Controller and Auditor General prepares an annual audit report in English and Swahili. The report is made public and is examined by the Public Accounts Committee of the National Assembly. The principal secretaries to the ministries of government, or their deputies, can be called before the Public Accounts Committee to discuss the report's findings and to answer questions. Afterward, the committee can issue directives for suitable remedial action.

Although the Office of Controller and Auditor General has been able to bring flagrant maladministration to public attention, its work has been hindered by financial constraints and its inability to attract, train, or keep suitable staff. This problem has worsened as private sector growth in Tanzania has resumed and offered more rewarding employment to professionals. As a result, the controller and auditor general is now faced with even higher turnover in staff and increased difficulties attracting new employees.

The Need for Stronger Anticorruption Mechanisms

The limited achievements of the organizations tasked with addressing corruption in Tanzania reveal that all need strengthening and, in some cases, refinements to their mandates to better shield them from conflicts of interest and the influence of their political and public service masters. All need better funding to provide them with the means to improve the quality and reach of their services and to attract staff with appropriate training and qualifications. Because of these weaknesses, these organizations have been unable to fulfill their mandates, with the result that public accountability in Tanzania has been weak in many key areas and has left the public sector vulnerable to a great variety of corrupt practices.

As the controller and auditor general of Tanzania himself wrote in 1993 (Aboud 1993, p. 199):

The Executive must take early and adequate steps to overcome weaknesses in several areas of public administration, right from the stage of planning to the final stage of completion. The design, management and operation areas should be substantially reoriented towards public accountability, and the monitoring and control system effectively strengthened. Absence of financial discipline (fraud, waste and extravagance), abuse of privilege and the insidious cancer of corruption and similar other ills in public bodies have led to a crisis of accountability.

These have to be tackled as a war with vision, foresight and earnest-
ness in the interests of the welfare of the nation and of the generation
to come.

The Role of Parliament

As noted earlier, in 1971 Parliament repealed the Prevention of Corruption
Ordinance and replaced it with the Prevention of Corruption Act, which
increased the fines for violations and stiffened jail penalties from 7 to 10
years. The new act also gave the attorney general the power to prohibit the
transfer of property or assets that were improperly acquired. In 1974 Parliament acted again to strengthen the Prevention of Corruption Act through
amendments that established a stronger institutional framework for its
enforcement, mainly by creating the Anticorruption Squad. In 1991 Parliament sought to give the squad a new and more powerful image by renam-
ing it the Prevention of Corruption Bureau.

Although much of Parliament's approach to fighting corruption has involved the enactment of laws, this body has also played a role through its
debates, its questioning of government officials, and the work of its committees. In 1988 Parliament passed legislation that provided it with
parajudicial powers to summon and interview witnesses in a very wide
range of matters. In the following years, parliamentary committees investigated a number of diverse issues, including some of the most widely pub-
licized corruption scandals.

For example, in November 1994 a member of Parliament asked the finance minister about a statement by the Norwegian ambassador that Nor-
way had frozen development aid to Tanzania because of widespread
irregularities in the payment of taxes and other duties. After initially denying any knowledge of the truth of the allegation, the minister was forced to
acknowledge a substantial loss of tax revenue over the course of 1994. Parliament strongly criticized the Ministry of Finance for failing to collect taxes
owed to the government—a failure that was clearly linked to corruption
and bribery on the part of those who sought to avoid Tanzania's high taxation rates. As a result, the president shuffled his cabinet and replaced his
finance minister. Several ministry officials were forced to retire, and criminal proceedings were launched against others.

During this period, the Constitutional and Legal Affairs Committee investigated the accusation that Mohammed Enterprises Company Ltd. had
imported and sold adulterated food that was, in some cases, unfit for human consumption. The committee discovered that although the
government's chief chemist had found the food unsafe, the owner of the

company had colluded with officials, as well as with Radio Tanzania Dar es Salaam, to cover up the finding. The company continued to sell the food to consumers, even though government officials and the company's owner knew it was not safe to do so.

The Finance and Economic Committee also probed the accusation that V. G. Chavda had misused funds provided for the Debt-Conversion Program and intended for the development of seven sisal estates in Tanga. The committee discovered not only that Chavda had misused funds in collusion with government and parastatal officials, but that high-ranking officials had also helped him obtain a class A residence permit although he was not a citizen of Tanzania.

Another committee investigated the Wildlife Department in the Ministry of Tourism, Natural Resources and Environment. The committee was able to substantiate accusations of favoritism in the creation and allocation of hunting blocks. The permission granted by the government to Bregadie Mohammed Abdul Rahim Al-Ali to hunt in the Loliondo area was determined to be contrary to the benefit of the nation and the people and to have been granted over the objections of villagers whose views had not even been considered. The committee also found that although the Wildlife Department had issued hunting licenses, it had little idea, if any, of the number or condition of wildlife in the area because it had not conducted the censuses required by law. The committee also noted that presidential hunting permits were illegally issued.

The findings of these parliamentary committees exposed corruption in Tanzania to national and international view at a pivotal time—before the 1995 elections and in the period when the donor community was exerting its greatest pressure on the country to deal effectively with corruption. The reports submitted by the committees were discussed openly in the legislature in February 1995. The work of the committees demonstrated Parliament's ability to carry out thorough investigations and make sound recommendations. The Mkapa government congratulated the committees, agreed with their findings, and assured members of Parliament that it would follow up on their recommendations.

Still, there is cause for concern. It is not yet clear how effective Parliament can be as a guardian of public ethics. Many of the candidates running for political office have been tainted by corruption, and bribery of potential voters has been widespread. At first it appeared as though only the ruling party was involved in such bribery, but now all parties are implicated to a greater or lesser extent. Given these realities, it is clear that parliamentary ethics need to be strengthened if Parliament is to play a role in the fight against corruption.

With the advent of a multiparty system, Parliament has never been in a better position to exercise its power and represent the popular will. Multiparty politics should strengthen the people's voice in Parliament and serve as a check on the powers of the executive. Indeed, Parliament can now impeach and remove from office a corrupt president and pass votes of nonconfidence in the government. However, the use of these powers can be exercised legitimately only by a body whose own integrity and honesty are above reproach.

The Judiciary and Law Enforcement

The judiciary and the police can be powerful allies—or enemies—in the fight against corruption in any society. Unfortunately for Tanzania, its legal profession and police force lost much of their integrity during the 1960s and 1970s.

One problem was the role of the party as the supreme authority. The legal profession was encouraged to have sympathy for the aspirations of the people, as defined by the party, and President Nyerere encouraged judges and magistrates to attend party meetings. Party offices were established within the judiciary, and the 1977 Constitution formally subjugated the judiciary to the party. The police were in a similar situation. Until 1992 the police were an institution of the party, and no one could become a police officer without first being a party member.

During this time, corruption in the legal profession grew apace with corruption in Tanzanian society at large. The outcomes of many cases were entirely unpredictable: the courts often rendered incomprehensible decisions that bore hardly any resemblance to the most fundamental sense of justice. Corruption became so widespread that even Tanzania's chief justice openly acknowledged its pervasiveness. The police, for their part, relied on bribery and extortion to supplement their declining incomes.

This began to change in the 1990s, as Tanzania began its transformation to a more liberal, multiparty state. The legal profession has responded positively in a manner that suggests a fundamental change in the way it sees its function and views the role of laws within a society. For example, the judiciary has upheld the right of the individual to sue the government and to hold the state accountable to the rule of law. It has also upheld the right of citizens to run for Parliament without membership in any single party.

At the same time, the legal profession has been restrained in its criticisms of the judiciary and its sometimes corrupt practices. The reluctance to be too vocal stems, in part, from the substantial power still wielded by corrupt judges to discipline lawyers, smear their professional and personal reputations, and ensure that cases handled in court by outspoken lawyers meet with regular failure.

Tanzania's police forces have also undergone a transformation in role and operation during the 1990s. Since 1992, recruits are no longer required to be members of the ruling party. In fact, police officers are not allowed to belong to *any* political party. For perhaps the first time, the police are no longer viewed as an instrument of party power but as a force for upholding the laws of the country in a fair and objective manner. Other initiatives have been undertaken to reduce the risk of corruption within police ranks. Salaries and incentives for police officers are reviewed annually to remove one of the most powerful inducements to corruption—underpayment—and police training now incorporates strong anticorruption messages.

Clearly, after years of economic decline, increased poverty, and the rampant spread of corruption, there is strong momentum for change in Tanzania. There is also a growing awareness that corruption on such a large scale cannot be dealt with piecemeal or through a single institution. Instead, it must be addressed in an integrated fashion through a strategy that involves and draws on all sectors of Tanzanian society. In 1995 the Tanzanian government, the Economic Development Institution of the World Bank, and Transparency International jointly sponsored a workshop in Arusha to devise just such a strategy.

The National Integrity Workshop in Arusha

The National Integrity Workshop on August 10–12, 1995, brought together leading Tanzanians from government, business, the judiciary, academia, and the media to discuss the crucial issue of corruption. The workshop's main objective was to develop, in general terms, the outline of a national integrity system geared toward fighting corruption. Organizers of the workshop invited participants to:

- Discuss the needs of post-elections Tanzania in the context of building a workable national integrity system and in light of contemporary corruption
- Prepare an outline document, drawing on best practices, that could serve as a focus for informed public discussion and political debate before the elections

- Determine how Tanzanian society as a whole might participate in a continuing debate on integrity and how it might work creatively and constructively with like-minded political players
- Establish ownership of, and commitment to, the conclusions and action plan developed by the workshop participants.

The workshop's themes were wide-ranging, including the administration of justice and the roles of government, Parliament, civil society, the media, the private sector, the police, professionals, the National Electoral Commission, and the controller and auditor general. The workshop concluded with the agreement that urgent action was required on a broad front to counter the menace of corruption and noted that the coming elections provided a historic opportunity for all Tanzanians to unite in tackling the problem. Workshop participants called on all candidates for office to sign the Arusha Integrity Pledge, committing members of civil society to doing all that they can to stop corruption.

Workshop participants acknowledged that a clean start could occur only if political parties ran clean candidates in the election. Moreover, voters would have to be encouraged to choose honest candidates over those with tarnished or suspect reputations. The workshop recognized, too, that committees in the new parliament—particularly, the Public Accounts Committee—would need greater power if they were to be able to hold the executive to account. All committees would also have to include fair representation of opposition members.

The workshop identified a number of institutions that would require restructuring, including the Office of Controller and Auditor General, the senior judiciary, the Office of Attorney General, the Office of Inspector General of Police, and the Permanent Commission of Inquiry. It also called for a clear definition of the roles played by the president, the National Assembly, the judiciary, and the civil service.

The role of the media was deemed vital as well—particularly because it was common knowledge that many journalists participated in the corruption of past decades (and, as it transpired, in the corruption of the October 1995 elections). The media, it was agreed, needed to self-regulate more vigorously, provide fair and objective coverage, and refuse to accept bribes for favorable reporting or the suppression of unfavorable news. Workshop participants also recommended the removal of all unnecessary restrictions on a free press, as well as the passage of a Freedom of Information Act.

In addition, mandatory disclosure of wealth and sources of income was recognized as critical to success. The workshop recommended that such disclosure be required for political leaders, senior civil servants, the judiciary, and senior police officers. The workshop concluded with a detailed plan of action, which included a proposal to hold a similar workshop after the elections and invite newly elected political leaders.

The following important themes emerged from the workshop:

- The government must lead the fight against corruption and become a role model through its own example. It must act in a transparent manner and be accessible to the people it serves. It must rid its ranks of all corrupt elements to create transparency and accountability in all the institutions that are critical to Tanzania's integrity. Only a corruption-free government can restore hope among the people.
- An informed public is a strong countermeasure against corrupt tendencies and practices. The government institutions charged with fighting corruption must work in concert with civil society to educate Tanzanians about the costs of corruption, citizens' rights and duties, and the redress they can seek in cases of maladministration and injustice.
- The private sector has been complicit in corruption and must refrain from continuing to corrupt officials. This will help set the stage for renewed growth in the economy, which will benefit the business community far more than is possible through the favors bought by corruption.

The 1996 Presidential Commission Report on Corruption

In January 1996 President Mkapa appointed a commission to examine the problem of corruption in Tanzania and make recommendations on how to combat it. The nine-member commission, headed by former Prime Minister Joseph Sinde Warioba, submitted its report on December 7, 1996. The Warioba report stated that the colonial-era law on corruption, which was adopted in 1958, was full of loopholes and that the public institutions charged with wiping out corruption, including the judiciary, were corrupt. According to the report, the trend of growing corruption in Tanzania stemmed partly from low wages and inadequate fringe benefits that failed to satisfy workers' needs. Public servants were forced to demand bribes in order to make ends meet—a situation that could be corrected by better income and wages.

Ministries and departments singled out in the report as being corrupt included those of education, health, home affairs, treasury, judiciary, attorney general's chambers, trade and industry, lands, natural resources, tourism, and public works. The report blamed unscrupulous businesspeople who corrupted top officials to evade taxes and win tenders and favors. High-ranking ministers under the previous government of President Mwinyi were named as corrupt and accused of resorting to corruption because they wanted to accumulate wealth (Presidential Commission of Inquiry against Corruption 1996). The report did not spare the media from criticism either. The report affirms that the Tanzanian media, which should in principle help expose corruption, has been infested with "checkbook journalists."

The Domestic Response

Although President Mkapa said the Warioba report gave only scientific findings about how to deal with and eradicate corruption, the public and media have gone further and called for measures to be taken against the top officials cited as corrupt in the report. The report itself suggested that the president should investigate those individuals, and that to further clamp down on corruption, all top government officials should declare their property.

Following publication of the Warioba report, the Prevention of Corruption Bureau's budget, salary levels, and staff were increased, along with those of the military and police. Legislation passed in the fall of 1997 increases the PCB's investigative capacity and allows it to undertake prosecutions. A joint police/security department/PCB task force was also formed immediately after publication of the report to pursue certain investigative leads provided to the president by the Warioba Commission. This led to the referral of 12 corruption cases to the director of public prosecutions. The PCB has also collected data from other parts of the government on the magnitude of corruption, the reasons for it, and suggestions for abatement. Furthermore, the bureau received authorization for 70 new positions countrywide.

Some Tanzanians have suggested that the PCB should be made entirely independent of the executive branch by placing it under Parliament, as is the case with a counterpart organization in Uganda. The Tanzanian government does not appear to be contemplating this move at present. Other steps under consideration are giving PCB investigators the power to administer oaths, which would strengthen the weight of their findings in court, and changing the law on burden of proof so that persons charged with illicit gain bear responsibility for proving that they obtained their assets legally.

While these changes are being considered, the PCB is concentrating on improving its public image and sensitizing the population to the evil effects of corruption through a weekly radio program, publications, and a telephone hotline. Meanwhile corruption remains a prominent issue, meriting almost daily front-page articles in the Dar es Salaam newspapers.

For example, the November 11, 1997, edition of *The Guardian* reported President Mkapa's announcement at the opening of the fifth national conference of the CCM Party, "that over half of the veteran employees of the customs, sales tax and income tax departments, including key officials, were removed for suspicions of corruption and questionable integrity." Of 4,517 employees in the above three departments, 1,129 were "retrenched" and an additional 139 were not confirmed in their positions after the six-month probation period, according to the article. Smaller numbers were identified as having been removed from other ministries and departments. President Mkapa was quoted as stating that "these actions were taken after being satisfied that available evidence on suspicions of corruption would not allow conviction in court."

The Response from Abroad

To date, the bulk of donor anticorruption assistance to Tanzania has been in the form of financial and technical aid to the Prevention of Corruption Bureau for its efforts to raise consciousness about the subject and ways of dealing with it. The most recent support has been provided by the Economic Development Institute of the World Bank, the Department for International Development in the United Kingdom (formerly the Overseas Development Administration), the Danish International Development Agency, and Transparency International. These organizations, working in concert with the PCB and the Presidential Commission against Corruption, have supported a series of workshops bringing together members of the executive and legislative branches of government and elements of the private sector. The object of these workshops has been to inform and raise consciousness about corruption, motivate participants in a common cause, and encourage follow-through action plans specifying next steps, timing, and expected outcomes.

At present the United Nations Development Programme, the European Union, the World Bank, and Finnish Aid are developing plans for institutional assistance to strengthen the Prevention of Corruption Bureau. They are also exploring ways to bolster more immediate Tanzanian government efforts to further implement the recommendations of the Warioba report.

Conclusion

The strongest message emerging from Tanzania's anticorruption workshops and experience is that pervasive and systematic corruption can be curbed only through a broad-based campaign involving all sectors of society. A successful campaign requires the sustained political will of the country's leaders to create an atmosphere in which wrongdoing is not tolerated and causes and acts of corruption are addressed fairly and swiftly. Conversely, the absence of political support weakens any campaign against corruption, undermining the incentive and morale of those who seek to eliminate unethical behavior.

Effective use of the law is crucial for defining acceptable and unacceptable practices, as well as for setting out the penalties for wrongdoers. Strategies that rely on law enforcement must include safeguards to ensure that the law is applied fairly and that the agencies charged with enforcement have the powers, resources, and independence to carry out their mandate efficiently and effectively. However, reliance on the law and its enforcement cannot be the only answer, for the simple reason that law only comes into force when a crime has been detected. Though it may have a deterrent effect, law enforcement does not address the root causes of corruption.

The failure of the 1983 campaign against economic saboteurs to stop the spread of corruption points to the limitations of law enforcement as a means of checking corruption. The experience in Tanzania—where strongly worded laws against corruption have been on the books for decades—clearly demonstrates that efforts focusing only on the symptoms of corruption are ultimately ineffective.

A successful campaign against corruption must include measures aimed at its roots. This includes the reform of laws, regulations, and procedures that, because of their poor design, afford public servants opportunities or temptation for corruption. It includes public education as well, because an informed and angry public can be a vital tool in combating corruption, especially once people are aware of its costs to society and its impact on public welfare.

Civil service reform is also critical. Tanzania, like other countries, must reinstill within public officials a sense of service to their country and its people. This can come, in part, by providing decent wages for public sector work and by replacing patronage and cronyism with a merit-based reward system. The salaries and incentives offered—especially where opportunities for corruption are greatest (police and customs, for example)—should be reviewed regularly, and remedial measures undertaken so that civil servants no longer feel the need to augment their incomes through bribery and graft. Monitoring the lifestyles and incomes of public officials, as well as enforcing the leadership code—in particular, the declaration of assets requirements—can act as a strong deterrent to corruption.

References

Aboud, Muhammed. 1993. "Watch-Dog Organizations for Upholding Administrative Ethics in Africa: The Case of Tanzania." In Sadig Rasheed and Dele Olowu, eds., *Ethics and Accountability in African Public Services.* New York: United Nations Economic Commission for Africa and the African Association for Public Administration and Management.

Government of Tanzania. 1995. *The National Integrity System in Tanzania.* Dar es Salaam.

Presidential Commission of Inquiry against Corruption. 1996. *Commission Report on the State of Corruption in the Country* (Warioba report). Dar es Salaam: Government of Tanzania.

12

The Fight against Corruption in Uganda

Shahrzad Sedigh and Augustine Ruzindana

> *Where systems have broken down, the first control to go is accountability.*
> *Eventually, a feeling of immunity characterizes the system so that politicians*
> *and civil servants think that they can do anything without any adverse reper-*
> *cussions against the culprits.*

— Augustine Ruzindana (1994)

Uganda today is a society in transformation. After two decades of violent civil war, massive corruption, instability, and economic decline, Uganda now appears to be moving toward renewed economic growth and greater democracy. The press is now free—and boisterous. Elections have been held since 1996; a new Constitution was promulgated in October 1995 after several years of vigorous debate; a sweeping program of public sector reform is under way.

Enormous challenges still lie ahead. Independent Uganda has had no history of transparent, accountable government upon which to build the foundations of the new democratic state. Since the colonial period, repression and corruption have been the defining features of governance. The

British colonial administration was, by definition, unaccountable to the Ugandan people, and it did not conduct business according to modern-day norms of openness, transparency, and accountability. Colonial policies also heightened social and ethnic tensions within the country, thereby helping to stir the conflict that would define Ugandan politics over the next three decades.

From Independence to 1971

In October 1962 Uganda became an independent but fractured country with a political culture ill-suited to the survival of an open, democratic system of government. Political and ethnic conflicts had produced a semi-federal constitution and a prime minister who was supported primarily by poorer, less educated groups in the north but resented by a powerful and wealthy southern establishment. The indigenous political elite actively sought wealth, patronage, and privilege from the state. They were handsomely rewarded when President Apollo Milton Obote took power in 1966.

During Obote's first years in office, the rapid rise of parastatals heralded the rise of pervasive corruption in Uganda. At the time, most economists favored state-directed economic activities as the way to advance the interests of the people while reducing the power of the elite minorities who pulled the strings of the post-independence economy.

State-owned cooperatives took over the agricultural marketing and processing monopolies once held by large European firms, as well as the crucial activities of electricity supply, cement manufacturing, and tourism. Though nominally independent—in some cases, even classified as "private sector"—these cooperatives were state-subsidized, and their managers were appointed by the government. With direct control over producer prices, taxation of goods and services, import and export licenses, access to foreign currency, and a vast array of permits required for even the most mundane features of daily life, these parastatals and other state agencies were prone to corruption.

Although some semblance of a check on corrupt behavior was maintained in the early years, through institutions of democratic control, this evaporated in 1966–67 when President Obote abrogated the Constitution with the help of the army. Interestingly, in the period immediately before the repeal of the Constitution, Obote himself was implicated in a corruption scandal that also involved Idi Amin, then a deputy commander in the Ugandan army.

Idi Amin in Power

Obote's subsequent shift to the left alienated many of the elite and was a key factor in their decision to switch allegiance to General Amin during his 1971 military coup. Subsequently, Obote left the country and went into exile. The Amin regime, which lasted until 1979, completely dispensed with any pretense of democratic procedures, using the state's resources and institutions for its own gain and that of a tiny political elite. Military officers, assisted by some collaborating civilians, took over the reins of the state, and the public sector became little more than a source of funds for paying off the elite.

Misappropriation and outright plunder were unrestrained. Idi Amin expelled the noncitizen Ugandan Asians, seized their personal and business assets, and distributed them to soldiers, the political elite, and parastatals. After the Asians left, the economy was grossly mismanaged, industrial productivity fell sharply, exports shrank, and foreign credit and investment dried up. Due primarily to a lack of funds and managerial expertise, state-financed businesses became increasingly inefficient and could not provide adequate jobs, output, or resources. Imports became scarce, and Uganda's economic welfare declined rapidly. Inflation and loss of per capita income soon followed.

As urban sources of revenue shriveled, the regime raised taxes on farmers, lowering their return from export crops. The government tried to force increased output of coffee and cotton—the main export crops—through a repressive campaign to double production. Meanwhile, the cost of agricultural inputs rose while rural services deteriorated. In reaction, growers shifted from export crops into food production for local and regional markets, selling their surplus to private traders. Cotton and coffee production dropped, along with government revenues. In fact, the production of coffee declined so sharply that the state was unable to realize appreciable gains from the rising coffee prices of the late 1970s.

The real value of salaries and wages collapsed by 90 percent (factoring in inflation) in less than a decade. The income crisis was reflected in the emergence of a parallel economy, or *magendo*, characterized by people selling to smugglers and by economic activities that took place outside the purview of official marketing boards and price controls. People who had access to goods—for example, from parastatals—could sell them without restriction, and they could import goods without paying customs duties. Honest, aboveboard dealings virtually ceased to exist, and petty trading proliferated in the streets. Anything that could realize a cash value became a commodity.

Civil servants made up a large share of Uganda's wage earners, and the soaring rate of inflation forced many to seek additional sources of income. As in virtually every employment sector across the country, civil servants had to take on more than one job—a practice that continued until the mid-1990s. Many kept their civil service jobs only for prestige and for the transportation and housing they provided. Attendance at work slipped badly as the real business of making a living was done elsewhere. Civil servants could be found tending shops, driving taxis, hawking wares in the market, or setting up small family businesses. Many officials, in both the countryside and towns, spent part of the day cultivating food. Government allowances were abused by civil servants at all levels. Those with official motor vehicles used them for business unrelated to their civil service duties. Those in higher ranks traveled abroad on "official" business in order to submit claims that, for the price of a few days away from home, could equal a month's pay.

As civil servants devoted less time to their public jobs, essential services were either performed badly or not at all. In some cases, this helped to strengthen the *magendo* economy where services could be provided "on the side." Corrupt activities became routine. Civil servants charged fees for services that should have been performed without charge. Increasingly, officials viewed these extralegal fees and commissions as entitlements, and complaints were invariably met with a familiar refrain: "But how shall I eat?"

Some activities were clearly even more illicit. Government-owned supplies were sold privately. Public property was provided for private use for a fee, and kickbacks of 10 to 15 percent became routine on contracts with foreign businesses and in aid projects. With scant fear of prosecution, officials gave contracts for public works to private companies that they themselves owned, or that their families or associates did.

Some public institutions suffered more than others. For example, the judicial system, especially the lower bench, fell into disrepute. Poorly paid—often unpaid—magistrates and court staff became corrupt, and judges often accepted bribes to issue unjust rulings. The decline in ethical standards among the judiciary and the legal profession became one of the most debilitating aspects of corruption in Uganda, and one of the most difficult to reverse.

Change in Government

Eventually the people's faith in the ability of government to carry on its business eroded. In 1979, in response to an incursion into northwestern

Tanzania by Amin's army, Tanzanian forces launched the invasion that overthrew Amin's regime. A year of extreme instability and violence followed, during which several factions attempted unsuccessfully to form governments. Meanwhile, fraud, plunder, and embezzlement reached their highest levels. The corruption that gathered rapid momentum in the 1970s was to continue into the 1980s and even into the early 1990s.

In 1980 elections were held and "won" by Apollo Obote, who had returned from Tanzania. When Obote refused to share power with the other groups who had played an equal part in removing Amin, Yoweri Museveni (then leader of the Uganda Patriotic Movement) and a number of his colleagues formed the National Resistance Movement (NRM). A bloody five-year civil war ensued, which was characterized by economic mayhem and rampant corruption. Obote was finally overthrown, and an NRM government headed by Museveni took power in January 1986.

The Costs of Corruption

In Uganda the costs of corruption are virtually incalculable. The economy went into a free fall in the 1970s. State revenues collapsed as the military became an enormous consumer of government resources. Inflation skyrocketed, living standards plummeted, and productivity declined sharply. Levels of service and commitment in the public sector fell steadily, and the ideal of public *service* barely survived.

The diversion of public resources, services, and assets to private use generally results in deteriorating roads, poor medical facilities, dilapidated and ill-equipped schools, and falling educational standards. Furthermore, it can be argued that the direct economic costs of corruption are dwarfed by the indirect costs. Widespread, systematic corruption can undermine the legitimacy of the public sector and foment political instability. As corruption erodes confidence in political leaders and institutions, the government becomes less able to rely on the cooperation and support of the public, and it increasingly resorts to force and coercion. The resulting social unrest often leads to civil strife and a violent change of government that can subvert, or even reverse, decades of hard-won development progress.

Another long-term cost, often overlooked, is the effect on the environment. In Uganda many species of wildlife fell victim to corrupt and illegal practices. Between 1970 and 1985 Uganda reportedly lost more than 75 percent of the elephant population, 98 percent of the rhinos, 90 percent of the crocodiles, 80 percent of the lions and leopards, and numerous bird species. Much of this destruction was caused by indiscriminate shooting and poaching sanctioned, and at times carried out, by government leaders and soldiers. Foreign traders, often in collusion with corrupt officials, provided a steady demand for Uganda's exotic species. In 1987 more than 1,200 birds were smuggled out of the country, more than 280 tons of ivory were illegally exported, and 550 crocodile skins were sent overseas, mainly to France and Italy.

Approaches to Curbing Corruption

Soon after coming to power, the NRM administration made it clear that it viewed corruption as one of the evils inherited from the past and a key obstacle to progress in Uganda. In its Ten-Point Program launched in 1986, the NRM government stated its commitment to ending corruption: "Africa, being a continent that is never in shortage of problems, has also the problem of corruption—particularly bribery. Therefore, to enable the tackling of our backwardness, corruption must be eliminated once and for all."

President Museveni often spoke of the seriousness of the issue, contending that corruption threatened Uganda's stability and the possibility of bringing democracy to the country. Eight months after taking office, Museveni signaled the government's intent to stamp out corruption by creating the Office of the Inspector General of Government (IGG), with extensive powers to deal with corruption and human rights abuses. The government also launched a variety of other measures to curb corruption.

Empowering the Inspector General of Government

The mandate of the IGG, who is appointed by and directly responsible to the president, is far wider and deeper than that of a traditional ombudsman. The statute establishing the office charges the IGG with the "general duty of protecting and promoting human rights and the rule of law in Uganda, and eliminating and fostering the elimination of corruption and abuse of public offices." The IGG has specific powers to inquire into violations of human rights (including the denial of a fair trial) and "the methods by which law enforcing agents and the state security agencies execute their functions." With regard to corruption, section 7 (1) of the statute directs the IGG to:

(c) take necessary measures for the detection and prevention of corruption in public offices, and in particular,

i. to examine the practices and procedures of the said offices in order to facilitate the discovery of corrupt practices and to secure the revision of methods of work or procedure which, in the opinion of the Inspector General, may be conducive to corrupt practices;
ii. to advise the said offices on ways and means of preventing corrupt practices and on methods of work or procedures conducive to the effective performance of their duties and which, in the opinion of the Inspector General, would reduce the incidence of corruption;
iii. to disseminate information on the evil and dangerous effects of corruption and society;
iv. to enlist and foster public support against corrupt practices;
v. to receive and investigate complaints of alleged or suspected corrupt practices and injustices and make recommendations for appropriate action;

(d) to investigate the conduct of any public officer which may be connected with or conducive to:

i. the abuse of his office or authority;
ii. the neglect of his official duties;
iii. economic malpractice by the officer.

Uganda's new Constitution (1995) further recognizes and strengthens the central role of the IGG in combating corruption in Uganda. It empowers the IGG to promote and foster strict adherence to the rule of law and principles of natural justice and to seek to eliminate corruption and abuse of authority in public office. The IGG may also investigate any act, omission, advice, or recommendation by a public officer or other authority exercising administrative functions, either on its own initiative or in response to complaints by the public (whether or not the complainant has personally suffered any injustice as a result). In addition, the Constitution authorizes the IGG to hear and make legal rulings on cases involving corruption or abuse of public office; to stimulate public awareness about the activities of its office through the media and other appropriate means; to establish branches at district or other administrative levels as needed for the better performance of its functions; and to submit to Parliament, at least once every six months, a performance report.

With constitutional backing, the Office of the IGG has actively pursued its mandate. During a seminar held on November 2–3, 1994, at the World

Bank, Augustine Ruzindana, then the inspector general of government, gave a presentation about the corruption still prevalent in Uganda. He cited a number of examples, including the following.

CASE 1: MISDECLARATION OF GOODS CONTRARY TO THE UGANDA CUSTOMS EXCISE ACT. A local firm was importing goods under the cover of a European religious charity resident in Uganda that was exempted from paying import duties and taxes. The IGG investigated and had the police arrest the company director. The director was forced to pay all of the duties and taxes owing before being released from police custody, but he was not formally charged. The firm fired a number of employees involved in the racket, but they were not charged.

CASE 2: PAYMENT AUTHORIZED FOR WORK NEVER DONE. The government almost paid 150 million Ugandan shillings for the fictitious repair of a 50-kilometer stretch of road. This case involved collusion between the company that had won the contract, the area engineer who was supposed to supervise the work, and the engineer's superior officer in the ministry, who authorized the payment. Suspicion was aroused when the check requisitions were processed in a record four days. The IGG intercepted payment and seized the checks. The permanent secretary was demoted, the firm was blacklisted and never got another government contract, and the officers involved were disciplined.

CASE 3: FRAUDULENT CLAIM BY A CONSTRUCTION COMPANY. After more than 10 years, a company that had won a government contract to build an industrial research center abandoned the project at the foundation level. The company then put in claims to be paid $4.8 million for the work. When no payment was granted, the firm filed suit against the government. In this case, the law firm representing the company happened to belong to the incumbent minister of justice and attorney general. When the suit reached court, the attorney general's chambers quickly admitted government liability. The IGG objected, advising the attorney general on the correct sum owed and the proper defense to file in court. The IGG also advised the Treasury not to release the money in case an out-of-court settlement was reached.

The attorney general's chambers made a poor defense of the government's case—one of the witnesses summoned was known to have died a year before. The government lost the case and did not appeal. In the meantime, a new minister of justice and attorney general were appointed, and the government appealed the lower court's decision to the Supreme Court. The appeal was successful, and the firm received exactly the amount the IGG had recommended.

CASE 4: MISMANAGEMENT OF A COOPERATIVE TRANSPORT UNION. A state-run transport cooperative was riddled with corruption, fraud, and embezzlement. Senior officers were pocketing funds and manipulating the accounts to hide the problems from top management. The general manager had even appropriated a union truck and used union funds to pay for its repair and maintenance. Other officers had borrowed money with credit notes that were later destroyed. To make things worse, the union's auditors had also been corrupted, accepting large sums of money that were not reflected in the accounts. Following the IGG's investigation, some officials were disciplined and the police were considering charges against the others involved.

CASE 5: "GHOST WORKERS" IN THE PUBLIC SERVICE. In one ministry selected for investigation, the IGG's staff found 4,190 nonexistent workers for whom pay was being collected, out of a total work force of 11,710. The "ghosts" were found in 66 institutions of the ministry in one half of the country, while investigations were continuing in the other half.

CASE 6: MANIPULATION OF BIDS FOR PRESHIPMENT INSPECTION SERVICES. The Uganda Revenue Authority (URA) had called for tenders to introduce competition in the provision of preshipment inspection services, which the Swiss-based firm SGS had previously held as a virtual monopoly. Six international companies responded with bids. The IGG got wind of irregularities that were occurring in the bid evaluation, such as unexplained changes in rules and regulations. The IGG's investigation found that SGS had manipulated the tendering process from within the URA and other influential institutions, the evaluation team had given unreasonably high marks to SGS to make its position over the other competitors unassailable, and tendering procedures were changed after the evaluation exercise was completed and recommendations made by the evaluation team.

The IGG recommended issuing a new tender call through the Central Tender Board, with bids to be evaluated by a completely new team. However, the Ministry of Finance, which has the final say, decided to quietly drop the whole business. No new tendering was undertaken, and no tender award was given.

CASE 7: MISAPPROPRIATION OF AID FUNDS. Officials misappropriated funds for purchasing animal drugs using a Japanese line of credit. Nearly 90 million Ugandan shillings could not be accounted for.

These examples illustrate that corrupt practices still occur throughout Uganda. However, they also illustrate that in only a few years and despite modest staff and financial resources, the IGG has established itself prominently in the minds of the public, politicians, and administrators as the central instrument in the fight against corruption. As a result of the IGG's investigations, a number of officials have been dismissed or suspended because of their involvement in corruption. Some political leaders have also been relieved of duty following IGG investigations and the ensuing public pressure.

Despite these gains, the office suffers from serious flaws that limit its potential effectiveness. Until recently, its reports were of an advisory and confidential nature—sent to the president instead of to an open and more directly accountable forum such as Parliament. Resource shortages have confined the IGG's monitoring and investigative activities mainly to central areas, such as Kampala, while the rest of the country remains "out of reach." In addition, the office lacks enforcement power and must depend on the justice system to initiate prosecutions against offenders. As an external observer mission stated in 1994, "This might be appropriate in other situations if these other arms are efficient, [but] at present this does not seem to be the case. . . . The impression is that very little happens once the IGG has tabled an adverse report. In fact, of those cases that are passed on [to] the Director of Public Prosecutions, only a minority lead to convictions" (EDI and TI 1995, p. 13).

Developing a Strategy for Public Service Reform

The Public Service Review and Re-organization Commission, in preparing its 729-page report, consulted over 25,000 public servants throughout the country between 1989 and 1990. Defining corruption as "conduct or practice by a public official or private individual done in flagrant violation of existing rules and procedures for the realization of personal or group gains," the report was published, along with 225 specific recommendations, as a government "white paper" in 1991.

The new vision outlined in the white paper decreed that by the year 2000, Uganda's civil service would be smaller, better paid, more efficient, and more effective. Fair, simple, consistent rules and procedures would be implemented to foster discipline while promoting personal initiative. Levels of corruption would be reduced, thanks partly to an effective police and prosecutorial staff. Clear organizational goals would be implemented, workers would be fully responsible and accountable for their assigned duties, and individuals would be committed to achieving clearly identified objectives.

The first step in the reform process involved reviews of all government ministries to evaluate their roles and determine which activities should be privatized or shared. At the district level, similar reviews were conducted to reconsider the role of government, set objectives and priorities, agree on performance indicators, remove redundant staff, and focus more closely on capacity building. After a slow start, two overriding objectives were established for the reform process: the payment of a minimum wage to civil servants and the introduction of results-oriented management. Both were intended to improve service delivery to the public.

The next step involved the development of a 50-page document, *Management of Change: Context, Vision, Strategy and Plan.* Written by senior government staff and supported by a detailed action program, the document received political approval from the presidential cabinet in August 1993.

Reducing the Size of the Public Sector

The role of Uganda's government is being redefined and limited to those functions and services that must be undertaken by government. "Non-core" services will either be turned over to the private sector or abandoned.

Staffing has also been streamlined. The president appointed panels of senior citizens to implement new staffing levels for the restructured ministries. The panels conducted interviews to identify which positions should remain and which should be declared redundant. As a result, the civil service shrank from 320,000 employees in 1990 to 128,000 in March 1996.

Personnel reductions were achieved through a number of measures. For example, "overdue leavers" were dismissed. This category consisted of individuals who would have been weeded out much earlier if the civil service had been functioning efficiently: those past the usual retirement age, irregular entrants, and those identified through performance assessments as incompetent. By 1995 the list included 11 of the 32 permanent secretaries, 6,339 other employees in the central government, and 7,241 teaching staff.

"Ghost workers" were also identified and eliminated. By 1994 approximately 42,000 deceased, fictitious, or former employees who remained on the government payroll had been removed from the system. The "group employees scheme," which allowed senior managers to recruit their own casual, short-term workers without reference to the established job grades, was also abolished. This led to a further reduction of 30,000 workers.

Workers declared surplus as a result of the reviews in each ministry were laid off. Although these employees were competent, bona fide workers, they could not be deployed elsewhere in the government and received severance packages. In addition, approximately 4,500 employees accepted voluntary retirement by the end of 1994.

Integrating a System of Responsibility and Accountability into the Civil Service Machinery

A modern management system—results-oriented management (ROM)—is being introduced to the civil service to improve employees' efficiency and performance, create a responsive and accountable work force, and establish a system that will quickly bring to light corrupt and inefficient practices. Under ROM, each government ministry defines its objectives, sets measurable performance standards and targets, and conducts a service-delivery survey to establish baseline indicators. Each ministry also decides how each department or district-level unit—and ultimately how individual civil servants—will achieve the components of the reform plan. Progress is then to be measured against the standards and targets established for each type and level of government service.

Ministries will also be given new authority to plan and fully control their staffing and other resources through their program plans. Permanent secretaries "will operate as quasi-managing directors of their respective ministries and will be free to determine the optimum resources needed to meet their set ministerial targets. Permanent Secretaries will be assessed on the achievement of the set targets within the allocated resources over a given time frame. The implication of this monitoring system is that every accounting officer will seek to be as efficient as possible. This will, therefore, ensure improved value for money" (Wangolo 1995, p. 75).

The work of individual civil servants will also be evaluated against objectives and performance indicators or standards. Promotion will be clearly linked to performance, with incentives available to reward superior performance within individual salary scales. Employees who engage in dubious practices or don't measure up will be subject to disciplinary action including dismissal.

Aside from results-oriented management, more direct controls on financial operations have also been introduced and existing systems strengthened. For example, in its first three years of operation the central payroll monitoring unit for government employees, located in the Ministry of Public Service and Administration, led to a reduction of 25,000 from the ranks of the Ugandan Teaching Service. The computerized monitoring system, which verifies entry into and exit from the payroll and tracks all changes, should preclude a recurrence of the costly "ghost worker" phenomenon. Auditing functions are also being strengthened throughout the government, and the auditor general's office is free to examine government accounts more vigorously. However, the auditor general's resources are still inadequate, and auditing is often lax.

Finally, the authority once given to managers to hire short-term workers without higher approval—the cause of much overstaffing and nepotism—has been rescinded. A hiring freeze is in force throughout the public sector, and exceptions require the personal consent of the head of the civil service.

Making Salary Levels More Equitable and Transparent

Between 1990 and 1994, civil service wages increased by approximately 50 percent per year. Paying a living wage has been one of the most critical issues in the reform program, as low wages in the civil service have been directly linked to corruption. Indeed, at a Donor Consultative Group meeting in Paris in August 1994, it was agreed that falling behind on pay reform would be fatal to the entire reform program. If the momentum subsided, it was feared, support for the entire reform program would diminish among civil servants, and the pressure to obtain supplementary income would increase. In particular, the civil service would remain unable to attract and retain the most highly skilled professionals and technicians, to the detriment of general efficiency and all development assistance programs. As a result, donors concluded that donor-supported, stepped-up pay increases would continue to be necessary within a program of broader civil service, macroeconomic, and other reforms.

Even with donor aid, government salaries in Uganda remain among the lowest in Sub-Saharan Africa. For many occupations, public pay is well below the minimum wage in the private sector. In 1994, police officers and primary school teachers earned, respectively, the equivalent of $45 and $43 per month, even though the minimum required to sustain a family at that time was estimated to be around $60. At these levels of compensation, the government cannot attract the best people to fill civil service positions, nor can it combat corruption in the lower-paid job classifications. Furthermore, expecting civil servants at the bottom of pay scale to work solely for the civil service is somewhat unrealistic.

Nevertheless, the establishment of a minimum living wage is one of the chief objectives of the current round of civil service reform. The minimum wage will be set at the level of the lowest acceptable salary for the lowest civil service classification, based on a food basket/cost-of-living survey carried out in 1989–90. Scheduled increases will compensate for inflation and differences in urban and rural locations.

Reaching the minimum wage targets is jeopardized by the government's low revenue mobilization. In 1992, tax revenue in Uganda, as a percentage of gross domestic product (GDP), was the lowest among 26 African countries receiving World Bank structural adjustment credits. In 1995, tax revenues represented 11 percent of GDP (compared with 19.1 percent in neighboring Kenya).

To improve the chances of meeting its wage targets, the government announced in August 1994 that it would cut the civil service by an extra 5,000 employees—to 145,000 instead of the targeted 150,000 by 1995—and use the savings to sustain higher pay for those who remain. Actual remuneration has been made more transparent, thanks to the monetization of housing, health, and transportation benefits that have been made available to some civil servants. In addition, the various types of cash allowances that civil servants received according to their tasks and occupation have now been consolidated into fewer categories.

These measures are designed to improve transparency while controlling abuse. Job classifications and positions on the salary scale are also being reviewed and simplified in ways designed to improve incentives for better performance.

Promoting a Code of Conduct for all Civil Servants

To support other aspects of the reform effort, a code of conduct has been established for all civil servants. Each civil servant is required to take an oath of commitment to the code, and anyone dismissed for breaching the code will be prohibited from holding a public post for at least five years.

Based on the principle of selfless service, the code of conduct correlates to the standing orders of the civil service, which state:

> No officer shall at any time engage in any activity which could in any way impair his usefulness as a public officer or engage in any occupation or undertaking which might in any way conflict with the interest of the public service or be inconsistent with his position as a public officer; or make use of his official position to further his private interests or those of his family. (Government of Uganda 1994, p. 54)

Workshops have been held across the country to introduce the code to senior government managers and to focus on their role as leaders in civil service reform and results-oriented management.

Communicating Progress

The public, civil servants, and the donor community are being kept abreast of developments in the reform effort through publications and regular reports on progress in implementing the action plan. Direct, accurate, and timely information is intended to help achieve transparency and encourage continued progress.

A Leadership Code of Conduct

The Ugandan Constitution is based on the notion that the country's future prospects depend, to a very great extent, on the quality and honesty of its leaders. The Constitution calls for a new culture of leadership for both elected and appointed officials in the public sector. It outlines a broad concept of what constitutes leadership, emphasizes the role of leaders in setting an example, and identifies principles of good leadership: honest, impartial, and nondiscriminatory behavior; sensitivity to marginalized groups; developmental leadership; respect for democratic procedures and the rule of law; periodic testing; a sense of duty and conscience; and transparency and accountability (Government of Uganda 1995, p. 10).

The leadership code statute describes the expected, and prohibited, forms of conduct for government leaders. For example, it requires leaders to annually disclose their income, assets, and liabilities to the IGG. This disclosure must cover not only the leader but also his or her nominees (defined as anyone who controls or manages business or other activities that principally benefit the leader). Forbidden activities include seeking or accepting gifts or benefits in relation to the exercise of official duties and personal interests; failure to seek prior approval from the Leadership Code Committee to contract with the government or with certain kinds of foreign businesses; abuse of government property; and misuse of official information not available to the public.

In addition to setting a minimum standard of behavior, the code establishes penalties for transgressions, although no provision exists for its enforcement. The debate in the Constituent Assembly has focused mainly on the sincerity of those politicians who have objected to some provisions of the proposed code, especially the requirement that close relatives of government leaders declare their assets. Discussions have been marked by considerable rancor, conveying a clear impression that some of Uganda's politicians do not welcome scrutiny of their income and property.

Aside from the leadership code statute, the Constitution includes another provision to promote greater integrity within the public service and in political office. The provision proposes that Parliament establish a National Council of State to review the backgrounds and qualifications of individuals being considered for political office or senior positions in the civil service. If this proposal is implemented effectively, any candidate suspected of dishonesty or corruption is likely to be disqualified at the screening stage.

The Director of Public Prosecutions

Since the 1960s, Ugandan laws have provided police and prosecutors with the power to deal with corruption. For example, the penal code (1964 and 1987) specifies penalties for different corruption offenses. Other relevant pieces of legislation include the 1987 statute establishing the IGG, the Police Act of 1964, the Public Finance Act of 1964, the leadership code statute, Statute No. 8 of 1992, and the Evidence Act. In addition, the Prevention of Corruption Act of 1970 specifically calls on the Directorate of Public Prosecutions (DPP) to investigate and prosecute corruption and bribery and confers on it the right to search, seize, arrest, and interrogate suspects. A special section within the Directorate handles corruption and fraud-related cases and has preventive, investigative, and prosecutorial functions.

Uganda's director of public prosecutions, Alfred P. W. Nasaba, has observed that although the legal framework is generally adequate for bringing offenders to justice, "prosecutions in corruption cases have been hampered by the laws of evidence, particularly the accomplice rule. This rule states that evidence of an accomplice must be corroborated by independent evidence before a conviction can be based on it. In cases of corruption, both the giver and recipient are accomplices. If corrupt people are to be convicted, this rule should be changed to allow an accomplice to give credible evidence against corrupt officials or persons" (Nasaba 1995, p. 93)

It is vital that only those officials who are untainted by corruption be put in charge of corruption cases. The investigators, prosecutors, and judges involved should be persons of transparent integrity.

The Auditor General and the Public Accounts Committee

As in other countries, Uganda's auditor general conducts regular financial audits of government operations. The new Constitution gives the auditor general the authority to audit all rather than some public accounts. "Value for money" audits are now required to ensure that the government spends taxpayers' money wisely as well as prudently. Government departments and agencies must now submit their accounts to audit scrutiny and publication in Parliament.

The increased frequency of audits in recent years has helped identify poor accounting practices, and the auditor general's annual reports to Parliament have regularly documented corruption and inefficiencies. In 1992, for example, his report exposed a failure to account for 4,100 billion Ugandan shillings (approximately $4 million) in the government accounts.

The auditor general's reports are reviewed by the Public Accounts Committee of Parliament. After several decades of inactivity, this committee is now active again in investigating the misuse of public funds. However, the fact that no members of the opposition parties are represented on the committee weakens its effectiveness, credibility, and accountability. Moreover, the government is not yet obliged by law to implement the committee's recommendations.

To supplement the work of the auditor general, the inspectorate system in the public service has been reinstated after many years of neglect. Checks are conducted regularly within various departments to ascertain, for example, whether funds are being used for the purposes intended and whether the recipients of pay are actually working in the ministry.

Other Government Reforms

Public sector reform, through its contribution to a more disciplined, productive, and responsible civil service, is likely to have the most direct impact on corruption. However, other reforms—economic, military, and governmental—will also help reduce the scope and incidence of corruption in Uganda.

Economic Reforms and Liberalization

A series of macroeconomic reforms are gradually eliminating numerous distortions that encouraged corruption. Some reforms have ended quota systems and importation rights on certain products. Another step has been the elimination of monopolies, allowing the private sector to trade in basic commodities and compete with the state. Export monopolies in traditional commodities (coffee, cotton) have been abolished, export procedures have been simplified, and a new investment code encourages investment in export-oriented activities.

The privatization of parastatals has helped reduce state control over the economy, as have other liberalizing measures. These include the removal of price controls—direct and indirect—on major, locally manufactured products, the abolition of monopoly over the export of foodstuffs, the elimination of the Coffee Marketing Board, and the deregulation of foreign exchange markets. As a result, confidence in the shilling has returned, and funds held abroad are now flowing back into the country.

The government has also sought to change the delivery of services in order to "depersonalize" the transaction of public business. Customers should not have to contact any particular official for information that can easily be obtained through posters, notices, or other information bulletins.

Reduced Military Spending and Reduction in the Military Establishment

By paring down the military—and military spending—the government is seeking to free up funds and diminish the role of the military in political life. In fact, military spending was reduced from 35 percent of gross national product in 1990 to 16 percent in 1994 through demobilization and other measures. Under a plan approved in May 1992 by the National Resistance Council, the government trimmed the military establishment by 40 percent—to 50,000 personnel—over a three-year period, for a savings of $14 million per year.

Government Decentralization

Decentralization is important in the fight against corruption because public sector decisionmaking in Uganda has been conducted largely in secret by highly centralized institutions with little accountability. To ensure greater public accountability and reduce corruption, the government has embarked on a major program to decentralize the administration and delivery of many public services to the local and regional levels.

The success of this effort will depend on how responsive and answerable district-level structures are to the populations they are supposed to serve.

To this end, the channels of communication are being widened, citizens are being encouraged to speak out at District Resistance Council meetings, and regular consultations are to be held between local councilors, civil servants, and nongovernmental organizations (NGOs).

The Role of the Press

The role of the press is critical in fighting corruption and in informing the public about the reform campaign. The government of Uganda has recognized the value of a free press and has encouraged its development as part of a move toward greater freedom and democracy. The government-controlled media has also been fairly free to report on abuses of public office and has given the fight against corruption considerable prominence. The efforts of one paper, *Uganda Confidential,* have been especially striking, although some observers claim that the paper still lacks professional reporting and has had to pay substantial libel costs.

Despite the media's contributions, a number of factors have hindered it from realizing its full potential in combating corruption. For example, because the free press is a new phenomenon, professional journalistic techniques are lacking, and a biased approach is often evident in investigative journalism. In some cases, professionalism has been sabotaged as underpaid reporters and editors succumb to bribery and replace reporting with what could be viewed as slander. In addition, public officials have until recently been unavailable to answer reporters' questions. Journalists have therefore not been fully informed of the various anticorruption measures now being undertaken or of the details of the government's sweeping public sector reform.

An effort to improve the press's effectiveness in curbing corruption was launched in 1994 when the government sponsored two workshops on reporting, with the assistance of the IGG, the Ugandan Journalists Association, the Danish media, the Danish International Development Agency (DANIDA), the World Bank's Economic Development Institute (EDI), and Transparency International (TI). The workshops, which represented one of the first opportunities for journalists to question senior government officials, helped to inform the press of the government's overall reform program and provided journalists with some training in investigative reporting. Four themes were stressed: the need to promote professional awareness of, and insight into, corruption and the institutions fighting it; the importance of improving professional techniques for obtaining information ethically, respecting privacy, checking references, and avoiding litigation; the need to promote a sense of commitment and responsibility among journalists; and the necessity of informing journalists about the government's civil service reform program, its impact on the country's welfare, and its role in reducing corruption.

DANIDA, the Canadian International Development Agency, the Norwegian government, and others have sponsored subsequent investigative journalism workshops. In addition, leading Ugandan journalists have established a specialized media-training NGO.

The Role of the President

The leadership and strong support of President Museveni have been crucial to Uganda's fight against corruption. The president loses few opportunities to drive home the anticorruption message. For example, while opening the new international terminal facilities at Entebbe Airport in 1994, he berated the corrupt practices of customs and immigration officials—a speech that resulted in extensive media coverage.

The EDI/TI Mission

By late 1994 it was apparent that corruption remained widespread and deep-seated in Uganda, despite government measures to curb it. A change in Uganda's political atmosphere—signaled by the debate on the new Constitution in the elected Constituent Assembly and by the presidential elections planned for May 1996—combined with a growing economy, suggested that the time was ripe for the government to intensify its anticorruption strategy.

At the invitation of the government (specifically the IGG), a joint mission from the Economic Development Institute and Transparency International visited Uganda in December 1994 to assess the country's progress in containing corruption. The team met with high-level officials and prominent Ugandans and was able to hear the views of individuals from a wide cross-section of civil society.

The mission report noted the government's achievements in controlling inflation and promoting democracy. The transformation of the political environment into one of more freedom and considerably less repression was considered nothing short of remarkable, and the public sector reform program earned approval. However, the mission expressed serious concern about the continuing pervasiveness of corruption in the country:

> Many people we met—even from the public sector—did not hesitate to classify corruption as rampant. . . . Corruption is a major issue in Uganda, at all levels of society. . . . Unethical practices, [we] found, were rampant throughout all levels of the civil service, from the bottom to the top. . . . Corruption [is] primarily a means of survival on the part of junior civil servants and others; at the top, it involves spoilage and misapplication (even misappropriation) of funds on a large scale by senior civil servants and politicians. (EDI and TI 1995, p. 6)

People from outside the government expressed a common view in meetings with the mission:

> There was a feeling that the government may be taking steps to fight corruption but not effectively enough. . . . People argued that far too little was happening, too few were being successfully prosecuted and too many notoriously corrupt individuals were retaining high level positions in the Government. (EDI and TI 1995, p. 11)

Cynicism also marked the public's view of politics and politicians. During the debate on the Constitution, members of the Constituent Assembly were perceived to be dragging out the discussion in order to maximize their daily allowances. This jaundiced view was reinforced by the heated debate over the provisions of the leadership code—a code that had been in existence for two years but had never come into effect. In the words of the mission, "the general public clearly interpreted the debate as further evidence that most politicians had something to hide" (EDI and TI 1995, p. 11).

While combating corruption loomed large among the government's preoccupations, and the president considered it a matter of highest priority, the mission report noted that corruption also loomed large in the consciousness of the people, but in a different way. The general public seemed unconvinced that the leadership was serious about dealing with the problem, and this skepticism prevailed even though Uganda had taken more substantive and determined anticorruption measures than most countries.

Areas of Concern

The mission expressed particular concern about corruption in the areas of procurement, privatization, vote buying, and the judicial system.

PROCUREMENT. The team reported that "public procurement is, not surprisingly, a major area of fraud and corruption. We were even given the very specific information that the going rate on parastatal contracts was 8 per cent. The payments go to the project managers for distribution to those who participate in the proceeds" (EDI and TI 1995, p. 13). In the bidding of international contracts, the mission found, few Ugandans seemed to feel that grand-scale corruption was a problem, although there were clearly instances of it (p. 19).

PRIVATIZATION. The mission report (p. 19) noted that privatization seems to have been welcomed by many, particularly in the business community. Nonetheless, it is also attracting considerable criticism regarding the transparency, integrity, and honesty of the process and the possible benefits being reaped by some senior public figures.

VOTE BUYING. The mission team heard several accounts of vote buying and suggestions that this was a widespread phenomenon during the elections for the Constituent Assembly. Some candidates allegedly spent millions of shillings beyond their allowable and available means in order to win office. Those who lost must now service their debts, while those who won are now expected to make good on promises made to their backers.

THE JUDICIAL SYSTEM. Everywhere the mission traveled, it heard sobering views regarding the judiciary. Despite some outstanding exceptions at the magistrates' court level, all other players in the judicial system are generally regarded with contempt. The ethics of the legal profession are also seen as highly questionable, even by practitioners themselves. Lawyers were said to bribe each other. Magistrates arrived late for court or not at all. Judges were paid for delaying judgment and for the judgments themselves, and they were accused of accepting payment for granting bail while knowing the defendants would skip town. Court staff also accepted payments to "lose" files or influence magistrates. Police held prisoners "for ransom" until money was paid, or charged them for transportation to and from court.

A consistent pattern of corruption and unethical practice was found throughout the judicial system. In addition, the mission concluded that judges and magistrates have hindered the fight against corruption through their reluctance to use the provision in the 1970 Prevention of Corruption Act that reverses the burden of proof for accused persons with unexplained wealth not in keeping with their income.

The Mission's Analysis

By and large, according to the EDI/TI team, the root cause of corruption in Uganda appears to be the combination of low salaries and wide differences in incomes. Low levels of pay within the civil service also contribute to the generation of income by legal or illegal means. The mission heard of people with as many as four or five jobs who also had to have gardens to provide food for their families.

As for the effectiveness of the government's anticorruption campaign, the EDI/TI mission ascertained both a direct and an indirect impact. It noted that some senior civil servants involved in corruption were being removed from positions of real power or even being suspended pending the outcome of inquiries. It also noted that many individuals were growing increasingly cautious or actually refraining from corrupt activities as the risk of exposure—and punishment—increased. However, it was also clear that the general public remained unconvinced that the government's efforts were serious or that politicians were interested in providing a "clean" government.

In summarizing the situation, the mission determined that the scope of corruption in Uganda was influenced by the following main factors:

- Very low levels of civil service pay, which encourage civil servants to seek additional income through legal or illegal means
- The high cost of political campaigning, which forces politicians to rely on powerful backers who then demand special favors
- Lax enforcement of auditing systems within the government and the parastatal sector
- The manifest failure to implement or enforce the standing orders of the civil service, which, among other things, prohibit conflict-of-interest activities
- The inability to monitor the assets and liabilities of key decisionmakers in the public sector
- Manipulation of some kinds of aid flows
- An underresourced judicial system that has not yet fully recovered from the civil war years
- A substantial privatization program that is subject to constantly changing criteria for private investment.

The mission's primary conclusion was that although the government's efforts were remarkable and admirable, its campaign might falter or even fail without the involvement of the general public and a determined effort to convict people found guilty of corruption. The mission also noted that a significant body of opinion in Uganda wished to see the process go further and supported additional measures.

The EDI/TI report proposed a number of steps to strengthen the anticorruption campaign, including:

- *Strengthening existing enforcement mechanisms*. The office of the IGG should be strengthened by adding experienced investigators to the staff and by giving the IGG powers to initiate and conduct prosecutions within its jurisdiction. An alternative approach would be to follow the example set in some Asian countries (and most recently in Botswana) of creating a completely separate body, like the Independent Commission against Corruption in Hong Kong, China, with very extensive powers. Whichever path is chosen, the mission suggested a definite need to reallocate some of the IGG's resources toward monitoring and detecting systematic patterns of corruption and coping with an anticipated wave of new complaints once the public becomes better informed of its rights.

- *Taking stronger action against high-level offenders*. The credibility of the anticorruption campaign suffered primarily because of the government's reluctance to severely punish certain high-level offenders. Part of this reluctance reflected fears of upsetting national unity at a time when the government regarded reconciliation and harmony among previously contending ethnic, regional, and other interest groups as paramount. However, public attitudes will remain cynical unless corrupt individuals are brought to justice through prosecution and conviction in the courts.

- *Engaging the public*. The public should be involved in helping to identify and root out corruption and building a public ethos rejecting corruption and the corrupt. The mission recommended that a national anticorruption awareness campaign be launched, modeled on Uganda's successful anti-AIDS campaign. Such a campaign should include family and school-level education and enjoy the open and active support of the president. Key messages might include the following: that the public has a right to certain public services without further payment; that the public should resist and report any demands for such illicit payments; that those who enrich themselves at the public's expense are stealing taxpayers' money and should be objects of contempt and derision, not role models; and that neither grand corruption nor petty extortion form any part of African culture but only diminish and debase long-standing traditions of hospitality and generosity. In addition, citizens should be educated about available complaint mechanisms and how to use them. To help involve the public, the mission recommended the creation of a Public Complaint Commissioner (PCC) who would be independent of the bureaucracy and highly visible.

- *Targeting the judiciary.* One suggestion for reforming the judiciary was to consider the problem in a regional context and provide for the rotational service of African judges.

Policymakers' Seminar and New Proposals

For two days in December 1994, 26 senior policymakers from agencies involved in the fight against corruption met near Kampala to examine the situation in Uganda and design a program to enhance ethics, transparency, and accountability. Chaired by the IGG, Augustine Ruzindana, the workshop participants included members of the National Resistance Council and officials from the Office of the IGG, the Office of Auditor General, the Uganda Revenue Authority, and the ministries of Justice and Constitutional Affairs, Education, Local Government, Finance, Economic Planning, and Public Service. The workshop was supported by EDI and the British Overseas Development Administration (now the Department for International Development) and facilitated by members of the EDI/TI mission.

The outcome consisted of a four-point plan of action accepted in January 1995 as the official program of the government. The plan lays down measures to be undertaken in the following areas:

- *Public awareness:* A public awareness campaign will stress the evils of corruption, using media ranging from cartoon sketches to TV skits. Leading figures will be involved in its implementation. The office of a Public Complaints Commissioner will be created.
- *Enforcement.* The IGG's office will be strengthened and its investigative capacity increased. Additional resources will be provided to enable the IGG to extend its work throughout the country. For the time being, the government has rejected the idea of establishing an independent commission against corruption with special powers, along the lines of similar bodies in Belize, Hong Kong (China), Malaysia, and Singapore.
- *Preventive measures.* The government intends to strengthen the inspectorates in key agencies such as the Customs Department, the Uganda

Revenue Authority, and the key monitoring and enforcement agencies (the Office of the IGG, the DPP, and the police).
- *Improved coordination and cooperation.* The departments and agencies involved in the workshop resolved that they would work closely together to find more constructive ways to use available resources effectively in the fight against corruption. For example, the DPP and the IGG agreed to develop new procedures to ensure that those suspected of corruption are brought promptly to trial.

To oversee the implementation of the government's new action plan, a National Committee has been created. Initially under the leadership of the IGG, the committee has been assigned specific tasks to ensure that the above measures are put into effect within a reasonable time frame.

Conclusion

The new plan of action marks a major intensification of Uganda's anticorruption campaign and a positive surge toward real accountability and transparency. Uganda has already won recognition on the continent for the scale of its efforts to reform the public sector and stamp out corruption. No other African country has carried out a public sector reform initiative of this magnitude and with so many components.

On the anticorruption front, EDI has facilitated a series of investigative journalism workshops and assisted the IGG in organizing awareness-raising and institutional strengthening workshops for the judiciary. It has also organized a workshop to help the Public Accounts Committee exercise more financial oversight. In addition, two more national integrity workshops have been held, as has a parliamentary retreat on corruption and a major regional conference linking good governance to private sector development.

The restrictions placed on party electoral campaigning in the recent elections give reason for worry, as does the resurgence of violence in northern Uganda by the Lord's Resistance Army. Nonetheless, if the government maintains its commitment to curbing corruption and if Ugandans from all walks of life join that effort, the future looks promising.

References

EDI (Economic Development Institute of the World Bank) and TI (Transparency International). 1995. "Ethics, Accountability and Transparency in Uganda: Assessing Current Situation and Looking Ahead." Unpublished report on a mission to Uganda. Washington, D.C.

Government of Uganda. 1994. *Civil Service Reform.* Status report. Kampala.

———. 1995. *Civil Service Reform.* Status report. Kampala.

Nasaba, Alfred P. W. 1995. "Anti-Corruption Legislation in Uganda and Its Improvement." In Jeremy Pope and Petter Langseth, eds., *Investigative Journalism in Uganda I: Final Workshop Proceedings.* Mukono, Uganda: Inspectorate General of Government in cooperation with the Economic Development Institute of the World Bank, Transparency International, and the Danish Ministry of Foreign Affairs.

Ruzindana, Augustine. 1994. "Combating Corruption in Africa: The Case of Uganda." Address at a seminar at the World Bank, November 2–3, Washington, D.C.

Wangolo, A. M. 1995. "Civil Service Reform." In Jeremy Pope and Petter Langseth, eds., *Investigative Journalism in Uganda I: Final Workshop Proceedings.* Mukono, Uganda: Inspectorate General of Government in cooperation with the Economic Development Institute of the World Bank, Transparency International, and the Danish Ministry of Foreign Affairs.

13

The Fight against Corruption in Sierra Leone

Sahr J. Kpundeh

Today corruption is a way of life for Sierra Leoneans. Despite numerous changes in government, both civil and military, little has changed the rampant corruption and malfeasance that plague all levels of government. Malfeasance in both the public and private sectors has aggravated the country's severe and prolonged economic crises. Since the 1980s Sierra Leone has experienced the most regressive and repressive economic conditions in its history. Many people in positions of trust have put their own interests first and the general interest of the country last. The continued failure of previous reform strategies has been due largely to a poor understanding of the roots and dynamics of corruption. Past remedies have lacked coordination, political will, leadership, and public involvement.

The military government of Valentine Strasser, which took power in a bloodless coup in April 1992, established commissions of inquiry to identify public officials and businesspeople who were culpable of horrendous dishonesty, negligence, and abuse of public office for private benefit. The commissions revealed innumerable cases of rampant corruption, including so-called daylight robbery by politicians and civil servants, theft and cheating by government contractors, and conspiracy among foreign and local businesspeople, politicians, and transnational corporations. Individually and collectively, these offenders plundered the state of money, goods, and services.

Despite the talk of transparency and accountability by the Strasser Administration, little was done to translate promises into genuine commitment to detect and penalize unethical behavior. The government became inundated with widespread allegations, primarily because Strasser himself refused to facilitate the free flow of information between government officials and the people in whose interest they claimed to govern.

In April 1996 Sierra Leoneans democratically elected a government that, like its predecessors, claimed it wanted to fight corruption and restore integrity. President Ahmed Tejan Kabba appeared committed, but without a strong political base he had to rely on the support of the "old hands" in his party. To win the elections, promises had to be made and kept, and so the seeds of political patronage were planted. It began with the run-off elections. Kabba struck deals with other political parties, promising ministerial positions to some of the allied parties if they backed his candidacy. After winning, he delivered and appointed 45 ministers and deputy ministers. While politically he boasted of a government of national unity, he was creating a bloated government in a country with fewer than 5 million people, a dwindling economy, and a protracted rebel war draining public resources.

Kabba's reform efforts were disappointing. He created the National Commission for Unity and Reconciliation to "investigate and identify the causes which have alienated citizens from the State and created conflict and division within society" (*Sierra Leone Gazette* 1996). The commission released two reports, both recommending the reversal of previous reform strategies. Seizures of illegally acquired property, dismissals of corrupt government officials, and stiff fines for wrongdoing were all countermanded—the properties and money returned and some of the workers even reinstated with compensation. A senior government official guilty of selling $210,000 worth of passports to foreigners was told simply to pay back the money. These kinds of government actions demonstrated a lack of political will to do whatever was necessary to begin eradicating corruption. Several journalists who reported the story were detained or harassed, and some even faced legal action.

The May 25, 1997, coup d'état in Freetown was the third successful forced change of regime in five years and the most bloody and destructive in Sierra Leone's history. The soldiers who struck claimed to act in the interests of the nation as a whole. They gave populist reasons for intervention: corruption, the previous regime's tribal and regional favoritism, and overreliance on

Nigerian soldiers in ECOMOG (the military arm of the Economic Community of West African States), coupled with too little attention to the Sierra Leonean Army. But the rebels' motives and actions were almost wholly self-serving, and great damage was done in the days following the coup.

By all available evidence, Sierra Leoneans overwhelmingly rejected the takeover. Out of protest and fear, they refused the ruling junta's orders to return to work. The economy was paralyzed. Foreign governments rebuffed the junta's appeals for understanding, and the United Nations imposed sanctions. Sierra Leone was suspended from the Commonwealth of Nations, and the Economic Community of West African States imposed an air, sea, and land blockade of the country.

In early 1998, economic forces successfully intervened to push the military government out of power. Kabba returned from exile in neighboring Guinea and reclaimed his office as president of Sierra Leone on March 10, 1998.

The Causes of Corruption in Sierra Leone

Corruption undermines good government, and poor government provides an environment in which it grows. Most acts of corruption are attributed to individuals, while both private industry and governments absolve themselves of any responsibility. However, corruption is made possible, if not encouraged, by systemic problems. Lack of accountability in the political process, in the performance of civil servants, and in the control of public resources enables corruption to flourish. Furthermore, a lack of appropriate balance among the various areas of government—political, administrative, and judicial—may undermine the possibility of preventing or mitigating wrongdoing. Thus fiscal mismanagement cannot be analyzed in isolation from good governance and participatory democracy.

In Sierra Leone indications of widespread systemic corruption surfaced in 1982 when the first major scandal, Vouchergate, erupted. Subsequent scandals, Squandergate in 1984 and Milliongate in 1987, were also uncovered, but the government failed to develop strategies to deal with what had obviously become a distinct pattern.

The revelations of the 1992 corruption inquiries and the continuous decline of the economy illustrate the deep harm and persistence of the problem. Several very specific stimuli created the pattern of corruption; an examination of these demonstrates that good governance and strong public participation are fundamental to the development of solutions.

Lack of Economic and Financial Discipline

A lack of economic and financial discipline permeates the entire social structure, with junior government workers demanding a premium ("put for me" or *"mukofay,"* as locals say) before performing routine job responsibilities. However, many public servants such as health workers, teachers, and civil servants work for months without receiving paychecks. Not only is this demoralizing, but it forces most of these workers to moonlight. Those with skills marketable to the private sector who have public positions that do not require stringent work schedules are particularly likely to hold a "mammy coker"—a second job considered subsidiary to their government job. Absenteeism, a severe decline in the quality of government services, and a degree of "self-help" follow, particularly if the remuneration is inadequate. Consequently, professionalism has given way to greed and profit seeking.

Lack of Transparency and Accountability

The principle behind transparency demands that every public act be done in an open manner. Actions of a public officer must be seen to be above board, and every act that may generate suspicion must be explicable. Failure to conduct public duties openly presents opportunities for the dishonest to engage in extortion and favoritism while operating under a cloak of secrecy.

Democratic systems offer a mechanism to minimize corruption by introducing greater accountability and transparency into governance. In Sierra Leone, corruption is arguably linked to undemocratic politics, as evidenced by the widespread abuse and increasing number of scandals that followed the 1978 introduction of the one-party system and the subsequent erosion of internal accountability. Many of the institutions that might have exercised a check on government agencies were seriously weakened or eliminated. The all-powerful president headed practically everything, including the army, the state-run university, and the civil service, and he tolerated no questions on matters that should have required public explanation. In other words, transparency in public service was nonexistent, giving rise to public doubts and loss of confidence in the instruments of power, which in turn contributed greatly to fiscal mismanagement.

Some observers argue that if politicians had not tolerated fraud, any revelation of wrongdoing would have been accompanied by swift retaliatory measures. When the public expects as much from the government, misuse of funds is rare because the possibility of being caught is high, the penalties severe, and the potential gains uncertain. Conversely, when politicians indulge in wrongdoing and plunder and the public is passive if not equally self-indulgent, public employees often feel as if they might as well get a "share of the pickings."

Some of the disclosures from the 1992 corruption inquiries seem to support the notion that administrative and political corruption feed on each other. According to testimony at the commission hearings, from 1968 to 1992, when the All People's Congress (APC) was the ruling party, top civil servants embezzled government funds with the knowledge of complicit politicians (Sierra Leone News Agency 1992). In a system where those in high political positions connive with civil servants to defraud the country, transparency and accountability are difficult to achieve.

Lack of Political Will and Commitment

Political will is a critical first starting point for sustainable and effective anticorruption strategies and programs. Under former presidents Siaka Stevens, Joseph Momoh, and Valentine Strasser, the lack of political will to systematically fight corruption allowed abusive practices to continue and eventually become endemic—a way of life for Sierra Leoneans. Although corruption sometimes can distribute small benefits to a large proportion of the population and break through bureaucratic and political stalemates, more often it is a regressive influence benefiting the wealthy and the well-connected at the expense of the have-nots (Johnston 1982).

The commissions of inquiry revealed that corrupt practices led to the ravaging of the treasury and are contributing to Sierra Leone's current state of economic despondency. Additionally, some government officials have diverted valuable, much needed resources, such as medical drugs, books, and equipment, to the private sector (Zack-Williams 1990). Unscrupulous civil servants, politicians, and businesspeople have sought to raise their standards of living through bribery, which in some cases is more accurately described as extortion. A lack of leadership has resulted in the absence of adequate sanctions or the failure to enforce them. People weigh the advantages and disadvantages of following the rules and decide how they are best served. Thus, if the benefits outweigh the costs, more people than not will choose wrongdoing as a customary way of supplementing their income. Corruption then becomes institutionalized, as has been the case in Sierra Leone.

Politicization of the Government

There were periods in Sierra Leone's history when corruption was less of a problem, particularly during the early years of the Stevens Administration (1968–71). Gradually, however, Stevens' need to consolidate power and the greed of senior party leaders led them to practice political patronage and misuse state funds to ensure the APC's domination.

Governmental authority, especially during one-party rule, extended to the private sector. No industry was protected from interference, including banking, retail trade, and the import/export industry. The government was the country's largest employer, service provider, regulator, and contractor. The wider the scope of government in the affairs of society, the greater the opportunities for corruption. Dishonest people exploited these opportunities in the early 1980s, especially during the periods of foreign exchange shortages that subsequently led to a decline in imports. Officials in the banking industry and the Ministry of Finance became targets of bribery. Corruption not only grew but gathered momentum during this period.

Politicization of the civil service, which escalated during President Stevens' term of office, is primarily responsible for its inefficiency. The APC, the only political party from 1978 to 1992, totally controlled civil servants' political views and associations. From the inception of the one-party system, neo-patrimonial politics dictated that civil servants be APC members. For example, section 139(3) of the one-party constitution of 1978 provides that no one can be appointed or continue to be permanent secretary "unless he is a member of the recognized party" (*West Africa*, April 16–22, 1990). In advocating the inclusion of this section, Stevens argued that denying civil servants the right to take part in party politics meant depriving the best brains of a chance to express their views on matters of public interest and share in the responsibility of citizenship.

In return for their loyalty, civil servants were often shielded, pampered, and allowed to increase the range of their powers and pursue opportunities for self-enrichment. It was therefore understandable that civil servants put the APC's interests above national objectives.

Political Patronage

A significant reason for the complete lack of transparency and accountability is the patronage system that both Siaka Stevens and Joseph Momoh used to solidify the APC's dominance. For example, the secretary to the president under both Stevens and Momoh was also the head of the civil service. This arrangement ensured that top civil servants were political appointees who hoped to gain recognition and advancement by associating with state and party officials.

During Stevens' and Momoh's administrations, whom one knew—not one's job performance—was regarded as key to personal betterment. As a result, everyone remained sensitive to the power implications of changes in leadership and office (Hope 1985). In 1985, when Momoh replaced Stevens, top civil servants and ambassadors tried so desperately to meet the new president that Momoh, exhausted from all the traffic to his office, had closed-circuit television installed to monitor his visitors. In some cases, he even turned away his own ministers (*West Africa*, July 6, 1987). Unfortunately, a high level of patronage still persists today.

The Growing Personalization of Politics

During the 24 years of APC rule, government officials were accountable only to the president and the party officials who surrounded him. Momoh, whose administration was notorious for promoting tribalism and nepotism, appointed his "Ekutay" comrades to all the top government posts. The Ekutay group consisted of Limbas (a tribe from northern Sierra Leone) mostly from Momoh's hometown of Binkolo. They formed an impregnable fence around the president and advised him on virtually all matters. These appointees were concerned only with pleasing Momoh, and in some cases they conducted business dealings and transactions with both foreign and local businesspeople on his behalf. In testimony before a 1992 commission of inquiry, Hassan Gbessay Kanu, a former minister of finance, indicated that "in his capacity as head of the Binkolo hegemony, [Momoh was responsible for] a group that was drenched in sectionalism, tribalism, favoritism, nepotism, incompetence, ineptitude, treachery, indolence, wining, dining and womanizing, which inflicted the severest mismanagement of the affairs of this country" (*West Africa*, October 4–10, 1993).

While power brings with it the promise of employment, security, privilege, promotion, and the authority to delegate, it brings as well the temptation to engage in patronage and corrupt gain. A system of patronage and opportunity, coupled with loyalty, increases the power of the patron (politician). The client (civil servant) of a patron is loyal to the patron as an individual rather than to the administrator (minister) of a government department, and personal relationships tend to govern the vertical exercise of authority (Hope 1985). Thus what Sierra Leoneans witnessed under both Stevens and Momoh was a growing personalization of political power, primarily because the two men used the political apparatus and state machinery to foster their private interests and the domination of the APC Party.

Low Salary Scales for Public Officials

Low salaries encourage corrupt behavior. When poorly paid civil servants administer highly valued programs, budgets, taxes, customs regulations, and so forth, there is an almost irresistible temptation to levy a fee. In an August 7, 1992, interview, R. O. Davies, then Freetown's commissioner of income tax, showed me his pay stub indicating a monthly salary of Le 13,941 (approximately $28 at the rate of Le 500 to US $1). If Davies bought a bag of rice at Le 8,200 (approximately $16) to feed his family for a month and paid Le 300 (approximately $0.60) for transportation to and from work every day, his expenses would exceed his earnings. That meant that to feed, house, and clothe his family, he had to look for other avenues to supplement his income. One can well imagine what a junior civil servant or laborer earns and the extent to which he or she must go to get additional income.

Despite the almost irresistible—and understandable—urge among lower civil servants to accept bribes, the most serious cases of corruption have taken place at substantially higher levels. All the major scandals and disclosures of aberrant behavior, including the 1992 commission revelations, indicate that those earning high salaries, primarily government ministers and senior civil servants, have indulged in more fraud than junior workers or private citizens. The lack of leadership and discipline among politicians and civil servants is largely to blame for widespread corruption. In an August 4, 1992, interview, the deputy comptroller of customs in charge of Lungi Airport, stated:

> Corruption is not the main problem in this society. It is just that people, especially politicians, do it too much. To say that people are not bribed is a big lie because it happens. Some people are just unreasonable. The main problem is that the productivity of the average worker is low, and the government does not put measures in place to increase productivity.

Lack of Clearly Defined Roles

Ambiguity in the roles, functions, and duties of most public officials creates an environment ripe for abusive behavior. The absence of supervision and accountability gives workers opportunity and license to perform public duties according to their own rules and not in accordance with government procedures. This has led some senior government officials to assume extraneous tasks that put them in a position to change and influence matters for their personal interests. For example, Ben Kanu, the minister of state enterprises and industries during the Momoh Administration, decided to take charge of the Maritime Freights Levy Fund, formerly the responsibility of the Sierra Leone Shipping Company. After he seized control, it was alleged that hundreds of thousands of dollars were misappropriated and embezzled (*Progress*, August 8, 1992).

Weak Law Enforcement Machinery

Despite its diamonds, gold, and other precious metals, Sierra Leone is one of the world's poorest countries. Diamond smuggling by private citizens has gone unbridled. Local dealers export only a fraction of their diamonds through the Government Gold and Diamond Office (GGDO). One GGDO official stated that "businessmen smuggle ten times the amount of diamonds they export through our offices and the problem is that we can't do anything about it because they are in business with the military" (Gberie 1996). The GGDO is supposed to get 1 percent of the value of each diamond presented to them by licensed dealers, and the government 0.5 percent. The rest goes to the dealer, who pays a yearly licensing fee of approximately $1,000. But very little revenue from diamonds ends up in state coffers, primarily because government officials have long found diamonds the easiest way to make their fortunes.

The government is known to be soft on illegal mining, the law enforcement agency is weak, and punishment for those caught in unlawful activities is light. This has encouraged corrupt activities to blossom, often with the collaboration of top officials. Desmond Luke, a presidential candidate in the 1996 elections, observed: "It seems no one can control this industry and the result is that our fertile soil is laid to waste, our school-going kids drop out to seek quick wealth and yet everything is smuggled out for the benefit of the outside world, particularly Lebanon. This situation must be changed" (Gberie 1996).

Institutionalized Corruption

At one level, corruption can be seen as a problem of individuals with excessive ambition or greed. If this is the case, then throwing out the "rotten apples" ought to work. But whenever this action has been taken, corruption has not subsided. For example, corrupt government ministers have been forced from office without making an appreciable dent in the problem.[1] Exposure and prosecution or disciplinary action removes the offender, but it does not eliminate corruption; it works only as damage control. Malfeasance continues unabated because the organizational systems and culture remain unchanged—the circumstances that created a corrupt environment still exist.

Thus corruption must be understood as both an institutional and a systemic problem, wherein institutions foster a climate in which wrongdoing can flourish. Rooted in the institutions of society, it is the result of a dysfunctional structure. At the foundation of this faulty structure is an inefficient auditing system. Nearly every governmental department has an internal auditing section, yet few audits ever take place. In most cases, financial records are not examined until years after the actual misappropriations.

The income tax department, Sierra Leone's second largest revenue collection agency (customs is number one), has limited means to investigate and collect taxes, no computers to store data, and weak data processing capacity, so taxes are primarily assessed by manual calculations. Although the department has been in operation since 1943, it lacks adequate office space, the roof leaks, and there is never enough electricity for people to do their work. As one official stated in 1992, "You cannot expect efficient work in this type of environment. It is just too sickening to be in here for eight hours" (R. O. Davies, personal interview, August 7, 1992). Ironically, departments that generate far less revenue, such as the Sierra Leone State Lottery, are housed in buildings with adequate space and better physical conditions.

Widespread fiscal mismanagement during the APC's reign affected economic growth, undermined the party's legitimacy, and contributed significantly to demoralizing both public officials and ordinary citizens. Economic and political mismanagement during both the APC administrations led to the disintegration of the country's social system. Sierra Leoneans today live with bad roads, poor medical facilities and schools, declining educational standards, uncompleted public works projects, and deplorable terms

---

1. S. B. Marah was arrested and detained during the Vouchergate scandal, Chernor Maju was arrested at Lungi Airport trying to smuggle gold, Souffian Kargbo was forced to resign and repay the government Le 6.4 million for mismanaging the Magbass Sugar Complex, and Shamsu Mustapha was convicted of embezzlement.

and conditions for all workers. Foreign exchange earned from exports is not effectively repatriated, and national assets have been sold or ruined. For example, several senior government officials allegedly sold the Sierra Leone Chancery Building in New York and split the profits among themselves (*The New Breed*, May 27–June 2, 1992).

The National Provisional Ruling Council

The so-called revolution of April 29, 1992, saw the demise of the All People's Congress and the single-party-state. The National Provisional Ruling Council (NPRC), consisting of the military officers who initiated the coup, emphasized that the end of the APC era signaled the total dismantling of its system and its promoters. This included inaugurating new ways of thinking and behaving, thereby developing a new Sierra Leonean society.

Arnold Bishop Gooding, the first attorney general of the NPRC, stated in the June 16–22, 1992, edition of *Unity Magazine:*

> The government has embarked on legal measures to effect a major role of the revolution; that is to say . . . the eradication of the cesspit of corruption that has pervaded every sector of the society, which was one of the primary reasons for the NPRC to take over the reigns of government. . . . We do accept that corruption is everywhere in the world, but in our country, corruption has reached alarming heights and levels thus causing for us tremendous disaster. . . . It is the intention of the NPRC to reduce corruption to a tolerable level.

Although the NPRC proclaimed its determination to eradicate mismanagement and institutionalized malfeasance by initiating policies to infuse morality and discipline into the system, the new administration was plagued by accusations of corruption, especially among the senior military personnel, including the former head of state, Valentine Strasser. It is common knowledge that NPRC members were enjoying luxurious lifestyles and probably living more lavishly than the APC leaders had. The public's initial trust dissipated when people witnessed continued widespread abuse of power, disrespect for human rights, and a blatant lack of transparency and accountability.

The abuse of government funds began immediately after the coup, when the military mined diamonds in Kono in exchange for Belgian and Romanian weapons. It was while mining diamonds at Gandohun, Kono, that

Strasser's men were overtaken by Revolutionary United Front (RUF) rebel forces in mid-1992 (Reno 1995). The invading troops took advantage of the mining operations to mount an offensive to seize the Kono mining area, and the rebel war remains ongoing.

In fall 1993 it was alleged that Strasser's government privately exported 435 carats of diamonds to Sweden (Reno 1995). A Swedish newspaper, *Sunday Express,* supported this assertion with the headline "Sierra Leone's 'Great Redeemer' Becomes a Millionaire Whilst the People Continue to Starve" (September 26, 1993). The paper reported that Strasser sold $43 million worth of diamonds in Antwerp, traveled to London, bought a house, and invested the remainder of the money. The report also painted an image of widespread corruption by Strasser's NPRC colleagues Karefa Kargbo, John Benjamin, and Charles Mbayo, who reportedly also bought houses in either France or London (*New Breed,* October 13, 1993).

Just as disturbing as the theft of diamonds and other valuable national resources was the way the NPRC handled the situation, particularly since the council claimed to champion accountability and transparency. When a local newspaper reprinted the *Sunday Express* allegations, Strasser immediately ordered the arrest and imprisonment of the editor and some reporters. This incident destroyed public trust in the NPRC and forced acknowledgment that the council was not living up to its promises or playing by its own rules. Such revelations of corruption led people to believe the NPRC was attempting to get rich at the public's expense and steal the country's resources. Consequently, belief in and support of the NPRC leaders was seriously damaged.

The NPRC was accused of a hidden agenda—manipulating an endless transition by using the war with the RUF as an excuse. Critics have often cited the NPRC's inefficient and sometimes half-hearted prosecution of the war. Strasser's collaboration with foreign firms forced him into a position where his partners compelled him to continue battling rebel forces, rather than negotiate as some foreign advisors recommended. Efforts to start peace talks in December 1995 made hard-line military factions anxious. They feared that negotiations with rebels would create political pressure to expel the South African mercenaries supplied by the Pretoria-based company, Executive Outcomes, and thus jeopardize their own ability to participate in lucrative deals with foreign partners (Reno 1996). Even after the January 16, 1996, palace coup in which Strasser was replaced by his deputy Maada Bio, the arrangements with foreign firms continued. Hence the NPRC leaders exploited the war for their own profit.

The Costs of Corruption in Sierra Leone

Colin Leys, an expert on corruption, noted that "it is natural but wrong to assume that the results of corruption are always both bad and important" (Leys 1965). Indeed, some scholars argue that corruption is broadly beneficial, bringing economic gains by facilitating economic activity (Johnston 1982). Nonetheless, the costs of corruption usually outweigh its benefits and are paid by those who can least afford them.

In analyzing the costs, it is important to make a distinction between tangible and intangible costs. Intangible costs—loss of trust in democracy, in leaders, in institutions, and in each other—are usually the more serious. Tangible or direct costs relate to the impact on trade and investments, administrative efficiency, good governance, equality of citizens, and so forth. Although corruption is not to blame for all of the negative effects in these areas, it certainly contributes to a majority of the problems faced in Sierra Leone today. The tangible costs of corruption are usually perceived to include a lack of basic services, a general acceptance of bribery as a way of getting things done faster, numerous scandals, and luxurious lifestyles for public officials that are not commensurate with their salaries.

In a 1992 survey on attitudes toward corruption in Sierra Leone, respondents considered corruption the second most important problem in the country, next to the rebel war (Kpundeh 1995). This finding refutes the "cultural relativist" argument that corruption as a political issue just reflects Western misunderstandings of African society. Sierra Leoneans, although they have other significant concerns, view corruption as an endemic problem. The same survey demonstrated overwhelming agreement among respondents that bribery is harmful and rampant throughout the business community, the police, and the judiciary. People think that progress toward development and economic reorientation is hindered by an inefficient administration and corruption among some high officials and politicians.

Loss of Trust

One of the greatest dangers of corruption is that it weakens trust in government and in each other. It undermines the legitimacy of political leaders and their institutions. Revelations of misdeeds have led people to believe that public officials wish only to get rich at their expense, that the country's resources are being wasted and stolen, and that bribery is the quickest way to get things done. These attitudes have led to serious crises of confidence in both public officials and public institutions.

Impact on Democratic Institutions

Corruption adversely affects democratic processes. Illegal practices result in a lack of transparency in decisionmaking, because decisions are motivated more by private interest than the public concern. In Sierra Leone there are documented cases of nepotism in the civil service, violations in competitive bidding, corruption among law enforcement officers, and public money disappearing from the treasury—all indications of the disastrous costs of corruption to democratic institutions. Furthermore, people in general believe there is no equality before the law and that the benefits of society are reserved for the "haves" at the expense of the "have-nots."

Lack of Good Governance

"Governance," as used here, means the use of political authority and the exercise of control to manage resources for social and economic development. Good governance entails efficient and effective reciprocity between rulers and the ruled, with responsiveness incumbent upon the government (Kpundeh 1992).

The Sierra Leone government has a very poor record of good governance. According to the World Bank (1995), economic mismanagement in the 1970s and 1980s created widespread poverty. The country is endowed with substantial mineral wealth, fisheries, and a varied agricultural resource base with good potential for raising yields. However, Sierra Leone's social indicators are worse than those of other countries at similar levels of per capita income—a result of limited social and human resource development. Access to basic health services, safe drinking water, and sanitation are beyond the reach of the majority of the population, especially in rural areas, and the illiteracy rate is among the highest in the world (World Bank 1994).

Sierra Leone's poor governance record can be attributed to the personalized nature of rule, the failure of the state to advance and protect human rights, the tendency of honest, decent individuals to withdraw from politics, and the extreme centralization of power in the hands of a few. Consequently, the government's control of the economy has meant that the only way to get rich is through political office, intensifying the problem of corruption and inducing leaders to stay in power. This has been disastrous for the country's economy.

Administrative Inefficiency

Corruption is a serious obstacle to administrative efficiency. Decisions are made not to serve the public interest but to promote the interests of individuals involved in secret and immoral agreements. Productivity is low because patronage and nepotism tend to lead to the recruitment of inept and incompetent individuals. Small bribes are routine to expedite normal administrative procedures such as obtaining a driver's license or passport. The result is an inefficient bureaucracy where professionally competent civil servants are frustrated, intimidated, and subdued into silence.

During the APC regime, civil servants considered their public jobs their property. Such a proprietary attitude institutionalizes a pattern of bureaucratic behavior characterized by self-aggrandizement, usurpation of power, and the conception of public office as an avenue for wealth (Jabbra 1976).

Impact on Trade and Investment

Malfeasance leads to economic waste and inefficiency because it affects the allocation of funds, productivity, and consumption. Trade, for example, cannot thrive where the entire administrative mechanism does not allow free market competition. Kickbacks have propelled investment, especially in the mining industry (diamonds, gold, bauxite, and rutile), primarily because of those investors who can make huge profits. But although investments are up, kickbacks paid to government officials are unlikely to remain in the Sierra Leone economy because ill-gotten money is usually used for conspicuous consumption or transferred to foreign bank accounts (Kpundeh 1995).

Earlier Strategies for Controlling Corruption

Before proposing tactics to fight corruption, it is important to review and critically assess the measures instituted by previous administrations.

APC Government Strategies

Scandals and inquiries are not new in Sierra Leone, and it is surprising that previous administrations never seriously devised strategies to combat corruption. For example, after the 1974–75 "Kilowatt scandal" involving senior officials and meter readers of the Sierra Leone Electricity Corporation who misappropriated government funds, President Stevens expressed his concern with corruption by publicizing the wrongdoing. However, he did nothing to prevent a recurrence. His government was overwhelmed by scandals in the late 1970s and early 1980s. Similarly, President Momoh in 1986 appointed an anticorruption squad because, as he said, "The business community in Sierra Leone comprises people who are very vicious and unscrupulous when it comes to making profits, to the extent that the ordinary man is usually charged very exorbitant prices for essential goods" (*West Africa,* May 5, 1986). But the anticorruption squad proved ineffective.

Neither president ever attempted to understand the problem. As Dele Olowu, an expert on public administration in Africa argues, "one of the reasons why governmental corruption has grown to be pervasive in Africa today is primarily because much effort has been spent to remedy the problem rather than to understand it" (Olowu 1993, p. 227).

During Momoh's early years in office, he seemed effective in tackling corruption, particularly when his efforts were compared with Siaka Stevens' inability to control the fraud and bribery that plagued his administration. For example, in addition to the anticorruption squad, Momoh established an antismuggling squad to reduce the large quantities of gold and diamonds that left the country every year. Both squads made spectacular arrests and confiscated goods suspected of being smuggled and hoarded.

Following investigations of financial impropriety at the Ministry of Finance, the deputy minister and two other senior officials were dismissed and arrested in August 1987. They were found guilty of fraud and ordered to repay the money or go to prison for six years. In September 1987 several people were detained and questioned in connection with alleged fraud at the Ministry of Information and Broadcasting and at the Bank of Sierra Leone.

Momoh declared an economic state of emergency in November 1987 and announced 59 measures aimed at preventing the hoarding of currency and essential goods and strengthening the campaign against smuggling (Clapham 1992) The emergency regulations came in response to several strikes that workers called when the government, in its attempt to deal with a currency shortage, failed to pay them. Under the new measures, malfeasance was defined as a criminal offense, and people accused of any crime could be tried in absentia. Penalties were introduced to curb the publication of "defamatory" news articles. Private mail could be inspected and a censor appointed. Later that month, 22 people, including 15 foreigners, were charged with violating the emergency regulations. The deputy minister of development and economic planning, Shamsu Mustapha, resigned in January 1988 and was later charged with fraud. The ministers of information, transport and communications, trade and industry, and parliamentary affairs were sacked in a cabinet reshuffle that was apparently Momoh's answer to accusations of official corruption (Clapham 1992).

Despite Momoh's efforts, the 1992 commissions of inquiry revealed his record on corruption to be worse than those of previous presidents. Under Momoh, as had been the case with Stevens, general economic conditions were often so bad that people feared fiscal irregularities and the lack of accountability would bankrupt the country. Politicians fought for power while the poor scrambled for rice—the staple commodity that hoarders made sure was always in short supply. The black market thrived on large amounts of smuggled diamonds, gold, and agricultural products.

After the government pumped huge sums of money into the banking system, President Momoh's emergency economic measures scored a few successes, as he reported in his third anniversary message. In a later address in Makeni, Momoh warned against continued corruption: "Those still in the public service should hopefully have learned a lesson from the recent past. I shall continue to view with disfavor, any repetition of malpractice. . . . Court action will continue to be taken against those who break the law irrespective of position or association" (*West Africa*, April 16–22, 1990). However, Momoh could not back his threats with consistent action because fiscal mismanagement continued among public officials at alarming proportions—the patronage system was out of control.

Momoh needed the civil service to have a clean image to conform with the objectives of his "constructive nationalism" program. In 1990 he formed the six-member Tucker Commission to study, review, and appraise the recruitment and performance of the civil service and to make recommendations for improvement. President Momoh's attempts to strengthen the civil service were facilitated by a constitutional amendment that required corporate employees, public officials, teachers, and lecturers to resign at least 12 months before seeking election to Parliament. The intention of the law, as argued by E. T. Kamara, assistant secretary general of the APC, was to reduce the numbers of highly qualified civil servants who were resigning to run for office. Their loss was depriving the civil service of many of its most experienced and talented men and women.

In 1988 the Tucker Commission released two government-sponsored reports on the civil service and the Ministry of Education. The reports appeared to be the most critical since the 1968 Foster Commission exposed large-scale malpractice during Albert Margai's regime. The Tucker Commission brought institutional corruption to light. It found that nearly half the employees in several ministries had little or no work to do. Many reported in the morning and disappeared for the rest of the day to engage in other jobs. Yet they always returned at the end of the month to collect their wages. The commission also found that at least 28 schools operated illegally but received annual government grants, and it uncovered a well-established financial racket involving school inspectors, the Ministry of Education directorates, and the so-called proprietors of the independent schools.

NPRC Strategies

When the National Provisional Ruling Council took power in 1992, senior NPRC military officials stated their determination to eradicate mismanagement, institutionalized corruption, and bribery. Much like the short-lived Buhari Administration in Nigeria (December 1983 to August 1985), NPRC leaders maintained they would devise policies to infuse morality and discipline not only into the public bureaucracy but also into the socioeconomic framework. Several strategies were instituted to demonstrate the military regime's alleged determination to "clean house."

1992 CORRUPTION INQUIRIES. The 1992 inquiries, yet another attempt to instill a culture of accountability, revealed the absolute lack of responsible behavior. Citizens in both the public and private sectors were again found to be engaging in theft, bribery, and malfeasance. As always, the effects contributed to a deterioration of socioeconomic conditions.

PREVENTION—DECREE NO. 6. In 1992 the NPRC issued Decree No. 6, which provides for the prevention of corruption and related matters. For example, sections 2, 3, and 4 specify the punishment for giving and accepting bribes, soliciting or accepting an advantage, and engaging in corrupt transactions with agents. Section 5 outlines the penalties for possession of unexplained property and deals with the confiscation of assets. The remaining sections address the penalties for illegally awarding contracts, corrupt jurists, and so forth (*Sierra Leone Gazette* 1992).

Decree No. 6 proved ineffective in deterring corruption because there was no specific system in place to enforce it. Although government officials appeared to want accountability, the military government did nothing other than enact the decree. NPRC officials claimed they had plans to establish an independent anticorruption commission, revise salaries, provide incentives to public workers, and completely reorganize civil service, but they never translated much of their talk into action.

Another shortcoming of Decree No. 6 is its curtailment of the press. The decree censors the press by specifically banning "sensitive" publications unless authorized by appropriate government functionaries. Arnold Gooding, the NPRC's first attorney general, was critical of the press:

> The press has allowed itself to be used as a mouth-piece of counter-revolutionaries; it is not helping the NPRC government with ideas and prescriptions as how to lift the country from its present status as the least developed nation in the world. Instead, every newspaper is full of sensationalism. . . . Is it not time that we have papers like *The New York Times*? (*Unity*, 1992)

The promulgation of constraints on the press scared journalists and sent the wrong signals to the international community. For any democratic society, a free press is crucial. The press plays a vibrant role in helping to awaken the consciousness of citizens, especially by exposing corruption and mobilizing public opinion. Robert Klitgaard, an expert on anticorruption strategies, reminds us that more than one country has discovered that free elections and economic reforms do not immediately reduce corruption. Whatever the size and type of government a country chooses, there will always be threats (and acts) of bribery, extortion, influence peddling, kickbacks, fraud, and other illicit activities in the private, public, and parastatal sectors (Klitgaard 1991). And without media attention to such wrongdoing, public outcry is unlikely.

DISCIPLINE. The military administration tried to institute discipline among government workers by on-the-spot firing of civil servants who were late or failed to come to work. One military officer, Colonel Akim Gibril, stated in an August 14, 1992, interview:

> Indiscipline could be largely said to be responsible for government offices being left empty while civil servants are busy operating private businesses. Henceforth, they have to choose between their public office and their private businesses, and the new buzzwords are "accountability," "responsibility," and "discipline," particularly with civil servants.

Military leaders made unscheduled visits to various ministries, departments, and parastatals in order to catch idle civil servants. This strategy had many Sierra Leoneans jittery and reporting to work on time. The first deputy chairman of the NPRC, Captain S. A. J. Musa, stated that his spot-check visits to the ministries were to make civil servants cognizant that they must be dedicated: "I am actually working on getting a small but disciplined civil service that can work well to improve situations fast, because we want to go on developing the nation fast" (U.S. government's *FBIS Daily Report—Sub-Saharan Africa*, May 28, 1992).

The disciplinary campaign affected not only civil servants but schools and the general public as well. After only a few weeks in power, the military brought an end to children loitering during school hours. Students who drifted to entertainment spots during school hours were drilled by soldiers. Soldiers also discouraged tardiness by asking those late for school to do odd jobs (*Unity*, May 18, 1992). Moreover, since May 1992 the last Saturday of every month has been designated as a "general cleaning day," when all citizens are expected to spend the morning cleaning their immediate area. One military official explained, "For a system that was clogged with corruption, nepotism, and tribalism to be corrected, a lot of house cleaning has to be done" (*Unity*, May 18, 1992).

The military also issued a public notice warning motorists to desist from bribing servicemen and traffic officers at checkpoints. The announcement states that anyone caught in violation will be arrested and detained along with the serviceman or officer involved.

The Current Situation

Despite the Tucker Commission's reports, corruption is still a major problem. Bribery, theft, and fraud persist in many government agencies. For example, Brigadier-General Maada Bio, during his tenure as deputy chairman of the NPRC, dismissed 10 police officers in the traffic division for taking bribes and issued warnings to numerous motorists (*West Africa*, September 13–19, 1993). And the Sierra Leone State Lottery, supposedly one of the most viable parastatals, is plagued by dishonesty despite the NPRC's efforts to correct the situation (*The New Breed*, May 26–June 1, 1993).

The inquiries into corruption, however, have had an interesting impact on people's attitudes. Despite widespread belief that some of the "big fish" have escaped, the numerous revelations of wrongdoing have tarnished many of the erstwhile heroes of the 1980s and resulted in a growing acknowledgment of the value of honesty.

Furthermore, the economy showed signs of improvement under the NPRC, primarily because it exhibited a higher level of fiscal discipline than the APC. More government funds than ever before were at work for the people. Roads in rural areas as well as major urban centers were repaired; the National

Power Authority provided more electricity between 1992 and 1997 than during the previous five years; steps were taken to improve the educational system; gasoline queues disappeared; and the price of rice was relatively stable. However, some observers have pointed out that the status of the common citizen worsened because of the NPRC's slavish adherence to World Bank and International Monetary Fund programs.

Suggested Remedies for Controlling Corruption

Political corruption is a symptom rather than a cause of underdevelopment. The problem needs to be addressed at both the national and international levels if progress is to be made. At the national level, a holistic approach, including prevention, enforcement, new incentives in private and state institutions, increased public awareness, capacity building, and strong leadership, has a much better chance of success than a simple focus on individuals. At the international level, a coordinated approach among bilateral donors and international organizations is needed. Furthermore, partnerships with organizations such as Transparency International are useful in the fight against corruption. For example, Transparency International and the Economic Development Institute of the World Bank have jointly organized workshops on national integrity in countries such as Tanzania and Uganda. The aim of these workshops is to assist in building a national integrity system by ensuring some level of transparency and accountability.

Instituting Political Change

The structure of Sierra Leone's political system contributes significantly to the pervasiveness of administrative corruption. Because the military regime operated within the framework established by the APC, and implementing new methods and systems depended largely on the cooperation of a lethargic and underpaid civil service, it was difficult to effect meaningful change. To successfully fight corruption now, the political system created by Siaka Stevens and perpetuated by Joseph Momoh needs to be overhauled. The Constitution should not allow personal rule, which has proved fertile ground for political patronage—a system that stalls the democratic process primarily because it depends on loyalty to one individual. Until the entire political system has adequate restrictions to prevent abuse of power, the general direction of any new administration remains uncertain.

High-level administrators who violate the law must be prosecuted and punished to the full extent of the law to send a message that corruption will not be tolerated. But making an example of corrupt officials is not enough. Anyone who is familiar with government operations during the APC era knows that one of the real contributors to Sierra Leone's pathetic plight is an ineffective civil service. The military did not succeed in controlling corruption by imprisoning politicians and leaving the institutions and structure intact. Some argue that people, not institutions, engage in corruption. But in Sierra Leone, institutional remedies will contribute significantly.

Thus, to control corruption, innovative institutional strategies should be established that depart drastically from the old way of doing things. These strategies must complement morality campaigns and "quick-fix" measures. Removing the APC was simply a first step and not the end. More explicitly, the military leaders underestimated the "system" left behind by the APC.

This is not to suggest that the armed forces are incorruptible. The military in most African countries wages a serious campaign to promote itself as noncorrupt and the country's most disciplined entity. Yet several Sierra Leonean soldiers in 1992 were court-martialed for armed robbery (*The New Breed*, May 27–June 2, 1992). In fact, events in Sierra Leone after the military interregnum of 1967–68, as well as the experiences of other African countries, particularly Nigeria, show that attempts by the military to fight corruption have had dismal results. Military regimes have proved more corrupt than civilian administrations, even though they usually justify replacing civilian governments to end corruption. But military rulers can veil the magnitude of their own corruption by refusing to make information available to the public and, more importantly, by censoring the press. If the Kabba Administration is to gain public confidence, it must go beyond policy pronouncements about making accountability and transparency paramount.

Bringing Corruption into the Open

Corruption is a sensitive subject and, by its nature, hard to observe. It is inherently a secretive activity, and those who engage in it rarely admit wrongdoing. Even those in positions of trust sometimes believe it is in everyone's best interest to deny any knowledge of corruption, in order to retain public confidence in government institutions, uphold the reputation of their organizations, and personally vouch for the "cleanliness" of their immediate jurisdiction. Many also claim to have their own way of dealing with corruption that does not involve public disclosure. Indeed, premature whistle-blowing might defeat countermeasures. Additionally, some persons with knowledge of wrongdoing may be unable to disclose it fully because of overriding constitutional, legal, and official restrictions. Some informants may even fear retribution.

The government should encourage research and extensive media reports on corruption. It benefits everyone if the taboo on discussing the subject is removed. As long as the existence of corruption is denied, it cannot be tackled. Denials and blanket reassurances only confirm popular assumptions about officials' hypocrisy and trustworthiness and prompt suspicion that the situation must be worse than commonly thought. Once people publicly acknowledge corruption in their midst and feel free to express their concerns, it becomes possible to discuss solutions. Furthermore, corrective action is much more likely when allegations of misconduct are based on reliable, credible information instead of secondhand sources and hearsay.

Enforcing Penalties for Wrongdoing

The Sierra Leone government needs to get tough on corruption. Many laws already exist to severely punish culprits. Without adequate enforcement, however, there can be little success in the fight against corruption. Effective enforcement mechanisms should be established, including investigators, prosecutors, and adjudicators who will perform their professional duties in a transparently independent fashion. Furthermore, the laws must apply not only to Sierra Leoneans but to foreign culprits as well—individuals and businesses alike. If legal procedures and remedies are fair and consistently enforced, they can provide an effective deterrent to corruption. With this in mind, Robert Klitgaard (1991) suggests that the criteria for determining penalties (and those to be penalized) should be smashing what might be called the culture of corruption.

Making Civil Service Salaries Competitive

Some scholars argue that low salaries and insufficient incentives in the public sector contribute to corruption. In many African countries, civil service remuneration and conditions of service have continuously deteriorated over the years in the wake of structural adjustment processes and programs. Most salaries have not been adjusted to keep pace with high levels of inflation. Workers look for alternative ways to generate additional income; second jobs and moonlighting follow. Employees may not be dedicated if their salaries are inadequate, and perhaps only the spoils of office keep them there (see, for example, Pope 1996). Departments such as the police and customs, which have large numbers of low-paid workers who are in direct contact with the public, are especially ripe for corrupt behavior. In these vulnerable departments in particular, but throughout the civil service, the government should periodically review salaries and incentives.

Creating an Independent Anticorruption Commission

There is a pressing demand for a competent, independent, and powerful agency to deal with entrenched and institutionalized corruption within the public and private sectors in Sierra Leone. Such an agency would be particularly useful in ensuring the effectiveness of NPRC Decree No. 6 (the Prevention of Corruption Decree). The commission must be free of internal corruption and outside interference and capable of operating in both the public and private sectors. It should have preventive and educational components, as well as the ability to gather intelligence, process complaints, and advise government and private agencies.

Independent anticorruption agencies have achieved relative success in several societies, most notably Hong Kong, China. Sierra Leone's military government was relatively well placed to launch such a commission but lacked the political will and commitment to do so. President Kabba later established an Office of Transparency and Accountability to strengthen morality and accountability in government business, specifically procurement, but the office is still in its infancy.

Decentralizing Government

Another key step in controlling corruption in Sierra Leone is to decentralize power so that one individual or group does not make all the decisions. The relationship between the executive branch and other participants in government, such as the legislature, the judiciary, local jurisdictions, political parties, the media, the private sector, and nongovernmental organizations, needs to be broadly articulated.

Experience and theory both indicate that an organization is most vulnerable to corruption when agents enjoy a monopoly over clients, have sole discretion over the provision of a licit or illicit service, and take actions that are difficult to monitor (Klitgaard 1991). When local governments have some real power, they can not only address local interests more fully but also exercise a check on the operations of higher levels of authority. However, two key ingredients are needed for the potential gain to outweigh the costs. First, decentralization must involve real delegation of authority, including the authority to generate and reserve a portion of local revenues. Second, local authorities themselves must be accountable both to higher levels and to local groups. In addition, abuse of authority and public corruption are less likely to occur if the rules governing local officials are at least in part defined by local norms (Charlick 1993).

Mandating the Declaration of Assets

In answer to overwhelming public support for the declaration of assets by prominent officials, laws should be enacted to ensure that all government workers above the rank of senior assistant secretary complete a declaration of assets form and update it annually. These forms, along with all financial records of high-level government officials, should be filed with an independent commission and reviewed periodically to determine if new assets are commensurate with income. Such a practice inspires confidence in public officials and loyalty to the government.

Establishing a Code of Ethics

The government should have a comprehensive code of ethics that spells out appropriate and inappropriate behavior for politicians and civil servants. It should, of course, outlaw the most blatant forms of corruption: bribery, fraud, theft, and so forth. It should also, for example, prohibit government officials' involvement in business ventures that are potential conflicts of interest. Officials should be required to indicate whether they are related to any individual who owns or manages a private concern.

Furthermore, the code should cover misuse of state property. For example, it might stipulate that government vehicles should be used only for official business and should be parked only on designated government parking lots after hours. People must accept the reality that a government vehicle is public property and a civil servant's employment status is temporary. To ensure the effectiveness of this policy, the government could solicit information about government vehicles or property being used in an unsafe or unlawful manner. Rewarding complainants, if the charge proves true, is a good incentive.

Protecting Whistle-Blowers

It is extremely important to protect whistle-blowers. The military government began using suggestion boxes in 1992 to enable people to anonymously report suspected corruption. Citizens misused this device, however, to settle old scores with their supervisors. Developing new ways to protect whistle-blowers will erode the fear of reprisal and encourage more people to come forward.

Improving Communication

Sierra Leone's new leaders should demonstrate the political will to re-duce corruption. A publicity campaign could be extremely complemen-tary in helping the government reach its goals. Measures such as public announcements explaining the procedures and criteria for granting per-mits, licenses, and bank loans, approving building plots, and assessing taxes are likely to reduce corruption in some of these activities. The veil of secrecy that surrounds these matters often forces applicants to resort to corruption in order to maximize their chances of success with corrupt civil servants. Thus publicity campaigns, especially in countries with poor communication networks and high rates of illiteracy, such as Sierra Leone, will produce results in the long term.

Conclusion

In conclusion, the key to successfully controlling corruption in Sierra Leone—as elsewhere—is to have a democratic system that guarantees the rights of the individual and has the potential to reduce corruption while limiting governmental intrusion (Kpundeh 1993). The country, through its current leaders and nongovernmental organizations, needs to initiate the evolution of a new political culture that allows competition and participa-tion without hindrance.

Corrupt politicians and civil servants have created numerous problems, and the efforts of past governments to fight malfeasance were ineffective. President Kabba has the unenviable task of raising the living standards of Sierra Leoneans, eradicating bribery and fiscal irresponsibility, collecting taxes, and bringing an end to the rebel war. Rather than initially focusing on remedies, he must understand the roots and dynamics of corruption in the country before developing an institutionalized anticorruption strategy.

Such a strategy must formally integrate all institutions and policies to fight this malaise—investigative, prosecutory, research, and prevention functions—into a single body. That body should work hard to establish public confidence through regular press conferences that are extensively reported in English and local dialects. It must go beyond policy pronounce-ments about the importance of transparency and accountability. In other words, the press conferences should reveal the government's progress in reducing corruption and increasing accountability—reporting, for example, the number of people arrested and prosecuted during the previous month and the value of goods seized. Such disclosures will contribute to the public's willingness to cooperate. But the best way to make an anticorruption agency free from all extraneous and political pressures is to make it answerable to the Sierra Leone Parliament comprising members from six political par-ties. International donors call for the implementation of good governance practices, but few if any such reforms will be effective without comple-mentary preventive and investigative measures.

References

Charlick, Robert. 1993. "Corruption and Political Transition: A Governance Per-spective." *Corruption and Reform* 7(3):177–88.

Clapham, Christopher. 1992. "Sierra Leone Recent History." In *Africa South of the Sahara*. London: Europa Publications Ltd.

Gberie, Lans. 1996. "Sierra Leone Economy: Curse of Riches." International Press Service, March 11.

Hope, K. R. 1985. "Politics, Bureaucratic Corruption and Maladministration in the Third World." *International Review of Administrative Sciences* 1:1–6.

Jabbra, J. G. 1976. "Bureaucratic Corruption in the Third World: Causes and Rem-edy." *Indian Journal of Public Administration* 22 (October–December):673–91.

Johnston, Michael. 1982. *Political Corruption and Public Policy in America*. Monterey, Calif.: Brooks/Cole.

Klitgaard, Robert. 1991. "Strategies for Reform." *Journal of Democracy* 2(4):86–100.

Kpundeh, S. J., ed. 1992. *Democratization in Africa: African Views, African Voices*. Washington, D.C.: National Academy Press.

———. 1993. "Prospects in Contemporary Sierra Leone." *Corruption and Reform* 7(3):237–47.

———. 1995. *Politics and Corruption in Africa: A Case Study of Sierra Leone*. Lanham, Md.: University Press of America.

Leys, Colin. 1965. "What Is the Problem about Corruption?" *Journal of Modern Afri-can Studies* 3(2):215–24.

Olowu, Dele. 1993. "Governmental Corruption and Africa's Democratization Ef-forts." *Corruption and Reform* 7(3):227–36.

Pope, Jeremy, ed. 1996. *Transparency International Source Book.* Berlin: Transparency International.

Reno, William. 1995. *Corruption and State Politics in Sierra Leone.* New York: Cambridge University Press.

———. 1996. "Ironies of Post–Cold War Structural Adjustment in Sierra Leone." *Review of African Political Economy* 67: 7–18.

Sierra Leone Gazette. 1992. "The Prevention of Corruption Decree." Supplement to no. 47, July 10.

———. 1996. "The National Unity and Reconciliation Commission Act, 1996." Supplement to vol. 127, no. 38, June 25.

Sierra Leone News Agency. 1992. *Commissions of Inquiry Special Weekly Reports.* Various issues.

World Bank. 1994. "Sierra Leone: Public Expenditure Policies for Sustained Economic Growth and Poverty Alleviation." Western Africa Department, Country Operations Division, Washington, D.C.

———. 1995. "Sierra Leone: Policy Framework Paper, 1995–1996." Western Africa Department, Country Operations Division, Washington, D.C.

Zack-Williams, A. B. 1990. "Sierra Leone: Crisis and Despair." *Review of African Political Economy* 49:23–33.

Conclusion

Rick Stapenhurst and Sahr J. Kpundeh

The issue of high-level bureaucratic corruption has come to center stage. Recent trends toward democratization and the economic consequences of pervasive corruption have increased the pressure for accountability and transparency in the way reform-minded countries conduct public business. This volume illustrates the magnitude and specific dimensions of the problem and the importance of understanding its nuances in each country—a necessary element in devising appropriate anticorruption tactics.

Each country or region is unique in its history and culture, its political system, and its stage of economic and social development. Nations differ dramatically not so much in their inherent tendency toward corruption but rather in the extent to which mechanisms of accountability constrain public officials in carrying out their functions. In some countries the legislature, judiciary, civil service, and electoral system remain underdeveloped and even undeveloped. The legislative and judicial branches of government, in particular, need to be strengthened to ensure their independence. The case studies in part III refer to disparate events in different government institutions in a variety of political systems across dissimilar cultures. Although more research is needed to better evaluate, detect, and suggest solutions to the problem of corruption, common threads run through all the case studies, and experience in reform strategies can provide universal guidance in developing solutions, even if only to warn against instituting certain practices.

Implicit throughout this volume is the idea that economic reforms—deregulation and liberalization, budget and tax reforms, and privatization—are at the core of a policy to curb corruption. Well-designed and properly executed market reforms increase competition and decrease the incidence of corrupt practices. Fewer regulatory and trade interventions, macroeconomic stability, and moderate, simple tax regimes with little discretion do much to reduce the opportunities for corruption.

The chapters in this volume are instructive because they remind us that reform is a long-term process and that the frame of reference should be shifted from weeks and months to years. We are also reminded that the obstacles to success range from a lack of information to a misunderstanding of the government's role in society. Some of the chapters also highlight the crucial role of civil society in the fight against corruption. Enlisting the citizenry in the fight involves helping them to understand that they personally have a stake in controlling corruption and the power to do something about it.

The country experiences discussed in this volume indicate that the fight against corruption should concentrate on prevention and punishment. The prevention process has education, socialization, and communication at its foundation. Measures such as public announcements can help to inform the public about ways to reduce malfeasance. A strong political commitment complemented by wide-ranging publicity campaigns is extremely effective in reducing corruption.

The significance of credible institutions is also highlighted throughout the book. Institutions fill in the gaps left when governments are unable to ensure accountability or promote and protect the rights of individuals. Such institutions include an independent and critical press, an independent judiciary, a functioning parliament free of influence and interference from the ruling party, and an executive branch or head of state with a commitment to good governance. While groups such as the World Bank's Economic Development Institute (EDI) are doing commendable work to promote the rebuilding of national integrity systems, many governments must still grapple with practical issues of methodology—that is, knowing exactly how to devise an anticorruption campaign with the most effective steps in the most effective order.

Measuring Corruption and Understanding Its Mechanisms at the National Level

Measuring corruption entails the identification of vulnerable areas and signs of high-level misconduct.[1] Depending on the setting being studied and whether corruption is to be analyzed comparatively across countries or more in-depth within one country, different approaches to data gathering and analysis will be called for. A number of tools are at the disposal of analysts today, including surveys and expert assessments.

Surveys

Surveys are particularly useful in describing the characteristics of a large population or a particular subset of the population, such as the business community. Surveys provide insight into society's ethical standards, tell us whose views are similar to the official views or norms of behavior, show us how personal or universal standards evolve from an individual's perception of right and wrong, and instruct us about people's attitudes toward misconduct in politics and business. Surveys designed by local experts for use by public managers and policymakers can determine the effectiveness of government services and how well they are delivered. Consumer surveys and citizens' polls also give consumers a "voice" and a means of conveying strong messages to service providers. They focus on improving performance by defining it in terms of the public's experiences.

In Tanzania, for example, President Benjamin Mkapa's Commission on Corruption requested a Service Delivery Survey in 1996 to investigate the extent of corruption in the delivery of four key public services: the police, the judiciary, revenue, and land services. There was a general perception that corruption in these services was commonplace. The survey relied on indicators that could be measured again later to assess improvements made in response to complaints. Additionally, the Tanzanian government

---

1. This section is based on Daniel Kaufmann, "Revisiting Anti-Corruption Strategies: Tilt towards Incentive-Driven Approaches," in Sahr Kpundeh and Irene Hors, eds., *Corruption and Integrity Improvement Initiatives in Developing Countries* (United Nations Development Programme/Organisation for Economic Co-operation and Development, New York, 1998).

wanted to stimulate a dialogue on malfeasance and its solutions, engaging service providers and users at different levels. The survey strengthened political will by airing the views of senior officers at the local level, along with their suggestions for remedial action. The results were used as a mandate to design specific strategies.

Diagnostics

As valuable as opinion surveys are, it is equally important to gather information on and analyze the main correlates of corruption within a country (and across countries as well). The key variables to be analyzed include the following: respect for the rule of law and protection of property rights; administrative regulations and the extent of regulatory discretion and bureaucratic red tape; economic policies; political variables; civil liberties; professionalism and incentives in the civil service; financial and accounting systems; natural resources; and such population characteristics as size, ethnolinguistic fragmentation, income per capita, and income distribution.

It is also useful to think about developing twin networks of nongovernmental agencies and experts as sources of information and facilitators in analyzing and developing practical reform methods. Many of the more broadly descriptive strategies offered by scholars and policymakers need considerable tailoring to fit specific political, economic, and cultural circumstances.

Elements of a Successful Anticorruption Strategy

The Underlying Fundamentals

A CUSTOMIZED APPROACH. Because the forms and determinants of corruption vary from country to country and setting to setting, it is vital to identify the most important problems to be tackled in an action program. In other words, a country-specific understanding is imperative.

POLITICAL WILL. Political will is essential. It is a critical starting point for sustainable and effective anticorruption strategies and programs. No legislative or administrative changes can ever be effective unless there is commitment at all levels of government.

Accountability in Governance. The central lesson in this volume is the importance of accountability in governance—the idea that each government official must answer to someone else—which minimizes the opportunities and incentives for corruption. External monitoring systems or oversight boards act as mechanisms to ensure accountability and prevent the abuse of power.

Programming

A Focus on Priorities and Fundamentals. As already noted, the causes of corruption are complex, and the types of corruption vary from country to country. Identifying a small number of fundamental determinants of the main types of corruption in a country is often useful so that an anticorruption program can be tailored to the critical causes. Such diagnosis, through corruption surveys or other means, can result in the appropriate sequencing of anticorruption measures, bearing out the rule of "20/80"—that the most appropriate 20 percent of all possible measures will yield 80 percent of the impact possible from all measures combined. The alternative "shotgun" approach—covering a wide field with hit-or-miss effectiveness—may well result in an inappropriate set of measures that neglect the main causes of corruption, while the "Christmas tree" approach—trying everything possible—will result in much wasted effort and little improvement.

A Holistic Approach. Although anticorruption strategies should focus on priorities, they should also be comprehensive. All the agencies designed to fight corruption—prevention, investigation, research, education, and enforcement bodies—have to work in concert, harmonize their efforts, and complement each other to develop one strategy. A few key agencies or areas should be identified where anticorruption measures can be focused in the first year. This prevents duplication of effort and waste of government funds and allows the reform program to gather momentum and achieve some early success.

Legal Remedies

Legal reforms are only part of the solution. Their effectiveness is contingent on being coupled with measures that guarantee their implementation, maximize the accountability and transparency of the reform effort and the personnel involved, and minimize vulnerable areas.

Training

Developing countries should conduct training for civil servants at all levels, emphasizing clearly defined guidelines and rules of conduct and thoroughly reviewing each department's and agency's training needs.

Public Outreach

Public education is a key component; an informed and angry public can be a vital tool in any anticorruption campaign. Many times the people are unaware of the costs corruption levies on society and its impact on public welfare. One means of strengthening political will is to conduct focused public debates on malfeasance and its remedies. These can be via radio or television, in classrooms, during community activities, in the press, and in formal workshops. Public awareness helps remove the veil of secrecy surrounding misconduct. More importantly, education campaigns begin to personalize corruption, explaining clearly and explicitly how individuals are impacted. Public ire is easily expressed when individuals are subject to predatory abuses by agents of the state. However, it is also piqued when the public is informed about abuses at a higher level, such as the diversion of public funds or flagrant disregard for the law.

The Sequencing of Reforms

The fight against corruption is neither simple nor straightforward. The process has to be gradual, and programs that are too ambitious and call for overnight changes will not succeed. Yet reform programs must also be designed to achieve quick successes in order to win public confidence and support. Grandiose plans that cannot be accomplished right away should be deferred.

Participation by the International Community

International pressure can play a significant role in inducing states to take stronger measures against corruption. International financial institutions and bilateral donors can begin to link their assistance to progress toward improved governance. In addition, the international community must ensure that their practices and programs do not contribute to corruption in developing countries. Foreign aid organizations and business communities can help develop structures that work independently of governments to inject accountability and transparency into international business and aid projects.

Values and Perceptions

For any country embarking on reform, perhaps the most important challenge is to structure a program or action plan that has, at its core, the goal of changing public perceptions and values. In due course, corruption will be seen as aberrant and immoral, rather than as a necessary means of surviving and prospering in an environment where resources and opportunities are often all too scarce.

Suggestions for Further Reading

In addition to the sources cited in the chapter reference lists, the following may be of interest.

Alatas, Hussein Syed. 1990. *Corruption: Its Nature, Causes and Functions.* Aldershot, U.K., and Brookfield Vt.: Avebury.

Allan, P. 1992. "Empirical Knowledge on Strategies for Corruption Control." In *Proceedings of the 5th International Anti-Corruption Conference.* Amsterdam: Kluwer Law and Taxation.

Bayart, Jean-François. 1997. "Le « capital social » de l'État malfaiteur, ou les ruses de l'intelligence politique." In Jean-François Bayart, Stephen Ellis, and Béatrice Hibou, eds., *La criminalisation de l'État en Afrique.* Paris: Édition Complexe.

Botswana, Republic of. 1994. "Corruption and Economic Crime Act, 1994." *Botswana Government Gazette* August 19. Gaborone: Government Printer.

Brett, E. A. 1995. "Neutralizing the Use of Force in Uganda: The Role of the Military in Politics." *Journal of Modern African Studies* 33:129–52.

Chew, D. C. E. 1990. "Internal Adjustments to Falling Civil Salary: Insights from Uganda." *World Development* 18(7):1003–14.

Clapham, Christopher S. 1982. *Private Patronage and Public Power: Political Clientism in the Modern State.* London: Frances Pinter.

Clarke, Michael, ed. 1983. *Corruption Causes, Consequences and Control.* London: Frances Pinter.

Coolidge, Jacqueline, and Susan Rose-Ackerman. 1997. "High-Level Rent Seeking and Corruption in African Regimes." World Bank Policy Research Paper 1780. Washington, D.C.

de Speville, Bertrand. 1995. "Strategic Control of Corruption: A Quiet Revolution over Two Decades." Paper presented at the Seventh International Anti-Corruption Conference Plenary Session, Beijing, October.

Diamond, Larry. 1987. "Class Formation in the Swollen African State." *Journal of Modern African Studies* 25(4).

Ekeh, Peter. 1975. "Colonialism and the Two Publics in Africa: A Theoretical Statement." *Comparative Studies in Society and History* (January):91–112.

Elliot, Kimberly Ann, ed. 1997. *Corruption and the Global Economy.* Washington, D.C.: Institute for International Economics.

Gardiner, J. 1993. "Defining Corruption." In *Proceedings of the 5th International Anti-Corruption Conference.* Amsterdam: Kluwer Law and Taxation.

Hansen, Holger Bernt, and Michael Twaddle, eds. 1991. *Changing Uganda.* London: James Currey Ltd.

Heidenheimer, Arnold J., Michael Johnston, and Victor T. Levine, eds. 1997. *Political Corruption: A Handbook,* 4th ed. New Brunswick, N.J.: Transaction Books.

Heilbrunn, John R. 1993. "Social Origins of National Conferences in Benin and Togo." *Journal of Modern African Studies* 31(2):277–99.

Johnston, Michael. 1992. "Corruption as a Process: Lessons for Analysis and Reform." In *Proceedings of the 5th International Anti-Corruption Conference.* Amsterdam: Kluwer Law and Taxation.

———. 1993. "'Micro' and 'Macro' Possibilities for Reform." *Corruption and Reform* 7(3):189–204.

Kasozi, A. B. K. 1994. *The Social Origins of Violence in Uganda 1964–1985.* Montreal: McGill-Queen's University Press.

Kelman, Fritz F. 1994. "Should Foreign Bribery Be a Crime?" Unpublished paper. Transparency International, Berlin.

Klitgaard, Robert. 1988. *Controlling Corruption.* Berkeley: University of California Press.

———. 1991. *Adjusting to Reality: Beyond State versus Market in Economic Development.* San Francisco: International Center for Economic Growth.

Kpundeh, S. J. 1994a. "Challenges to Democratic Transitions in Sierra Leone: The Problem of Corruption." In *The Democratic Challenge in Africa.* Carter Center Working Paper Series. Atlanta.

———. 1994b. "Limiting Administrative Corruption in Sierra Leone." *Journal of Modern African Studies* 32(1):139–57.

Langseth, Petter, and Rick Stapenhurst. 1997. *National Integrity System: Country Studies.* EDI Working Paper. Washington, D.C.: World Bank.

Mauro, Paulo. 1995. "Corruption and Growth." *Quarterly Journal of Economics* 106(2):681–712.

Okanla, Moussa. 1996. "Benin: The Struggle against Corruption in Theory and Practice." In Patrick Meagher, ed., *Governance and the Economy in Africa: Tools for Analysis and Reform of Corruption*. College Park, Md.: Center for Institutional Reform and the Informal Sector.

Peil, Margaret. 1975. "A Civilian Appraisal of Military Rule in Nigeria." *Armed Forces and Society* 2(1):34–44.

Pope, Jeremy. 1997. "Involving Civil Society in Anti-Corrupt Practices." In Sahr Kpundeh, Margit van Ham, and Fiona Simpkins, eds., *The National Integrity System in Malawi: Final Workshop Proceedings, Lilongwe Hotel, Malawi, 25–27 November 1996*. Washington, D.C.: World Bank.

Pope, Jeremy, and Petter Langseth, eds. 1995. *Investigative Journalism in Uganda I: Final Workshop Proceedings*. Mukono, Uganda: Inspectorate General of Government, Economic Development Institute of the World Bank, Transparency International, and the Danish Ministry of Foreign Affairs.

Prevention of Corruption Bureau of Tanzania, Economic Development Institute of the World Bank, Tanzania Development and Research Group, and Overseas Development Administration. 1995. *The National Integrity System in Tanzania: Proceedings of a Workshop*. Dar es Salaam.

Rasheed, Sadig, and Dele Olowu. 1993. *Ethics and Accountability in African Public Services*. Nairobi: ICIPE Science Press.

Republic of Uganda. 1993. "Management of Change: Report on the Proceedings of the Seminar of Ministers and Permanent Secretaries." Civil Service Reform Program, Kampala.

Ruzindana, Augustine. 1997. "Building a National Integrity System in Uganda." In Sahr J. Kpundeh and Petter Langseth, eds., *Good Governance for Sustainable Development: Final Workshop Proceedings, 13–14 March 1997*. Washington, D.C.: World Bank.

Scott, J. C. 1972. *Comparative Political Corruption*. Englewood Cliffs, N.J.: Prentice Hall.

Tanzania Chamber of Commerce. 1995. *Industry and Agriculture, Corruption and Drug Trafficking in Tanzania*. Dar es Salaam: Popular Publications Limited.

Tanzi, Vito. 1994. "Corruption, Governmental Activities and Markets." IMF Working Paper. International Monetary Fund, Washington, D.C.

Theobald, Robin. 1992. "On the Survival of Patronage in Developed Societies." *Archives Européennes de Sociologie* 33:183–91.

———. 1994. "Lancing the Swollen African State: Will It Alleviate the Problem of Corruption?" *Journal of Modern African Studies* 32(4):701–6.

Tirole, Jean. 1992. *Persistence of Corruption*. Working Paper 55. Washington, D.C.: Institute for Policy Reform.

Tripp, Aili Mari. 1997. *Changing the Rules: The Politics of Liberalization and the Urban Informal Economy in Tanzania.* Berkeley and Los Angeles: University of California Press.

Wei, S.-J. 1997. *How Taxing Is Corruption on International Investors?* NBER Working Paper 6030. Cambridge, Mass.: National Bureau of Economic Research.

Index

Note: Page numbers in **bold type** reference non-text material.